Oxford Castaways

50 inspirational people select objects, paintings or books which have a special place in their lives

By Sylvia Vetta

with illustrations by Weimin He
Edited and designed by Tim Metcalfe

Published by OXPENS

Content originally published in
Oxfordshire Limited Edition
between 2008 and 2012

First edition March 2012

ISBN: 978-1-78018-520-0

The Castaways

1954, but those were less than four inspiring minutes in an altogether inspiring life. Moyra, his artist wife of 57 years, painted and sketched Roger and her children throughout those years. As the daughter of the first chairman of the International Monetary Fund, she received a letter of condolence from President JF Kennedy on the death of her father. 116

How about you?
If you were marooned on a desert island, which works of art, objects or books would you want with you? And if you can have only one what will that be? Begin, like the castaways, by making a list — and then make that difficult final choice.

Thanks and acknowledgements

Tim Metcalfe, the editor of Oxfordshire Limited Edition Magazine has worked with me on the castaway series since January 2008. He has been tirelessly supportive in helping to produce this book, for which he has my grateful thanks.

Thanks to Simon O'Neill, group editor at Newsquest Oxfordshire and Wiltshire for giving me permission to reproduce the 50 features with photographs.

I would also like to thank the talented photographers who have provided portraits of the castaways — Antony Moore, Jon Lewis, Ed Nix, Damian Halliwell, Mark Bassett, Mark Hemsworth, Andrew Walmsley, David Fleming, Marc West and Denis Kennedy

Grateful thanks to the artist Weimin He who has created the cover artwork and illustrations for this book.

I would also like to thank the Oxford Writers Group and Lady Moyra Bannister for their encouragement and Charles Jones, of WritersPrintShop, for his advice.

The best place to be marooned?

Sylvia Vetta reveals how the 'castaway' series began

While writing these features, I had a blinding moment of revelation — a vision of this amazing city of Oxford. It was not only of the beautiful buildings, the museums, libraries, theatres, parks, meadows and rivers — but the people thriving within this environment.

The 50 castaways have come from completely different backgrounds, often from other parts of the world but the atmosphere of Oxford has added a rich ingredient to their lives.

Oxford is rather a small city, but with each interview, a realisation grew that the lives of these wonderfully creative people have benefitted not only this county, but the rest of the UK — and often the rest of the world.

As you read about the lives of our 50 castaways, I hope you may come to a conclusion about what is so special about this place and its people.

We live in a time obsessed by the idea of celebrity. Because of their modesty, you are likely to pass many of our castaways without recognition in the street. I believe most of the castaways are happy with that situation and would hate to be called a celebrity.

A good example is Sir Roger Bannister. In 1954, he was the first man to run a mile in under four minutes, which made him one of the most well-known men in the English speaking world.

I discovered that he is as proud of his work as a neurologist as of the sporting achievements which catapulted him to fame.

So how did I come to meet them and be inspired by these intriguing people? It all began in the summer of 1998, with a telephone call from Tim Metcalfe seeking my advice. The writer of *Oxfordshire Limited Edition*'s antiques page was moving to London and they needed to find a replacement.

Why ask me? At that time I was Chairman of the Thames Valley Antiques Dealers Association and until recently had been a director of Oxford Antiques Centre, affectionately named by me and my business partner as The Jam Factory.

Situated in the former Cooper's Oxford Marmalade factory, we thought Marmalade Factory was a bit of a mouthful.

My first encounter with author Brian Aldiss was when he became a customer.

From the week of my arrival in Oxford in 1970, I became an avid reader of *The Oxford Times*. At that time, I was probably not aware of just how exceptional Oxfordshire's county newspaper is.

It was not just that I loved newspapers but was addicted to the printed word, and had been ever since I joined my local library, aged seven.

By 1998, I was inclined to think that if you read, you can also write. So Tim may have been surprised by my response. "I'll do it for you," I said.

The result of that impetuous promise is that every month, since August 1998, I have been privileged to write the antiques pages of the award-winning *Oxfordshire Limited Edition* magazine.

For the first two years I wrote a potpourri of features but decided that the best way to avoid repetition was to write a series.

My first series was *The Antiques Time Machine.* Starting with Gothic and moving through time, I looked at the way homes were furnished, in the broadest sense, and discovered what is available to buy from each period until eventually reaching the present. At that moment in 2002, I asked specialists to suggest what will be the antiques of the future. Art Glass was not a surprise but the just invented iPod did give me a jolt.

My next series was *Ask the Experts,* for which I interviewed specialists in everything from costume jewellery to fine art.

When handling antiques I always wondered who owned them and what kind of lives they lived. What drew me to appreciate antiques has nothing to do with their monetary value. Frankly, knowing what something is worth bores me.

I love history, art, design and storytelling and it seemed to me that they are all present in the world of antiques. Surely, I thought, every antique comes with a story?

That idea led to my next series, *Every Antique tells a Story.* This was 2007— well before Neil McGregor's wonderful *History of the World in a Hundred Objects* broadcast on the BBC.

In 2010, Dr McGregor had the benefit of the contents of the British Museum but I simply asked our readers to send me stories of their antiques. They were not as erudite as Neil's Radio 4 series but were fun.

For example, Dr Geoff Smaldon contacted me with the story of his collection of apple scoops. It turned out to reflect an aspect of social history we may wish to ignore — before modern dentistry and oral hygiene, people lost their teeth and could not eat apples unless they were shaved into soft little strips — hence the origin of apple scoops.

The problem for me was that many of the stories from readers needed supplementing to fill at least two pages so I wondered where to go next for inspiration. Like many readers

10

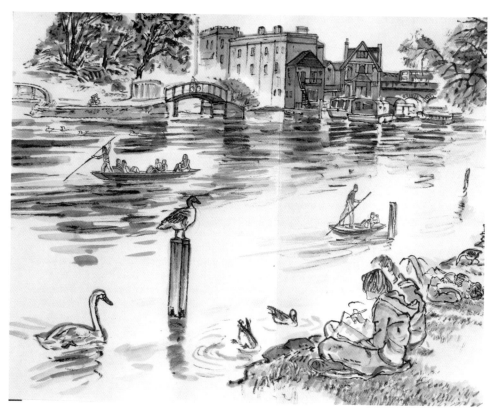

of *The Oxford Times*, I have enjoyed listening to Radio 4's long-running programme, *Desert Island Discs*.

I felt that the castaway's choice of luxury and book were more revealing than their choice of music. Eureka!

What if I asked castaways which antique, work of art or book they would like with them if marooned on a desert island? The formula could be similar to *Desert Island Discs* in that they can suggest various items but in the end choose one of them. And so, in January 2008, the castaway series began.

My choice of first castaway was not difficult. In Oxford we are privileged to have what is probably the world's first public museum, the Ashmolean.

Its energetic Director, Dr Christopher Brown, came to Oxford in 1998. In those days, the museum appeared closed to the public behind its huge blue front doors and you entered into a rather dark space.

Christopher had a vision of opening up the museum to the community, local, national and international — and amazingly he has achieved that ambition. When I interviewed him, the extensions to the rear of the museum

had been demolished and work on building the wonderful new Ashmolean was in progress.

The Ashmolean began life in Broad Street in the building that is now home to The Museum of The History of Science.

The original Tradescant collection included Powhatan's cloak, brought from Virginia in 1638. It is embroidered with delicate little shells and Christopher pointed out that a lot were missing. although the cloak had arrived in Oxford in perfect condition. The curators of the Ashmolean had nailed the cloak to to the wall of the museum — and visitors had helped themselves to shells as souvenirs!

A certain visiting German academician was horrified that not only the local farmers and tradesmen visited the museum on market days but even *women* were allowed in!

The Ashmolean although part of the University has always represented an overlap of town and gown. I hoped our castaway series could do the same.

Another area where town and gown overlap is continuing education. Reflecting that among the castaways are lecturers employed in that department and Sir Christopher Ball, a former

Master of Keeble College, who as a devotee of lifelong learning, was a founder of Kellogg College.

Gown is no longer just those colleges in the centre of Oxford but up the hill in Headington where the first female vice-chancellor of Oxford Brookes, Janet Beer, and its present chancellor, Shami Chakrabarti, both agreed to be castaway.

An organisation where the town overlaps with gown is The Oxford Preservation Trust, so the feisty Deborah Dance, who is its director, joined the castaways on the island.

The series has been a success and, in February 2012, the 50th castaway — Oxford MP Andrew Smith — was marooned on our island, taking his garden tools with him.

Since we were flexible in our interpretation of antique, some intriguing items have been chosen for the island. Within six months, the emphasis changed from the objects to the castaways themselves and the series has continued to evolve.

The castaway has also been able to choose the location for the photoshoot within Oxfordshire. That too has shown how lucky we are to live in this city and county.

I asked Tim Metcalfe, the editor of *Oxfordshire Limited Edition* whether he thought we could reproduce the features in a book and the rest — as they say — is history.

How to live a good life is one of those big philosophical questions but I hope that you can make some interesting reflections based on the journeys of these fascinating men and women to the desert island.

There are stories among them to inspire young people about to choose a career, and others, in midlife who maybe want a change of direction. For those about to retire, the dramatic new directions some castaways have taken after the age of 60 are motivating.

These are all positive and often surprising stories and I hope you enjoy reading them.

Ilustrations by Weimin He

Dr Christopher Brown

Director of the Ashmolean Museum, Oxford

The obvious place to begin the series was in the world's first public museum, a place second only to the British Museum in the range and depth of its collections. That place is, of course, The Ashmolean Museum, right here in Oxford.

Someone who appreciated the richness of the Oxford collections and realised that many of the treasures of the Ashmolean were poorly displayed is the current director, Dr Christopher Brown.

His dream of making the Ashmolean fit for pourpose for the 21st century came to fruition in November, 2009, when the new building, designed by architect Rick Mather, opened its doors to the to the public.

During the refurbishment of the building, half-a-million objects were put into storage. We asked Dr Brown to select just one item to take with him to our desert island. He gave the question a great deal of thought.

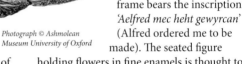

Photograph © Ashmolean Museum University of Oxford

"The museum owns wonderful collections of drawings by Raphael and Michelangelo. There is a fine one by Rembrandt of his father, but I decided to choose from one of the 244 items selected from all the departments for inclusion in our 'Treasures' Gallery," he said, explaining that this gallery was set up to showcase the museum's collections while the museum redevelopment was taking place.

Dr Brown added: "I was tempted by the elegant Turkish dish c1530-50 which has the particularly beautiful colour combinations of Isnik pottery. Fitting the pattern to the awkward shape was masterful. The Gulbenkian Museum in Lisbon has a fine collection of Middle Eastern artefacts including exquisite Mosque lamps.

"A recent visit there made me re- examine one of ours, the 14th century lamp from Cairo made for the Mamluk Sultan of Eqypt, Muhammad Ibn Qala'un, which was purchased with the help of the Friends of the Ashmolean. I admire it as an aesthetic object for the delicacy of the enamelling on glass. It is a sophisticated bronze of the Roman god of the home, Lar. Looking at the vigour of

the movement and the folds of his tunic, it is easy to see why there was debate between the so called 'Ancients and Moderns' during the Renaissance. They argued passionately about whether it was possible to surpass the achievements of the classical period.'

'In the end I will reluctantly leave all three behind and choose instead a piece that comes from close to home – the Alfred Jewel.'

Alfred was born in the village of Wanating, now Wantage. He was the youngest son of King Æthelwulf of Wessex, by his first wife, Osburga. Alfred is noted for his defence of the Anglo-Saxon kingdoms of southern England against the Vikings, becoming the only English monarch still to be accorded the epithet 'the Great'. Alfred was a learned man who encouraged education in his kingdom.

The Alfred Jewel's gold frame bears the inscription *'Aelfred mec heht gewyrcan'* (Alfred ordered me to be made). The seated figure holding flowers in fine enamels is thought to represent the sense of sight.

Dr Brown said: "The sense of sight is an allusion to its purpose as a pointer. The jewel is actually a handle of an 'aestral' for following the text of a manuscript.

"Alfred is famous for his love of learning and the Anglo Saxon Chronicles. This beautiful piece is from what is conventionally known as the 'The Dark Ages'. The device may have saved illuminated manuscripts from the greasy fingers, but we are probably rash to dismiss the period in that way.

"This jewel alone raises questions. It was found in 1693 at Newton Park in Somerset, an area associated with Alfred. It was bequeathed to the Ashmolean by Nathaniel Palmer in 1718 and was a very early exhibit," Dr Brown added.

"On a desert island, it would transport me back to England, to Oxford and the Ashmolean in particular. It evokes memories of my family, too. I remember showing it to my children. My wife is curator of 19th and 20th century literary manuscripts at the British Library. The jewel's use in reading would make me feel close to her as well."

Dr Christopher Brown was educated at Merchant Taylors' School and St Catherine's College Oxford (BA Hons in Modern History) 1969

His PhD at the Courtauld Institute of Art in 1986 was 'Carel Fabritius and other studies in 17th century Dutch painting.'

He was appointed assistant keeper with responsibilities for 17th-century Dutch and Flemish paintings at the National Gallery in 1971 and chief curator in 1989. He becaame director of the Ashmolean Museum in June 1998.

He was elected as a fellow of Worcester College in 1998 and became Visiting Professor, University of Amsterdam in 2002-3. He is also a trustee of the River and Rowing Museum at Henley-on-Thames .

He was invested as a Commander in the Order of Orange-Nassau by the Ambassador of the Netherlands in 2002.

Dr Brown has written extensively on Dutch and Flemish paintings of the 16th and 17th centuries. His books include: *Carel Fabritius:Van Dyck :Rubens'Landscapes:Rembrant :The Master and his Workshop*.

He has also somehow found time to publish more than 40 articles in respected journals and has lectured at museums and galleries around the world.

Dr Jim Bennett
Director, Museum of the History of Science

When the Ashmolean moved to its present site in Beaumont Street, its original building in Broad Street became home to the Museum of the History of Science.

It holds the world's finest collection of Mediaeval and Renaissance scientific objects. Sometimes we don't properly appreciate what we have on our doorstep.

Dr Jim Bennett's task when coming here, from Cambridge, was to find a balance between its academic functions and its role as a public museum.

He has succeeded in using the research to enrich what the MHS offers the public. He has mounted a succession of successful exhibitions, including ones on Hooke, Einstein and Marconi. There are family friendly activities and public lectures.

Dr Bennett grew up in Belfast and went to school there but developed an odd notion, as it seemed to his friends, of going to university in England. After a BA and PhD in Cambridge, where he discovered the history of science, he was a lecturer in Aberdeen and an archivist in London before finding his love of museum work as Curator of Astronomy at Greenwich, looking after the Royal Observatory and its wonderful collection of instruments and clocks.

From there it was back to Cambridge, where there is also a museum of the history of science, and to Broad Street and the Old Ashmolean in 1994.

Out of all the fascinating exhibits in the museum, I wondered which he would choose to take on our desert island. Dr Bennett said,

"There are a number of famous objects that are very tempting. We have the only spherical astrolabe in the world. It is Islamic, beautiful and unusual but it was essentially a bad idea.

"The reason there is only one is because it was a failure and it is unlikely that many more were made. The astrolabes that succeed are flat like maps.

One of the most famous is here. It was presented to Elizabeth I by its maker Thomas Gemini. He was a shrewd businessman because Gemini was not his real name. England under Elizabeth I had ambitions to become a world power but our knowledge of mathematics was poor," Dr Bennett added.

"That knowledge was brought here by immigrants like Thomas, who came from the Netherlands. He set up shop in London and since no one could pronounce his name correctly and he made scientific instruments including astrolabes he called himself Gemini."

Jim smiled as he showed me another famous exhibit — the large elaborate silver microscope made by George Adams for George III.

"This celebrated item is superb, but also absurdly over the top," he said.

Then he delved into the back of a cabinet and pulled out a not impressive looking wooden 'mat' about four inches by six inches.

"I shall leave all the famous items behind and chose one of the most obscure," Jim said. "I shall take this wooden Horary Quadrant. It will be very practical on the desert island because as long as I know the date and the latitude I can use it to tell the time anywhere in the world.

"Portable sundials of many kinds remained in use until the invention of the radio. A watch can tell the time but cannot find the time and there was a need to find the time in order to set a watch."

This piece of advanced technology was made in 1558 and Jim said

"It is particularly special for me because I researched its origins myself. I shall be able to recall that journey. It is part of the collection of Louis Evans which founded the museum and he purchased it in a shop in Paris.

"It is rare, not because it was rare at the time but because it has survived although made of wood.

"The ones made with metal were treasured and preserved, most humble wooden sundials perished. One side finds the time in Italian hours and so this was the first clue to its origin. In Latin it is inscribed Miniato Pitti of Florence made this," Dr Bennet said.

"I traced him to the monastery of San Miato al Monte in charge of the Olivetan order. I visited the monastery in Florence where he had been Abbot and so they still knew about him. They told me he was a nobleman related to the family who owned the Pitti Palace and was close to Cosimo I de' Medici, the Grand Duke of Tuscany.

"Powerful men often had their names on pieces but did not actually make them. In this case, according to contemporary records, Miniato enjoyed engraving them with his own hands. In this example he made a small error.

"On one side in Roman numerals he carved MDLVIII but on the reverse he missed out the V and scratched it in above when he noticed his error," Dr Bennett revealed.

Miniato Pitti was obviously a renaissance man because his interest was in both the arts and sciences. He arranged the map room in the Palazzo Vecchio and befriended Giorgio Vasari helping him find a publisher for *The Lives of the Artists*.

Dr Bennett said "His letters to Vasari mention conversations with Michelangelo. So as I hold this quadrant I am not only in touch with the man who engraved and coloured it but also with the great renaissance artist and writer.

"I can imagine him, his life and the people he met and maybe wonder how it ended up in the shop in Paris. There is plenty to hold my interest for it is both technically challenging and aesthetically pleasing."

Bill Heine

Broadcaster and author

Bill Heine's life journey brought him from the plains of Illinois to the hub of power in Washington DC. He marched with Martin Luther King, worked in the home of Robert Kennedy and spent three years in the Peace Corps in Nicaragua and Peru. He studied law at Balliol and built a media career in Oxford.

Bill was quite keen to become a castaway on our desert island. He said:"I love sand and sea and would enjoy being on a desert island away from TV, radio, microphones and clocks.

"I grew up in a small town. Batavia, Illinois was a place where you knew everybody and the Chief of Police relaxed doing crochet work.

"It gave me a childhood of wonderful freedom but could be claustrophobic. I would sometimes escape up a tree and read Shakespeare. So, I think I would be all right on my own for a while, but I would like my object to root me in a time and place," he said.

"My choice must enhance the time I spend on the island. I want something a little quirky and unexpected. If it is washed up on the beach, it must be indestructible.

"My first thought was to have something that would link me to my life in Oxford. One thing that will capture a time and a place is the shark in my roof. The shark dominated a significant part of my life before Michael Heseltine, gave it the green light to remain." Bill said.

"The council, when battling with me for six years suggested I put it in a swimming pool. On the island, it could float in the water like Damien Hirst's shark floats in formaldehyde, but that is not the point of it. The house and shark cannot be separated. They came together at the time of the US bombing of Libya. But do I really want a shark on a desert island . . . coals to Newcastle comes to mind."

As well as the shark, the Oxfordshire artist, John Buckley (*pictured with Bill*) created other memorable images in Bill's life. He created the Can-Can legs for the 'Not the Moulin Rouge' cinema in Headington, and the Al Jolson hands for The Penultimate Picture Palace on the Cowley Road. So it was not surprising when Bill decided he would like to take a piece by Buckley to the desert island.

Bill said: "I admire his 'Atlas'. The naked man has a bath in place of his head. It represents the height of domesticity.

"We carry all of this junk around literally and in our heads to make our lives and our families' lives seem real but it is his nakedness that is real.

"I love its quirkiness. It is also a fountain. The bath fills up with water which keeps running over and leaking out. The drops would feed my fantasy on the island."

"But as I can have only one piece, I have decided to take John's sculpture entitled *The Embrace*. It is a monumental but intimate piece.

"Are these two people caught or are they choosing to be there bound inseparably together? Do they want to be bound or do they want the opportunity to break free? It has love, hate but also vulnerability because they are caught up in an embrace. It is about protection and yet it is also a little claustrophobic Do they want to cut the bandages that bind them?"

Bill's enthusiasm for the island has limits.

"I would enjoy life on the desert island for a while," he said. "But I would also think about escaping. *Embrace* is about the hope of escaping and also the contentment of being where you are. The tension might connect with my life as a castaway.

"Conversations play a large part in my life and work and looking at it would remind me of some long conversations with John. We imagined this sculpture on top of the Berlin Wall, an arid, frightening and disturbing place with nothing natural and green. Mounted on top of the wall, it would represent the people of the two halves of Germany, the love between them and yet the lack of freedom the wall represented."

Postscript
Since this feature was printed in 2008, Bill has published two books, Heinstein of the Airwaves-about his Radio Oxford years and Hunting the Shark about its creation and battle for survival. Embrace never made it to the Berlin Wall as it came tumbling down in 1989. I suggested to John Buckley that there is a wall, much closer, that would be equally appropriate-The Belfast Wall. Imagine how delighted I felt when John and Bill contacted the Mayor of Belfast!
Film-maker Philip Hind has made a documentary called The Ultimate Survivor (2011) about the history of the Penultimate Picture Palace, featuring Bill and John as well as Ian Hislop and writer Brian Aldiss.

BILL Heine grew up in Batavia, Illinois, corn-belt country in the Mid-West of the United States. At the entrance to the town was a sign 'No steel wheels or lugs'. He has never seen either, but that sign has fired his imagination ever since.

In 1963, he left for Georgetown University in Washington D.C where he worked as an intern for Senator Paul Douglas, a Professor from the University of Illinois.

He spent a short time in the home of Robert Kennedy at Hickory Hill, Virginia, helping with social functions including everything, from setting up the piano for Roberta Flack, to lifeguarding at the family swimming pool, before becoming involved in the War on Poverty Campaign. In 1965, Bill took part in the Civil Rights march from Selma to Montgomery, Alabama, where one of the marchers was murdered. Bill came to Oxford in 1967 to study law at Balliol College but his studies were interrupted by the United States government inviting him to join the Vietnam War effort. He opted, instead, to join The Peace Corps and was sent to Nicaragua at the height of the Somoza dictatorship.

Disillusioned, he resigned and wrote a report which resulted in him being interviewed for a week in Washington "to see whether or not I was a subversive element in this august institution" Bill explained. Once they decided he was a straight talking guy he was transferred to Peru where he worked in a communal hacienda before returning to Balliol to complete his degree.

He remained in Oxford, opening two art-house cinemas, The Penultimate Picture Palace and Not the Moulin Rouge. Bill has left his mark on the landscape of Oxford with John Buckley's is the shark sculpture protruding from the roof of his house in Headington.

The six year dispute with Oxford City Council which followed its erection by sculptor John Buckley, in 1986, was eventually resolved by the then Environment Secretary, Michael Heseltine, whose verdict was that it should stay.

The shark rapidly became a tourist attraction and has recently been renovated.

Professor Janet Beer
Vice-chancellor, Oxford Brookes University

Professor Janet Beer is Oxford Brookes University's first female vice-chancellor. Her answer to my question 'If you were shipwrecked on a desert island which antique or work of art would you like to find washed up on the beach?' revealed a major influence on her life.

Professor Beer explained: "As a scholar of late-19th/early-20th century American literature and culture, and having a particular obsession with the life and work of Edith Wharton, I have always felt powerfully drawn to the painting of John Singer Sargent and in particular his portraits.

"So many of his subjects had a relationship with Edith Wharton, either they were her friends and acquaintances, or she knew about their lives and transformed the spirit — if not the letter — of those lives into her fiction," she said.

"One of my particular favourites, a strong contender for the desert island slot, is Sargent's 1913 portrait of Henry James, held in the National Portrait Gallery in London.

"Edith Wharton's relationship with Henry James was central to her sense of herself as an artist, living the life she wanted to lead, among people who inspired her. When James died she wrote in a letter that '*His friendship has been the pride & honour of my life*.'

Another friend of Edith Wharton painted by Sargent is Theodore Roosevelt, then president of the United States of America.

Professor Beer said: "The portrait, painted in 1903, hangs in the White House in Washington DC. Edith and the president were regular correspondents, he greeted her with the words: "*Well, I am glad to welcome to the White House some one to whom I can quote 'the Hunting of the Snark' without being asked what I mean!*"

"The portrait catches the big-stick carrying man of action at the turn of the staircase, ready to go — up or down — and clearly intolerant of the usual poses of the sitter.

"Wharton said of him: 'he was so alive at all points, and so gifted with the rare faculty of living intensely and entirely in every moment as it passed'. Something of this energy is communicated in the painting, but the energy seems to derive from his impatience," Professor Beer added.

"My final choice has to be *The Duke of Marlborough Family*' held locally at Blenheim Palace and, for me as a Wharton scholar, almost over-burdened with significance.

"In *The House of Mirth* (1905) Wharton has her heroine, Lily Bart, take part in a *tableaux vivants* in which she dresses as Mrs Lloyd by Joshua Reynolds," Professor Beer explained.

"In Reynolds' painting, Mrs Lloyd, inscribing her husband's initials in the bark of a tree in a carefully composed pastoral setting, is showered with light, a light which foregrounds her womanliness as she poses clad in clinging Grecian folds.

"Wharton used the moment at which Lily is revealed in this pose as the turning point in her heroine's life. She becomes what she seems to be — a woman whose display of self has breached the code which decrees that women and their portraits must have a sponsor, if not a master.

"Painted to update the family story from the Reynolds portrait of the 4th Duke of Marlborough and his family, Sargent's *The Duke of Marlborough Family*' positions the sponsor of the portrait interestingly to the side and lower than his wife, the American heiress, Consuelo Vanderbilt, elements of whose story Wharton was to dramatise in her final, unfinished novel, *The Buccaneers* (1938).

"Their marriage, one which brought to the British landed aristocracy a substantial infusion of American wealth and beauty, was publicly acknowledged to be unhappy and it ended in divorce," Professor Beer said.

"Interestingly, in her own autobiography, *The Glitter and the Gold* (1973) Consuelo commented on Edith Wharton's marriage: *'her husband seemed more of an equerry than an equal, walking behind her and carrying whatever paraphernalia she happened to discard. Indeed Edward Wharton could not hope to do more than fetch and carry for a personality so far removed from his orbit.'*

"This is an accurate picture of the disastrously ill-suited Whartons — who were especially incompatible intellectually and divorced in 1913," Professor Beer said.

"They did have one passion in common, small dogs, dogs very much like those which sit and stand in the Marlborough family portrait and which feature in numerous pictures of the Whartons.

Professor Beer believes that themes that pervade Wharton's life and work can be drawn from this painting, its painter and its subjects.

She explained: "Born into the leisured classes Wharton tried all her life to find an alternative world — the 'land of letters' where she could be happy; she knew what it was to be pressured by a domineering mother into a suitably prestigious marriage, she knew what it was to be disappointed and unhappy in that marriage.

"Like Consuelo and Sargent, she lived in Europe for most of her adult life by choice, and all three moved in some of the same circles.

"As with Sargent and Henry James, Wharton's subjects moved in a transatlantic world, they crossed and re-crossed the Atlantic and were heirs to some of the most seismic shifts in the structure of women's lives — the new possibility of divorce being simply the most obvious. On my desert island, the portrait could summon up so many different strands of Edith Wharton's life and add to it some of my own — most importantly my move to Oxford, coming into proximity with so many wonderful houses and gardens, not least Headington Hill Hall.

"Shortly after moving to Oxford, I had a birthday and spent that day, with my husband and children, at Blenheim Palace. The painting would remind me of my family on that glorious sunny day."

Korky Paul
Illustrator

Hamish Vigne Christie Paul-better known to his many fans as Korky was born in Harare, Zimbabwe in 1951 one of seven children. At an early age he was reading comic books and in his words, 'scribbling cartoons'. Nowadays, his scribbles bring smiles to the faces of children, thanks to the world of fantasy evoked by his unforgettable illustrations.

Korky's scribbling led him to art school in Durban and from there to Greece. He also spent time in California before ending up in this city of dreaming spires.

Korky's first children's book was a pop-up called *The Crocodile and the Dumper Truck* published in 1980, with paper engineering by Ray Marshall.

In 1986, Korky Paul met the editor Ron Heapy, at Oxford University Press, who commissioned him to illustrate *Winnie the Witch*. It won the Children's Book Award in 1987 and has been published in more than 10 languages and sold more than three million copies worldwide.

So, from his experiences in three continents what would he choose in answer to my question: "If you were shipwrecked on a desert island which antique, work of art or antiquarian book, would you like to be washed up on the beach and why?

"As a child I was wild about American comics by Stan 'the Man' Lee; Marvel, *Spiderman* and *Batman*. I loved the illustrations and they inspired me to draw," Korky said.

"My mother encouraged me to read but she was happy whether it was comics or books as long as I read. I was half in love with all things American. I guess 'Coke' is an American icon and I have collected coke bottles. The most unusual one was bought as an airport road souvenir in Tanzania and is carved from ebony.

Korky also revealed that his grandmother had a big influence on him and gave him her water colours, brushes and her famous '303' drawing nibs.

He said: "As she did not own a camera, she sketched her children, the farm and the bushmen of the Kalahari.

"Wherever we go, my wife and I look for interesting rocks and stones. Susan (who is also an artist. She paints under the name Susan Moxley) turns some into jewellery and I wear one around my neck so I guess that would be with me anyway. I could spend time searching for new ones on the desert island so I think I will leave my quirky collections behind."

Free to explore the bush, Korky described his childhood in Africa which imbued him with energy and zest for life.

"I enjoyed a wild and privileged childhood in the African Bushveldt," Korky said.

"My father bought a two-tone Chevrolet Impala. The body was grey but the roof, bonnet, bumper and wheel hubs were white and the leather upholstery was red. I was fascinated by the indicators which winked like eyes.

"My mother hated it because it was so flash but it was my father's pride and joy. I found a die-cast model of it in the Summertown Oxfam Shop and I am tempted to take that," Korky said.

It evokes memories of happy times and some amusing ones. Lots of us piled in it to go to the swimming galas, but it did rather rock-n-roll which meant one boy could not come with us because it made him travel sick."

"On a visit to South Africa, Susan bought me a present of a model of a sewing machine made from old wire. It reminds me of the Shona people who were gifted at recycling waste material.

"I also have a handmade Heath Robinson construction barbeque I would love on the

island but it is rather heavy. It is made from a recycled water tank so has unique features. I could even use my favourite Jamie Oliver frying pan on it because I love to cook. I don't think that is quite what you have in mind so I could take a painting by Susan."

"But, since I can only take one thing, I think it has to be a children's illustrated book because they loom so large in my life. There is one that caught my imagination as a child and has inspired me ever since. It is *Struwelpeter* by Dr Heinrich Hoffman.

"It was first published in English, in 1848, and called *Shock-headed Peter*. Every fortnight my mother took me to the library and it is a habit I have never lost," Korky said.

"I was amazed by this book and its illustrations and borrowed it many times. It is anything but politically correct. As you can see from this extract, it is really quite gruesome."

'The door flew open and in he ran
The great, red- legged scissor-man
Oh children see the tailors come
And caught out little suck-a –thumb.
Snip! Snip! Snip! The scissors go
And Conrad cries out –Oh! Oh! Oh!
Snip Snap Snip! They go so fast,
That both his thumbs are off at last.

"On another page, three yobbos who taunt a black boy get dunked in a large inkwell. Growing up in Southern Africa I knew about racism. I read this book so many times, I was given a brightly coloured 1930s edition as a present.

"Nowadays, I teach illustration at Cheney School on Tuesdays. One evening I noticed a damaged 19th-century version in a box of books given to the school for sale or use. I asked if I could buy it.

"The colours in this one are more pastel and the paper finer. This is the version I want to take to the desert island. I would never get bored with it.

"And I could grumble to myself about the crazy restrictions in children's publishing today I can't remember being tempted to cut off any thumbs because I read *Struwwelpeter*. So I will be able to let off lots of emotions, evoke memories and marvel at the pictures."

Postscript
When Kennington library was threatened with closure, I recalled Korky's passion for libraries and invited him to lead our 300 yard Pied Piper Procession to deliver 600 letters and 100 children's posters to the leader of Oxfordshire County Council. He accepted and you can see him on savekenningtonlibrary.blogspot.com

Sir Peter Moores

Founder, Compton Verney Gallery

Sir Peter Moores was born in Lancashire, in 1932, and will always be associated with the city of Liverpool because of his father's business, Littlewoods. But he has strong and enduring links with Oxford.

He read Italian and German at Christ Church and later, believing that it was crucial to provide business teaching at undergraduate level, his foundation's donation, in 1991, to Oxford's School of Management Studies which paved the way for the development of the Said Business School.

Here the post of the Peter Moores Dean, and the Peter Moores Professorship of Management Studies are testament to his vision. Another far-sighted initiative resulted in a new post at the Business School, the Peter Moores Lectureship in Chinese Business Studies. It is a word not used much nowadays but Sir Peter is a philanthropist in the tradition of Carnegie and Rowntree. It was another of his charitable initiatives that prompted my invitation to Sir Peter to be our castaway.

Just north of Banbury, he created an art gallery of which any city would be proud. That place is Compton Verney and it opened its doors to the public in 2004. Only Sir Peter would have the vision and courage to house major international art collections in a gallery apparently in the middle of nowhere but actually just 90 minutes' drive from half the population of England.

The possibility of the roof of the Grade I listed 18th century mansion collapsing was actually an advantage when he sought

planning permission to build a state of the art display area within the grade one listed exterior walls. I wondered what would inform his choice: of objects for the island his love of Italy, of opera or art?

"I first discovered the visual arts as a wide-eyed teenager in Cologne, so I want Compton Verney to be for art virgins like I was then — something to stumble on and be inspired by," Sir Peter explained.

"After that initial exposure, I spent years learning to look and gained an eye for medieval sculpture and painting.

"I had grown up with my dad's cupboard full of operas on old gramophone records and I wanted to see them performed. So after Oxford, I worked as a production assistant with the Vienna State Opera. When on tour in Italy, I saw the work of Neapolitan artists of the Golden Age and loved them."

"I receive advice on acquisitions for Compton Verney but they are influenced by the emotions I have experienced when encountering art. The reason there are no labels next to our pictures is because I don't want the experience to be verbal. Visitors don't have to like what they see but I want them to be relaxed, look and see and then make up their own minds. We hope our leaflets from each room will be taken home to reinforce people's personal experience."

"Assembling the collection has been a physical and mental journey across continents so it is hard to choose one piece. For sheer beauty I would take the Tilman Riemenschneider Limewood carving of a Female Saint (1460). Another possibility is Lucas Cranach's *Lot and his Daughters* because it would remind me of that moment in Germany which started me on the road to Compton Verney," Sir Peter said.

"My life was enriched by Italy and Naples in particular, the home of my late wife. I saw Italy rather like travellers on the Grand Tour who brought back pictures like Gaspar Van Wittel's *Prospect of Naples.*

"But the painting that reminds me most of a city I love, where you can go into a café anywhere and be assured of good food, is the *View of Naples from the West with Peasants Gaming* by Pietro Fabris (c1765).

"It shows Vesuvius had two summits before one disappeared in a large eruption, but you also see the people enjoying a meal and each other's company. On a desert island, it would probably have me salivating for the good food I would be missing in Italy and here in Compton Verney.

"In 1984 in Boston, Massachusetts, I visited the Arthur M Sackler Museum at Harvard University where they had four or five superb Chinese bronzes on display.

"The bronzes knocked me sideways. They were so ancient and yet so powerful. I returned to England and in the British Museum met Jessica Rawson, former warden of Merton College. At that time she was curator of Eastern Art so I discussed with her what I had seen.

"She encouraged me in my choices for the China Gallery. We bought the bronzes within a relatively short period of time but I am told that alongside the British Museum it is one of the three best collections in Europe.

"There are two that particularly appeal to me: a ritual wine vessel and cover from the Shang Dynasty-Anyang phase, 12th century BC that I call the dodo because of its wonderful beak-like head. It is actually a bottle-horn dragon's head.

"The other bird which drew my attention came up for sale by auction in New York. An owl's head is depicted on three sides of the late Shang Dynasty ritual wine vessel or fangyi, (1500-1050 BC). Although more than 3,000 years-old, it is a sophisticated work of art.

Above, *View of Naples from the West with Peasants Gaming* by Pietro Fabris (c1765)

"Americans were livid when we bought it," Sir Peter recalled. "They were not happy to see it leave the country. There is something monumental in the body but its saucer like beady eyes look knowingly at you from 1,000 years before Christ.

"I think that is the piece I would want on the desert island. You may have to arrange for it to be washed up in an airtight container because bronzes corrode in sea air!"

John Ballam

Author and director of the Undergraduate Diploma in Creative Writing

Think of the low-budget horror movie *The Blair Witch Project* and you will have an idea what John Ballam's birthplace looks like. The film was made in the woods near his family farm in the quaintly-named village of Harmony in Maryland, USA.

Born in 1963 in Frederick, Maryland, John lived in Harmony (near Myersville) until 1988 when, at the age of 25, he moved to England.

He graduated from York University with First Honours and then read for his PhD at the University of Bristol.

He has taught at various UK universities since 1994 and held various posts at the University of Oxford since 2004, including visiting Fellow at Harris Manchester College; Chair of Examiners in Creative Writing and Departmental Lecturer in Creative Writing. He was appointed director of the Undergraduate Diploma in Creative Writing in 2008.

Dirk Bogarde described J.D. Ballam's autobiography *The Road to Harmony* as "a book to cherish", and Joanna Trollope likened it to *Cider with Rosie* and *Angela's Ashes*.

His latest book, a novel entitled *The Toymaker,* is set near his birthplace in the Appalachian mountains. It is a story of "witchcraft, murder and Blue Ridge Mountain magic".

John's grandfather was a British Army boxing champion who put down roots in the Appalachian mountains. His grandson made the reverse journey and is now a British subject and director of the Undergraduate Diploma in Creative Writing in the University of Oxford's Department for Continuing Education.

John said: "I am fascinated by the ways they connect us to people who lived very different lives long ago."

So I wondered which side of the Atlantic would evoke the response to the question.

"If you were shipwrecked on a desert island which antique, work of art or antiquarian book would you like to be washed up on the beach?'

Would he be inspired by his life among the dreaming spires, or the setting of his books *The Road to Harmony* and the recently released *Toymaker*, both set in the Appalachians?

"My first thoughts were that I would like something practical on this desert island, John said. "I grew up living with and using antiques. Our iron frying pan was cast from iron ore dug by hand out of the mountain under our home.

"Tools forged and carved by my family were still in use. Parts of old machinery were remodelled and reused. Maybe I should take one of those?

"Still, although antique tools might be useful, they would not enrich my life," he added.

"My next idea was something diverting and nostalgic. My family had an enormous Philco radio, as big as an armchair. It made sitting around and listening to it a family event. We also had a giant phonograph on which we played 78 rpm records by Elvis Presley and Hank Williams.

"In the 1940s, my grandfather built a television set. No one in Harmony had even seen one before. It had a 12-inch screen and the community gathered around to watch programmes that connected us with a world beyond our valley.

"But there won't be electricity on this island, and while they will remind me of former times, they would stimulate ideas of escape. So instead, I have decided to go for a small cardboard box.

"The contents came with me from Harmony and all of them were found on our farm. Some may be 250 years old, others may be thousands of years old. They are stone arrowheads. I think they are aesthetically pleasing and each is as different as its maker.

"Before the coming of the Europeans, our farm was part of the nomadic life of one of the Six Nations, the Tuscarora. Like the Mohicans, they were driven out by the middle of the 18th century and are now almost a vanished people.

"I have a clear picture in my mind of why the arrowheads were found in the valley because my family hunted deer in the same place.

"At the same time each year the deer behave in a similar way, coming down the mountainside and along the valley where the Tuscarora braves would have been waiting, ready to shoot their arrows.

"Handling them has always been a marvellous mystery, connecting my experiences to the earth I once farmed and the place of my childhood memories.

"With them on the desert island I would feel that I had not completely lost contact with the past.

"I enjoy having and using antiques and I am intrigued by the materials being used — especially to the ways they connect us to people who lived very different lives long ago.

"I suppose, going back to my first thoughts, the arrow heads could also be practical: I could use them to hunt. In some respects, life in Harmony included the aspiration of self-sufficiency. Old timers used to boast that if they had 20 dollars in November, they could survive until March.

"Perhaps, life on a desert island might not be very different from life in Harmony, where we hunted for mushrooms, berries, nuts and fruit; where hunting, fishing and cooking in the outdoors during the summer were all normal. The main difference would be that I would have to imagine so many people who gave my old life its shape and its rhythm."

John Forster
Archivist to the Duke of Marlborough

John Forster may have retired as head of the Blenheim Palace education service but he has not retired from Blenheim. He is now archivist to the Duke of Marlborough, but I sensed that he loves storytelling and enthusing children of any age.

Maybe that is not surprising because for much of his life John was a teacher and a headmaster of a grammar school before taking up his post at the palace.

When we shipwreck John on our desert island, what tales of Blenheim and the Marlboroughs and which of John's personal memories will come with his choice of objects and art?

He took me first to the Long Library and pointed to the largest thing any of my castaways has considered and said

"There may be problems transporting this to the island. The Willis organ, built in 1891, and the largest musical instrument of its kind in the country needs to be played regularly and it has been my pleasure to do just that. As Head of Education, I ran Victorian themed tours of Blenheim. In my preparation pack for schools, I suggested the children learn the musical hall song *Daisy Daisy* prior to their visit. In front of this beautiful organ, I talked to them about home entertainment and played the song at full volume. So, playing the Willis organ on my desert island, I can picture fifty children singing and swaying with surprised but pleased adult visitors joining in. Arthur Sullivan played *The Lost Chord* at the inaugural concert and was the first of many distinguished organists to have filled the palace with sound.

"One recital I shall never forget, I watched with seventy cathedral organists on a short break from a conference in Oxford. They chose a brilliant virtuoso, David Briggs, to perform for them. He did something very challenging on an instrument of this size and complexity, he extemporised, to the admiration of all of us. I could not be bored playing it on the desert island but the problem is likely to be powering it. Nowadays it runs on electricity although originally it was powered by water so there would need to be a hill and a fast flowing river on the island. Maybe, I should consider taking something smaller?

"If I were to choose one picture it would

be the 'Mantilla Portrait' of Sarah, the first Duchess of Marlborough. It was painted by Charles Jervas soon after the death of her younger son, Charles in 1692. Sarah was a 21st-century figure born in 1660 when women were regarded as chattels of their husbands," John said.

"Researching the history of Blenheim, I came to admire the feisty women connected with its history but among them all, the power of Sarah's personality dominates. Without her determination, it is unlikely the palace would have been completed.

"She and John's marriage was one of opposites attracting," John explained. "He was a courtier while she was reputed to have a fiendish temper. On one occasion when they disagreed, Sarah became angrier and angrier but John calmer and calmer until in a fury of frustration she took her sewing scissors and

Photograph: Richard Cragg by kind permission of Blenheim Palace

cut her hair. After his death, those locks were discovered in a secret drawer in his desk!

"She was beautiful, capable and mean. Despite the restrictions on women, through her own acumen she became the richest woman in Europe," John added.

"She shrewdly left most of her wealth to the fourth generation. It was the fourth duke who commissioned Capability Brown to layout the glorious landscape that created, arguably 'the finest view in England'.

"The Duchess's forceful personality was also her downfall, ending her close friendship with Queen Anne, who had granted Marlborough the Manor of Woodstock in which to build a house as a monument to his victory at the Battle of Blenheim. Wherever you stand

looking at this portrait, Sarah's withering gaze assesses the viewer. I am not sure that it would be a comfortable experience, so I think my choice has to be something equally significant but possibly less judgmental." John said.

"My choice commemorates the battle which according to Winston Churchill 'changed the political axis of the world'. The French were so thoroughly defeated at Blenheim that England was free to rule the world's trade routes and that resulted in the largest Empire the world has known.

"I shall take the silver centre piece of Marlborough on horseback after the victory writing his famous dispatch to the Duchess," John said.

"It was commissioned by the Londonderry

family on the engagement of their daughter, Frances. It was made by the court jeweller Robert Garrard. The firm continued to serve the Royal Family, re-setting the crown for the Coronation in 1953.

"I wrote to the firm seeking more information on the centrepiece. They had deposited their archive safely away from Hitler's bombs during World War Two. Sadly the depository flooded and all the records were lost! Looking at it would remind me of the reason for the building of the palace and of those two personalities I have come to know so well. It will also remind me of Francis.

"The palace is a home and during the time of the fifth and sixth dukes it was an unhappy morbid place. Francis and the seventh Duke had 11 children and filled the palace with life and fun. Through her, it will remind me of Winston Churchill who was born here but neglected by his parents. He was taken under her wing," John added.

"To me it represents family life and above all I am a family man so on the island it would remind me of my own family, too.

"It is also a remarkable piece admired by the world's silver experts for its detail and complexity. I could run my fingers over it feeling all the various textures, the moss, the horse hair and the smooth drum. Should the island be inhabited, I imagine the value of one hundredweight of silver would be realised and make my life secure."

Postscript
Since this article appeared, John's wife Margaret Forster's book on Francis the 7th Duchess of Marlborough, entitled Churchill's Grandma, has been published by The History Press.

Rita Ricketts
Historian

Blackwell's is more than a bookshop. It is an Oxford institution with its own historian — Rita Ricketts. A bookshop is an appropriate home for her, as she is a natural storyteller.

A visiting scholar at the Bodleian, Rita is also director of the official fringe for the *Sunday Times* Oxford Literary Festival as well as the originator of the World Writers group at Blackwell's.

I wondered what object could inspire her to tell stories to herself when she is marooned on our desert island? Which antique, work of art or antiquarian book would she like to find washed up on the beach?

"In the cemetery near my childhood home was a beautifully sculptured angel with outstretched arms," said Rita. "Inscribed on its chest was 'Jesus called a little child'. At the age of five, I loved the statue but didn't think it a good idea to 'call' little children, even to heaven. That carved angel was the first significant 'antique' in my life.

Rita continued: "Visions of growing up appear in the form of a statue of General Wolfe on Blackheath, at whose feet I would sit before careering down the hill on my bike, passing the Greenwich Meridian and visiting my favourite painting in the National Maritime Museum, *The Death of Nelson* by Benjamin West.

"Describing it now sounds rather morbid but they were days of illicit freedom. Crossing the Greenwich tunnel to play on the Isle of Dogs, even though our parents forbade it.

"Life in my twenties and early thirties was as a student, teacher, mother and feeder of poets and writers," Rita explained.

"Some are long dead, like George Fraser, and some were already famous like Seamus Heaney (fed on whiskey and Irish stew) and Fay Weldon (on chocolate cake — I had burnt the pizza for the main course!)

"That was also the time I inherited a marquetry box made by my grandfather, who had died when I was six. I remember my surprise when I opened it and found inside the letter I wrote to him asking him to get well.

"In 1981, we set sail for New Zealand. Arriving in cold wintry Wellington and feeling lonely I cried with the early settlers buried in the cemetery, which had been cut through by a motorway," Rita said.

"An iconic painting of a bird flying over that road by an outraged artist, Rita Angus, would remind me of Wellington. But the antique that would root me to the New Zealand soil is further north in Auckland — a huge sculpture of a Maori Elder opposite the ferry terminal.

"He is part of that landscape and practical too, because he acts as a windbreak. This giant 'father' would listen while I reminisce about times spent at the one-roomed, bunkbed-lined wooden beach hut with a stove where we stayed with Booker prize-winner, Keri Hume, author of *The Bone People*. She took my five children out to sea armed only with a machete!" Rita recalled.

Awarded the New Zealand 1990 Scholarship, by the European Commission, Rita set off to the European University in Florence.

"From its monastic terrace in San Domenico I could look down on the whole of Florence," Rita told me. "This view is my antique of the mind — 'a mind with a view' — one I can always own."

After a period of struggle in England finding solace in work and teaching variously in an inner city comprehensive, a college of further education and part time at UCL, Rita eventually found her 'turrangawiawai' (a place to stand) in Blackwells. Rita had written a history of people associated with this family firm called *Adventurers All*.

"My research in New Zealand had involved collecting stories of those affected by the big economic change brought about by Britain's membership of the EU. Now I was inundated with more stories; of scholar's manqué making their way against the odds," Rita said.

"The room I work in was where Sir Basil sat on his mother's knee looking out of the window as the circus paraded down Broad Street. The wallpaper, hand printed in 1872 by William Morris, is called 'Powdered'.

"I think the Broad Street shop is itself an antique, filled with the spirit of books and the hunger for learning of those that love them. The early Blackwells had little formal education. The first nonetheless became Oxford's first public librarian. The second founded the famous bookshop on Broad

"This is a beautiful book – an antique we could all afford if only it was still in print. Its characters would remind me of Blackwellians, those devoted and well informed booksellers, and of all the people with rich stories who walk through Blackwell's doors."

Street. The third, Sir Basil, was the first in his family to go to university.

"With the help of Reg Carr I created a tripartite link, between Blackwell's, the Bodleian and the university admissions, for prospective students, with an aim to widen participation, Rita explained. "New Zealand is a place where anyone who makes the effort, irrespective of formal qualifications, can go to university.

"Despite popular prejudice, Oxford deserves a better press for the encouragement it gives schools and teachers in the state sector. It has an open door, to a world of ideas and imagination, through books," Rita said.

"The Bodleian too will open its doors more widely when the renovated Gilbert Scott Building transforms it from a fortress to a fairway.

"Libraries, local public ones, and bookshops were and are my Arcadia. And so my final choice has to be a book.

"In the Blackwell archives I find treasures galore, many of which are now in the Merton Blackwell Collection and a larger collection, together with the working Library of Sir Basil,

(generously donated by Julian Blackwell) will soon be lodged in the Bodleian. The one I have chosen was printed on the Kelmscott Press so it will also remind me of the room I work in," she added.

"In 2004, to celebrate 125 years of 'Blackwell's of the Broad', I persuaded the Bodleian to mount an exhibition of selected editions of Chaucer's *Canterbury Tales*. The show included Caxton's mid-15th century version, an illustrated 18th century edition and William Morris's 'Kelmscott' Chaucer curled around with Pre-Raphaelite maidens disporting themselves in finery.

"But that is not the one I want on the desert island. Producing finely printed books was Basil Blackwell's iconoclastic act, staying the hand of mass production. His (Shakespeare Head) Chaucer was also printed on the Kelmscott Press.

"This is a beautiful book — an antique we could all afford if only it was still in print. Its characters would remind me of Blackwellians, those devoted and well informed booksellers, and of all the people with rich stories who walk through Blackwell's doors."

Rt Rev John Pritchard
Bishop of Oxford

Saint Cuthbert, who strongly resisted becoming a bishop, is one of Rev John Prichard's heroes — and as it turns out, the current Bishop of Oxford has followed in the footsteps of his favourite saint.

The Rt Rev Pritchard was born in Salford (in the shadow of the Old Trafford floodlights). He went to Arnold School in Blackpool, and then read law at St Peter's College, Oxford. His summer job was as a Blackpool tram conductor, so he has seen Blackpool Illuminations more times than anyone could reasonably need to.

While at Oxford, he recognised a calling to the priesthood and, after his degree, went on to do a Diploma in Theology at Oxford, and then a Certificate in Pastoral Theology at Ridley Hall in Cambridge. He was ordained in 1972.

Rt Rev Pritchard was a curate at St Martin's in the Bullring in Birmingham until 1976, when he became youth chaplain to the diocese of Bath and Wells. From there he moved in 1980 to become priest in charge of a large and lively parish in Taunton, contributing regularly to local radio and newspapers.

In 1988, he became Director of Pastoral Studies at Cranmer Hall, the Church of England's theological college in St John's College Durham.

He became Warden in 1993, and had responsibility for training men and women for ordained and other ministries. In 1996, after eight years in Durham, John became Archdeacon of Canterbury and Canon Residentiary of Canterbury Cathedral. But returned to Durham in January 2002 to be consecrated as Bishop of Jarrow .

Rt Rev Pritchard completed an M.Litt. in Pastoral Theology during his first time in Durham, and co-wrote Practical Theology in Action for SPCK in 1996.

He is deeply committed to the encouragement and care of the clergy. He enjoys a wide teaching ministry in this country and abroad, and relishes making the Christian faith accessible and attractive. In the Diocese of Durham, he recently led a successful bid for the twin site monastery of Wearmouth-Jarrow to be the UK's 2010 nomination as a World Heritage Site.

He set up a Spirituality Network in the north east and had responsibility for ordinands and curates, Readers, the Board of Education and the Council for Ministry, Hospital Chaplains, the Lesotho Link, College of Counsellors, Spiritual Direction, the Region.

Rt Rev Pritchard was installed as Bishop of Oxford in June 2007, and relished getting to know one of the largest dioceses in the Church of England and the complex sociological fabric of the Thames Valley. His national commitments include work with the Ministry Division of the Church of England, the Church Army, Church House Publishing and the Guild of Health.

His vocation took him to the north-east for 12 years and to Canterbury for five — in addition to time spent in Birmingham and Taunton before returning to Oxford as Bishop.

So, when marooned on our desert island, he will have memories of most regions of England. Which antique, work of art or antiquarian book would he pick for inspiration?

Pointing to a simple but beautiful oak rocking cradle that has been in his family for about 250 years, the Bishop of Oxford said: "On the desert island that would be a poignant reminder of all the people I love who I have left behind.

"Being the Pritchard family cradle, it would make me reflect on who I am and where I come from. In a sense I am what I am because of what they were. I see myself as a product of their lives, the good and the no-so-good, the mixture that is in all of us.

"As well as helping me reflect on my identity, the cradle would be a constant reminder of the people I would want to remember and pray for on the island; the two most recent being my grandchildren of ten months and five months who lay in it before their Christenings.

"I spent 12 years in the north-east and its people made a strong impression on me. In the history of the Church in England, the area has given us some remarkable people.

" I immersed myself in the stories of St Cuthbert, Aidan, the Venerable Bede and Hilda of Whitby. In fact, we named our cat 'Whitby' short for Hilda of Whitby — on a bad day she becomes 'Synod of Whitby'.

"Bede's time (673- 735) is often regarded as the Dark Ages. If so Bede was a bright light. He was a mathematician, a scientist and an historian as well as a biblical scholar. He was the first to make the English think of ourselves as a nation.

"He also gave us our means of ordering time before and after Christ, BC and AD. His master work was his History of the English Church and People. The illuminated version is in the Bodleian Library

"In it he wrote about Cuthbert who resisted becoming a bishop and who when finally he accepted the post, soon left for Lindesfarne where he received visitors in the peaceful rugged surroundings of the island. I wear his cross, the original of which is in the Treasury at Durham. After he died, just two years later, his body was carted around the country before it finally came to rest in Durham Cathedral where Cuthbert is buried at one end of the cathedral and Bede at the other.

"They are both important figures to me. If I had Bede's History of the English Church and People with me on the desert island, it would remind me of all the Celtic saints of the north east and I would of course have the pleasure of reading it," Rev Pritchard said.

"Were I to leave behind the antique and the book, the work of art I would take would be a Carravagio. I remember going to the Exhibition at The National Gallery in 2006. There were two versions of *The Supper at Emmaus* on display.

"The first was painted in 1601 when he was the toast of the town in Rome. That version hangs permanently in the National Gallery. The second, on loan from Milan, was painted in 1606 after he had killed a man in a duel and went on the run.

"In the first, Jesus looks young, boyish even androgynous. Although the second picture was inspired by the same story it is much darker, the face of Jesus is drawn and marked by his suffering.

"In the Bible story, Jesus joins the two disciples as they were leaving Jerusalem and talks with them on the road to Emmaus but they do not recognise him.

"They invite their companion to supper and the moment when he breaks bread is like a revelation, they recognise him as the risen Jesus. I would like one or both of those paintings with me.

"If I have a theme for my life as a Christian, it is the desire to share the love of Christ. Being alone on a desert island would, I think be one of the bad times when I would need reminding of what being a Christian was really about.

"That is the journey of my thinking on what to take to my island, but as I can only take one of these three I think maybe the Venerable Bede may prove to be better company than the brilliant but troubled Carravagio, so I shall opt for the Bede.

"I hope that a photo of my family may be in my pocket when I am swept up on the beach so, that way, I won't need the cradle."

LG 'Bob' Martin
Air Commodore

Air Commodore LG (usually known as Bob) Martin's life has included so many near misses that one suspects he has a guardian angel. His first brush with death, came in 1940 when he was on leave and his home in Dulwich, London, was bombed.

He took shelter under a heavy mahogany table while the house collapsed on top of him.

When, in 1951, Bob met, fell in love and married Hilde he discovered that she was the daughter of the air-raid warden who pulled him from the wreckage. The family like to think Hilde's father, Paul Rosenberg, who was later killed in the Blitz, saved Bob for her.

Bob was on active flying duties for 25 of his 36 years in the RAF, surviving three wars, three aircraft crashes and three friendly fire incidents.

At the end of his active service he was seconded to the Foreign Office and, in 1972, was appointed Air Attaché at the British Embassy in Bonn.

Retiring from the RAF did not end his dance with death. When Bob and Hilde were attending the 1984 Conservative Party conference in Brighton, they stayed at the Grand Hotel. They needed to leave early to catch a plane to Germany and thus narrowly avoided the IRA bomb which killed 5 and injured 34.

So Bob, now 88, is definitely a survivor - but how would he do on our desert island? I asked him "If you were shipwrecked on a desert island which antique or work of art would you like to be washed up on the beach to remind you of your long and eventful life?"

"I think it probably has to be something to do with flying because as long as I can remember I wanted to fly." Bob said " I recall being in a field near Birmingham in 1933

desperately wanting five shillings to pay for a five minute flight. I didn't have five shillings.

"I tried to join the RAF in 1938 but, as I was under 21, my parents had to give permission and they refused. The war swept aside conditions like that," Bob said.

Bob, who was born in Kilkenny, was 19 when he joined up. "In 1940, Winston Churchill, desperately wanting to train as many pilots as quickly as possible advocated 'Makie Learnie' or learning on the job . This was pretty hairy when it involved flying - and my apprenticeship was on Wellington Bombers alongside four other young pilots. I was one of only two of us who survived.

" In 1941, I came to RAF Kidlington and after six months proper training, I received my wings as a night fighter pilot. This area has so many rich memories for me including, at that time, walking into Oxford to get a social life.

Bob was posted to the Middle East (Italian front)Desert Air Force before the end of the war and was, briefly, commanding officer of RAF Crete.

"I may have flown the last sortie of the war in Italy," he said. "Near the end, Germans were escaping by ship from Venice and my orders were 'to beat the hell out of it.' It was a clear and sunny day and this was my first sight of the beautiful city of canals. There were no ships in sight and I like to think I saved Venice by choosing not to attack it with the Mosquito's cannons.

Bob was Commanding Officer in Cyprus before returning to England in 1947.

"I was posted to Spitalgate near Grantham where I was detailed to escort the Mayor, Alderman Roberts, his wife and his daughter to a Mess Ball. I was briefed that she was an aspiring politician. She was a good looking young woman and in my youthful chauvinistic opinion she was more likely to be married than succeed as a politician.

"During my diplomatic career, when I met her as Margaret Thatcher, the Prime Minister, I am glad she didn't recognise me.

Post-war Germany played a big part in Bob's life.

"In 1972, I was appointed Air Attaché at the British Embassy in Bonn and became President Luftwaffen Attaché Verband (President of Foreign Air Attachés.)

"Maybe I should take the medals I was awarded 'Das Grosse Verdienst Kreux' (the German Order of Merit) by President von Weizacker and the Europakreuz by the Bundesrepublik.

"They are the only medals I have that didn't involve wars killing people and if I took them to the island they would remind me of my involvement in the Anglo German Association.

"The general impression of the diplomatic service is, I think, misleading," Bob explained. "Hilde and I did indeed drink quite a lot of Champagne at that time entertaining over 1,500 people but there was a good reason behind it. It is about networking and knowing who to approach when any problem or project arises.

"One of the aims was to persuade the Germans to buy the Tornado instead of the American planes on offer. We made the agreement that secured thousands of British jobs and billions to the Exchequer.

"I was in Germany when the Berlin wall came down — and joined in its destruction. I have a souvenir of that remarkable moment in history," Bob said.

"The West Berlin side of my piece of the wall is creatively coloured and the eastern side is just plain concrete symbolising the difference between east and west during the Cold War.

Bob commanded 151 and 85 Squadrons during the Cold War, serving at Leuchars, West Morling and church fenton.

"I was serving on All-weather Night Fighter Squadrons during the Cold War and it felt decidedly hot," he recalled.

"We flew top secret missions, we called 'Exercise Unmentionable' because we were not allowed to tell even our wives. Soviet bombers often tried to fly over our airspace and we intercepted them with orders to fire on them if they behaved in a hostile manner.

"Hilde and I have probably spent more time in Oxfordshire than anywhere else. I was Commanding Officer at RAF Abingdon when approximately 8,000 people worked and lived on the base. At that time Abingdon provided all parachute training for the Army.

"To understand the nature of parachute training, I decided to experience it for myself. Standing in the open door and leaping out was quite something for me as I had always been taught not to jump out unless the aircraft was out of control or on fire. It left me with great respect for our Parachute Regiments.

"The souvenir that could remind me of RAF Abingdon is an unusual baton I was given as a 'thank you'. General Kong Le of Laos wanted to set up a similar parachute training school as ours and, after his visit, he gave me his embossed silver topped baton inscribed with good luck symbols.

"Maybe his luck ran out when he handed it to me because he was killed in a coup soon afterwards.

"When Hilde and I semi-retired, we came to live in Kennington, in 1976. We soon realised that Kennington is a very convenient village with a population who are friendly and community spirited and so hope to live out our remaining years here.

"I became a Vale Councillor and served on the Parish Council for ten years but I think my final choice has to be about my passion for flying rather than my diplomatic life.

"I have photographs of most of the forty plus aircraft types I have flown. I am tempted to take them in an album together with a model of the Gloucester Javelin which I flew when stationed in Scotland. It was one of the first supersonic fighter planes," Bob said.

"I remember journalists being excited by it and disappointed when they experienced a flight and it glided smoothly and silently through the sound barrier. I suggested that in future we should 'Give the stick a good shake' and devised a membership certificate to the Big Thunder Club for those who had flown through the sound barrier.

"I signed it on condition that a 'voluntary' payment to squadron funds was made.

"So I will take this elegant model and the photos which will remind me of the excitement of flying and that other world in the skies and perhaps I could somehow attach the piece of the Berlin Wall to the album?'

In recognition of his nine lives maybe we can find a way of combining the three…

Jane Tranter
Senior television executive

Most of us are privileged to be taught by at least one inspiring teacher and in my case that was Donald Tranter who taught me history at Westminster College. At that time his daughter Jane was attending primary school in Oxford.

Now, most readers of *Oxfordshire Limited Edition* have enjoyed the fruits of her labour while perhaps not knowing her name as Jane is controller of fiction at BBC television.

She may not appear on our television screens herself but she is responsible for delivering top class drama from *Cranford, Oliver* and *Larkrise to Candleford* to cutting edge contemporary thrillers like *Warriors, State of Play* and *Criminal Justice*.

Jane went to school at St Helen's in Abingdon until, at 16, she transferred to Kingswood Methodist boarding school. After A-Levels she returned to Oxford, attending secretarial college. Memorably, she typed the script of Susan Hill's *Woman in Black*.

This was followed by studying for her degree in English at Kings College in London where she chose to study early literature from Chaucer to the Victorian novel.

In 1985, she took up a job as a secretary in the radio drama department at the BBC. She transferred to a similar post in television. Here she was able to get production training as an assistant floor manager, and then as script editor on an early series of *Casualty*. Later she worked in the BBC's Single Films Department.

In 1992, when Carlton Telelvison took over Thames, Jane moved to commercial TV and witnessed a TV station being born, working on a new soap *London Bridge* and the now oft repeated *Bramwell*. Returning to the BBC in 1997, she worked as head of in-house drama

series and serials.

In 2000 she was made the BBC's first ever drama commissioner and commissioned all the drama across the BBC's four television channels, overseeing new work as well as her hallmark classic adaptations.

Her late father was a theatre enthusiast. I remember taking part in a production of Jean Anouilh's *Joan of Arc* stylishly directed by Donald — and he has passed on to Jane his passion for the theatre and history.

Nowadays she commutes into London from her home near Henley and, as she was a regular customer during the ten years I was director of Oxford Antiques Centre (the Jam Factory), I was curious to know how she would answer my question. If you were shipwrecked on a desert island which antique or work of art would you like to be washed up on the beach?

Like me, she admires the work of Antony Gormley because she began by saying "It would be magnificent to have the *Angel of the North*. On that tiny island it would remind me of the island I have come from and make me feel part of something bigger. But I have decided that I really want something personal that would remind me of different parts of my family life which is so important to me.

"My husband, TV and film director, David Attwood, is passionate about Picasso. Together we travelled in France and Spain to all the places associated with the artist including a memorable viewing of Guernica. Picasso is my favourite artist of all time and I bought David two photos of the artist at work.

"Even before she could walk, my daughter, Maddy loved drawing and she also admires Picasso. There is a print of *The Girl with a Dove* on her bedroom wall. If I took any painting by him to the desert island I would be in the

presence of, in my opinion, the greatest artistic genius of the 20th century but it would also connect me to my family," Jane said.

"On holiday in Cornwall, David introduced me to the work of the Persian born artist, Partou Zia. I love the colour, depth and symbolism of her paintings. David bought two of them before her tragically early death. We chose semi abstracts of Newlyn ice house. They would remind me of our holidays in Cornwall as well as of home.

"They would also be a poignant reminder of a life cut short and youthful potential not allowed to blossom into maturity. So maybe I should take some pictures by my six and half year old twins which would invoke happier thoughts.

"The twins love painting and drawing but their style is very different. Joseph loves ideas based detailed sketches and his favourite subject at the moment is *Doctor Who*. He could be useful on the desert island if he came to life as if from a magic brush. It could also be a reminder of my time at the BBC. Maddy is a confident and talented little artist in all media. She never stops drawing. Her ability comes from the Attwood side of the family — David did an art foundation course just after he studied film in Paris.

"In the end if there is one thing that I just couldn't leave behind, my choice has to be the Briget Riley print entitled *Start* which David bought for my birthday — significantly on the millennium year. It was then that we made a decision that has changed our lives. It is a picture of endless possibilities. You can never stop looking at it. It hangs at the bottom of our bed and so *Start* is the first thing I see in the

morning, a time when the kids often join us. They talk about it a lot. I can visualise Maddy asking 'Why White?' Although she admires Briget Riley's work, Jane says there were personal reasons that inspired the purchase.

"For a long time we had wanted to have children and that was the year we told ourselves that we must deal with this. We began to undergo fertility treatment and decided to move out of London.

"At first the picture hung on the wall of our Victorian house in the East End until we bought it here to this very contemporary space. Buying it bought us hope. We wanted it to be the start of something new and it was. It ushered in an intense period in our lives but a happy one.

"I sometimes think the movement in the painting is like that of wriggling sperm but it also has sharp edges and pieces that are torn apart. The timing evokes strong emotion for other reasons too. It was that year my father was diagnosed with cancer. It could have been a dreadful time but he would not let it be like that so most of the memories from those early years of this millennium are happy but intense. Looking at it on my desert island it would remind me of different areas of family life."

Postscript

Jane received a special achievement award. At the ceremony, in April 2009, the Chair of the BAFTA television committee, John Willis said: "She is one of the most gifted television executives of her generation." Since Jane resurrected 'Doctor Who', the lead character has had three rejuvenations - including the memorable depiction by David Tennant. Jane has recently been involved in Torchwood.

David Fickling
Publisher

David Fickling believes reading, especially for children, should be a delight. For him storytelling is as old as mankind and he believes today's children have an appetite for a story well told.

Most of David's working life has been spent with some of the greatest children's writers of our age, writers such as Philip Pullman and Mark Haddon, whose books appeal to young and old alike.

And, in the age of the Internet and computer games, David also dared to launch a new comic, *The DFC*.

So what item would he like to see washed up on the beach when marooned on our desert island?

"Although I am not a Christian, I would be tempted to have a copy of the Bible on the island because Jesus was a storyteller and one of the greatest stories ever told is that of the Prodigal Son.

"As with all good stories you are left wondering what you are meant to think. I believe that literacy and reading in our childhood is the basis of our culture and our morals.

"I sometimes despair at the desire to censor danger out of children's literature. The Bible is full of violence and tragedy but it does not turn us into killers. Agatha Christie mysteries are about murder, but her readers do not become assassins. Scary stories are important to children because they help them deal with the world and their own emotions.

"Cave paintings, Egyptian hieroglyphs, the Mahabharata, the Koran and the Bible and all storytelling ever since help give structure to ideas and meaning to our lives," said David.

"As a child, I remember being on the edge of my seat enjoying a comic serial called *Wrath of the Gods*, full of amazing, startling artwork. I did not know then that it was based on the Greek myths, but it was very exciting.

"Some of the oldest stories written can be found in Homer's *Iliad*, but I believe they began life as oral story telling and the

stories of the siege of Troy are thrilling but full of graphic violence. The first copy would probably have been on papyrus.

"The earliest surviving copies might come from the Byzantine Empire, I suppose. I was lucky to read medieval history at university; history is nothing if not stories. I remember that the sacking of Constantinople in 1453 was a turning point.

"Choosing an antiquarian edition of the Iliad would be wonderful but creates a problem — I can't read ancient Greek! I shall need to read on this island. If I took an early copy I would also want a means of learning the language. Of course, I have been privileged to publish some cracking good reads and it would remind me of those fine authors if I took a DFB book but how could I choose only one from all our authors?" David said.

"So, I think my choice has to be what some people might regard as trash literature, a comic. I strongly disagree with that judgement.

"One of the reasons boys are reading less is, I think, because of the dearth of comics to fire their imagination in print.

"Comics did not die because they were not successful but because the business model failed as they were taken over by bigger and greedier companies. There is something very English about the combination of pictures and stories.

Pictures that tell a story like Hogarth's *Rakes Progress* or the Pre-Raphaelite paintings in the Ashmolean are particularly English.

"Good artwork in comics makes children want to draw — and good storytelling makes them want to write. The comic serial has all the excitement that comes from having to wait for the next episode to see what happens next," David said.

"That is why we have launched the DFC. No, it isn't an abbreviation for the David Fickling Comic but stands for something different every week. 'Decidedly Forgetful Chicken',

'Disagreeably Flatulent Cherubs' and so on.

"Philip Pullman and John Aggs have created The Adventures of John Blake and I hope they give children today what Billy Binns and his Magic Specs did for me as an eight-year-old.

"As a child, comics made me want to read, not have to read but gave me the desire to read and experience the magic of being shown something new and never wanting a book to end but nevertheless be brought back safely to the world. I could ask to take the first copy of the *DFC*, the illustrations are so imaginative it would be endless fun looking at them and, maybe, I could even try copying them in the sand. But it would make me feel sad being away from my life in Oxford and working with the *DFC* creative team. They are amazing and young, and the *DFC* is nothing if not a team effort.

"I have to take something that will bring delight so my final choice is a comic called *Boys' World*. I don't have any copies in my possession, although as an eight year-old it inspired me more than any other comic. I think it was first published in 1963, but it only lasted for 18 months so copies are valuable," said David.

"The reason it ended then was not because it was not any good but because it was bought by *The Eagle* who absorbed it for a while and then dropped it.

"I was upset, to say the least, when it disappeared from my life so suddenly. Every Monday I had eagerly awaited the next instalment of *The Human Bullet* and *The Steel Claw, Billy Binns and his Magical Specs* and *The Wrath of the Gods*. I really could not believe that joy of expectation was all over.

"So, on my desert island I want to relive those 18 months. I would like a weekly delivery of the *Boys' World*, please."

A bound set maybe, but a weekly delivery?

"A bound series would lose that sense of waiting for the next episode of the serial. In fact it would bring back the magic of childhood if it could be delivered by different means each week — washed up in a bottle, brought by Man Friday one week and Robert Louis Stevenson the next and air-dropped on another.

"The suspense would keep me alive. Nothing makes me want to live more than wondering 'what will happen next' and that is the golden rule of storytelling."

Dr George McGavin
Entomologist and broadcaster

D r George McGavin was famously seen on television with leaches hanging from his legs — after allowing himself to be bitten by mosquitos and fleas. He is currently the media's expert of choice when it comes to championing the cause of insects.

If you heard Radio 4's recent broadcast of the Earthwatch *Irreplaceable* debate from the Royal Geographical Society you will have experienced his persuasive powers at first hand.

He championed bees, while other experts backed primates, fungi and plankton as the most important species for the health and wellbeing of our planet. Dr McGavin won the debate convincingly.

Despite being a sociable man, Dr McGavin may not feel as lonely marooned on a desert island as most of us. He is likely to be at ease with the millions of creatures sharing his new home — after all he has several insect species named after him.

I wondered how this entomologist's view of the world would affect his choice of the object he would most like to see washed up on the beach?

Dr McGavin began our conversation by explaining why he is fascinated by the scarab beetle a fascination shared by ancient Egyptians.

"The beetle was a symbol of good luck and rebirth, the symbol of the sun god Khepri. It is even suggested that the process of mummification was modelled on the scarab. When Egyptian priests excavated the buried balls of scarab beetle dung and unravelled them they discovered pupae inside — the next life of the dung beetle.

"In the British Museum's Egyptian galleries there is an incredible carving in granite of a scarab beetle from the Ptolemaic period circa

200 BC. It is not the size of a beetle — it is huge and heavy. To do it justice I would have to haul it to a high place on the island, and that might prove difficult!" Dr McGavin said.

Dr McGavin is particularly impressed by the antque globes at Oxford's Museum of the History of Science.

"There are some beautiful globes on display," he said. "I thought it could be interesting to have one and study the world as its maker visualised it at that time. But it could also make me feel sad, isolated and trapped on my desert island.

"I assume it is a tropical island with a clear view of the stars. I am interested in astronomy, so I could take one of the museum's exquisite astrolabes as I shall have plenty of time to figure out how it works, and it could be useful if I tried to escape. I am a social animal and I do enjoy an audience so I would miss people on this desert island, however interesting it is to explore. My next thought was to take a book because you are never alone if you have a good book. A copy of the complete works of Shakespeare or at least his sonnets would fit the bill. I could read and re-read those and still get a huge amount out of them.

"But I have decided my choice has to be something that would remind me of my time in Oxford, where I worked for 25 years at the Oxford University Museum of Natural History in South Parks Road.

"For me, it is the most amazing building in the world. If I could take a special place it would be the whole thing, or at least the Huxley Room. The museum was built in 1860, at a time when the whole world was about to change."

"I would like to take something that would remind me of the tremendous event that took place in the Huxley Room in the museum — almost while the paint was still drying on the walls.

"Before 1859, everyone in England believed that God created the earth in literally seven days. Late in that year, Charles Darwin published *The Origin of Species* and it shook those certainties to their foundations.

"The first and second print runs sold out in days, but his theory was met by expressions of shock and horror.

"The controversy over the book came to a head here in Oxford, on June 30, 1860, when the museum opened its doors, ornamented with carvings of creatures from the natural world, to a meeting of the British Association for the Advancement of Science.

"The association had invited Darwin to come and speak, but he was ill and unable to attend, recording in his diary that he was 'utterly weary of life', Dr McGavin said.

"But the packed audience included many of his admirers including Thomas Henry Huxley, after whom the venue of the debate is now named. On the other side of the argument was the Bishop of Oxford, Samuel Wilberforce.

"If I could choose to return to one moment in time and be a fly on the wall, that is the event I would attend. We have reports of the excitement and ferocity of the debate, but no word-for-word accounts.

"The room has since been divided and the uppermost section houses part of Oxford's insect collection. I looked after the Huxley Room for a quarter of a century. It was ground zero for the theory of evolution. But, as I can't take it with me, I shall take something from the Museum of the History of Science which will remind me of someone who was, by chance, present that day.

"His name was Admiral Robert Fitzroy and he was captain of the *Beagle* on the voyage when Charles Darwin was a passenger. It was his observations on that voyage around the world which led to the publication of *The Origin of the Species*.

"Admiral Fitzroy attended that meeting and paced up and down clutching a Bible and waving his fist yelling 'Blasphemy, blasphemy'.

"On that warm afternoon, he realised that he had been responsible for taking Darwin, as he saw it, on that fateful journey. Some say it was a feeling of guilt that he had unwittingly caused the upheaval that led him to commit suicide a few years later," Dr McGavin revealed.

"It was sad that a man who wanted to use science and engineering to save the lives of sailors should end his life that way.

"Fitzroy designed barometers and wanted every sailor to be able to predict the weather. He designed a storm barometer which bears his name. Each instrument gave clear instructions on how it could be read.

"The Museum of the History of Science has one. It is an object of beauty and could also be of use on my desert island.

"It would make me feel connected with my life and times in Oxford. It would remind me of Fitzroy, who clung to his beliefs because his somewhat closed mind wanted to fit the evidence to support them, and Darwin, who used that five-year voyage on the *Beagle* to analyse the evidence.

"There are Fitzroy barometers on the market, but I would like one which the Admiral handled so it would evoke that meeting 149 years ago when 700 people gathered in the Natural History Museum.

"Many years ago I helped the museum to obtain a grant from the Museums and Galleries Commission to restore The Huxley Room to its former glory, as it looked on June 30, 1860.

"Using Fitzroy's storm barometer on the desert island I shall remember the inspiring times I have experienced in the Oxford University Museum of Natural History."

Simonetta Agnello Hornby
Novellist

Novellist Simonetta Agnello Hornby was born into an aristocratic Sicilian family and brought up in Palermo. She might have continued to live a life of cosmopolitan comfort indefinitely had she not been sent to Cambridge to learn English.

Here she she met and fell in love with her future husband, Martin Hornby (who was studying astrophysics), and started work on a law degree, studies which eventually led to the establishment of a pioneering law firm in London.

Her first novel *La Mennulara (The Almond Picker)* published in 2002, saw her life take a new direction. The book, which she wrote in Italian, is set in her native Sicily.

But when I first met Simonetta in Kennington, in 1970, writing novels was not even on the horizon. She was still working on qualifying in English law.

I can still picture her with a huge volume of The Law of Tort on her knees and her little son, George, playing at her feet.

After qualifying — and the birth of her sons George and Nicolas — she exchanged a glamorous job in a City law firm to work as a childcare lawyer.

Not long after, she set up her own practice in Brixton, specialising in childcare and domestic violence cases. Then, finding time from her day job, she wrote her first novel. Despite literary success, Simonetta, now in her sixties, is down-to-earth about her new career.

"I can't understand the fuss," she said. "I am a better lawyer than a writer!"

Her second book, *The Marchesa*, is based on the life of one of her 19th century ancestors.

"When I was a child, I would stay at my grandfather's palazzo in the small town of Siculiana. I was allowed to go up and down between floors, and loved to listen to my great-aunts' conversation.

"Whenever there was a woman who was ugly, dirty, unkempt, greedy or stupid, one of them would say: 'She's like the marchesa'.

Simonetta's interest was further piqued by Luigi Pirandello's novel *The Three Widows*, which was loosely based on the life of her ancestor.

"The story Pirandello tells is partly true," she said. "But I got cross about the way he talked about her.

"She was red-headed and considered ugly on account of that. She spoke Sicilian and not Italian. She liked to cook, and did so as a married woman. She liked the company of servants."

In her novel, Simonetta reinvents the

marchesa as a victim of a dynastic system that would not tolerate women who did not know their place. Simonetta said she hoped that her portrayal of this remarkable woman would change perceptions about her relative.

Knowing how much Simonetta enjoys contact with her family and friends (she has four grandchildren), her exile on a desert island will be hard. So I wondered what antique, work of art or antiquarian book she would like washed up on the beach to remind her of her life in London?

"At 19, while I was studying law at the University of Palermo, I used the first month's earnings from my first paid job (teaching a young man English) to buy an exquisite semi-circular embroidery from Albania which now hangs in my eldest son's house," Simonetta said.

"The second month, I went to an antique shop that specialised in small silver items and my eye was drawn to a delicate 18th century writing set made in Naples. I bought it and have taken it with me everywhere — to Zambia, the USA and England. It has two ink pots, one for the red and one for the black ink, a pounce pot to hold the powder to dry the page, a holder for the quills and a little silver bell.

"On the desert island, I could make coloured inks and should be able to find feathers to write with. But I would enjoy the bell the most. The noise of the birds and the sea on this island would not be enough for me. The bell would resonate with the ingenuity of human sound."

As you will gather, Simonetta has been a connoisseur of antiques from an early age.

"I like things that appeal to different senses. For example, on the island I would like to be creative. So a Swiss Army knife would be useful.

"A well-made knife is a pleasure to handle, and I could use it to cut bark from trees to make paper, to write and inscribe on wood and stones, and to make walking sticks. A traditional craft in Sicily is carving beautiful geometric patterns on walking sticks made out of branches from olive trees. It would bring back childhood memories and smells. The bark of olive trees from our farm, Mose (near Agrigento), retains its perfume for a long time. Carving will thus reward three senses," she said.

'Sicily is at the crossroads of the Mediterranean, and has been ruled by everyone from the Greeks to the Arabs. The architectural remains in Palermo prompted my interest in Islam. On a trip to Istanbul with Martin (Simonetta's ex-husband) we bought a pair of old Kashmiri miniature paintings.

"When we separated each of us kept one. Mine shows a teacher and his student, their eyes locked. To me, this is possibly the most profound relationship. Passing on knowledge and ideas is an act of love between the generations. After buying the miniatures, I read the Koran for the first time.

"But if I am allowed to take with me only one thing, it has to be the Japanese miniature cabinet painted with flying cranes on a golden background. Its drawers contain lots of tiny boxes. It was given to me by my Aunt Marjory.

"I was very fond of her and she represents to me a certain generation of plucky women. She was engaged to be married but when she contracted TB her fiancé's family terminated the engagement.

"She remained single and kept herself teaching in a girls' dancing school. Her life was poor but dignified without ever a word of complaint or regret. She loved beautiful things and her pupils gave her nice presents, such as this Japanese cabinet.

"When my boys were little, I called it 'the pagoda of dreams', remembering the Tibetan Buddhist stupas where pilgrims attach their prayers. At first I filled its boxes with sweets and nuts and allowed them to take some each day.

"When they were older I suggested they write their wishes and thoughts on a small piece of paper and fold it up and put it in one of the boxes. I promised I wouldn't read them."

"Many of my young clients were sad young things. I recommended that they do the same thing. They were surprised but loved doing it. I would read their notes only if they allowed me, and I respected their wish to keep them secret, always.

"On the desert island the cabinet would remind me of Aunt Marjory, my children and the many children whose lives have touched mine as they passed through my firm. It would also have a practical function. It would help me mark the passage of time.

"Each day I could put a seed in a drawer and after 100 days replace them with a larger seed or pod. This would help me count the days until I am rescued."

Debbie Dance
Director of the Oxford Preservation Trust

With spring in the air, you may decide to sample the delights of a walk by the water meadows at Kennington, climb Shotover or Jarn Mound, have a family outing to Oxford Castle, picnic on South Parks or wait for a friend on the steps of the restored Martyrs' Memorial.

Some readers may not realise that the freedom to wander in these places is because of the foresight of the Oxford Preservation Trust. In fact this month's castaway, Debbie Dance, in her ten years as director of the trust, has touched the lives of most Oxford residents.

As well as trying to prevent carbuncles and protect beautiful views, the trust is a creative force. Like its director, it is a forward looking organisation with a vision of a better environment for everyone who lives and works in Oxford.

Under Debbie's leadership, the trust 'unlocked' the 11th century Oxford Castle giving access to St George's Tower and the Castle Mound.

When I first moved to Oxford in 1970, the council was about to demolish St Ebbes and erect the Westgate Centre. To meet Debbie in the trust's office, I walked down Turn Again Lane, the one street of Old St Ebbe's that remains.

Turning my back on the ugly car park, I appreciated this little part of the area that the trust succeeded in preserving.

Debbie attended St. Helen & St. Katherine's school in Abingdon and her MSc in Historic Conservation is from Oxford Brookes University. She is a qualified chartered surveyor and she says she is a 'buildings and place sort of person'. Would this I wondered be reflected in her choice of antique, work of art or book to be washed up on the island?

Debbie's first suggestion is a historic symbol of Oxford.

'The Oxford Preservation Trust's logo is based on The Oxford Crown, a silver coin of Charles 1 which was minted at Oxford — in New Inn Hall Street— during the English Civil War when Charles was resident in the city.

"It has connections to the early days of the trust, when the legendary archaeologist, Arthur Evans was a trustee — he gave an amazing Jarn Mound at Boars Hill to the trust. The Ashmolean has one in its coin gallery. On the desert island it would make me think about Oxford's long and significant history and the city's many stories," Debbie said.

"One of those stories that I love is of Matilda escaping from the castle across the water meadows to Wallingford, some of which is now in the trust's ownership for the people of Oxfordshire to enjoy. On the day she escaped, the Thames was frozen.

When the Castle was being redeveloped we found a single little medieval skate made from bone which is now on display in St George's Tower, and it is such a romantic image to think that this may have been used to save her life.

Many of the most famous view points of Oxford are owned by the trust, including the spot where the poet, Matthew Arnold, admired the 'dreaming spires' and including 'the signal elm' which we bought from All Souls.

"Not far from here our greatest painter JMW Turner surveyed Oxford from North Hinksey. That picture is in the Manchester City Art Gallery but they have kindly given us the right to use the image which we have made into a postcard. It has everything for me, the setting, the buildings and the work of a great artist.

"One of the trust's early acts was to give South Park to the city with covenants ensuring it is preserved for the enjoyment of the people. The artist Eric Gill was commissioned to carve the obelisk stone at the foot of the hill. If I took that to the island it would probably suit the surroundings but also remind me of South Parks and my illustrious predecessors including the poet John Betjeman. Eric Gill provides a link to a special area in Wolvercote where he also carved a memorial stone to mark the gift to the trust of a plot of land opposite The Trout. Today this land is run as a community orchard by the locals in return for an annual rent to the trust of a basket of apples!.

"Eric was an artist inspired by William Morris who was the founder of the conservation movement of which Oxford Preservation Trust is one of the earliest local societies.

"As a young man, Sir Michael Sadler, founding trustee, met William Morris when he was up at Oxford, linking him to the opening lines in the trust's first annual report 'guiding change, not stopping it'. This rings as true today as it did then, recognising the needs of Oxford in the 21st century but balancing this against the duty to keep and protect the best of our buildings, places and views for future generations."

A prime example of how the trust manages change is the project that has revitalised the area around Oxford Castle.

Debbie said: "Oxford Castle involved a £3.8 million Heritage Lottery Fund grant and we are proud of the results and the links to education. It is a place for everyone and has changed the face of the city for the better.

"To see the public spaces used for all kinds of music and cultural events is a great pleasure and all this comes together in one moment for me — sitting alongside the Dean of Christ Church one cold December evening, watching the children of Pegasus School of Blackbird Leys, perform a play they had written on Oxford saints and Saint Frideswide whose shrine is in the cathedral, town and gown united!

"The castle has also given us the opportunity to connect with the public so much more and my passion for breaking down the barriers between town and gown has led to our biggest local scheme Oxford Open Doors.

"People laugh when I say that I do not believe the barriers exist, that they are in people's minds only. If you want proof that it can be done, 24,000 visits took place across one weekend throughout town and university last year."

Debbie shares ownership of a watercolour of the Martyr's Memorial which hangs in the Meeting Room in the trust's offices.

"Taking this painting to the island would be a poignant reminder of restoring the Martyr's Memorial, and of working with my trustees. The trust was helping to acquire an early painting of Oxford Castle by Rooker for the Museum of Oxford. In the same auction, Richard Carter Jonas, twice chairman, spotted this early watercolour and we bought it together," Debbie recalled.

"The restoration of the memorial marked the 75th Anniversary of the trust. We had thought of commissioning a piece of public art, but on my way to the meeting, I passed the memorial, sad and neglected and behind security hoardings.

"It gave such a gloomy appearance to St Giles and no one really had ownership of it because it was built by public subscription. We agreed to work with Oxford City Council to raise money and restore it and it is amazing to think that this was five years ago and that so many people since have enjoyed sitting on the steps watching the world go by."

Debbie's next choice could not be more up to date - Antony Gormley's Iron Man on the roof of Blackwell's Art and Poster Shop.

Debbie said: "If I took that to the island it would link the past, present and future, which is what the trust is about. It would also remind me of my time working in Birmingham; I was there when they were revitalising the public spaces when The Iron Man was installed in Victoria Square.

"Birmingham has none of the advantages of Oxford but has oodles of civic pride. The people there are just so proud of their place and I guess that is what I want for my place, Oxford, to generate civic pride."

I reminded Debbie that she must choose just one item from her fascinating suggestions. She found that a difficult task, so, in the end, opted for a book.

"When Queen Elizabeth 1 visited Oxford she was presented with her own illustrated guide book! This rare book and beautiful book is kept in the Bodleian. It would encapsulate the sixteenth century city but perhaps it is too fragile to survive on the desert island.

"But I have an out of print book by Christopher Hibbert published in 1988. It is called The Encyclopaedia of Oxford. I look at it all the time. It is my Bible and includes all of the places I have mentioned. It pulls everything together. I would love to see it reprinted. I wonder if I can challenge some one to take it on!'

Shami Chakrabarti

Director of Liberty and Chancellor of Oxford Brookes University

Chancellor of Oxford Brookes University, Shami Chakrabarti, is probably better known for her role as director of Liberty, also known as The National Council for Civil Liberties, which was set up 75 years ago to champion the rights of ordinary people and hold the powerful to account.

This is obviously a formidable and daunting task, yet Shami Chakrabarti has displayed a determined spirit to stand up for Liberty's founding principles since taking on the role of director in 2003.

"The image of a university chancellor is of a grey-suited man, possibly overseeing the credit crunch. Considering a Sun columnist once described me as: 'The most dangerous woman in Britain', it was brave of the university to consider me. "

She is featured in a new open-air photographic exhibition being staged this month in the run-up to the reopening of Oxford's Ashmolean Museum — a collection of more than 40 portraits taken by photographer, Theo Chalmers.

So, given her support for Oxford's great museum, what antique work of art or antiquarian book would she like to see washed up on our desert island?

Shami describes herself as 'more into books and words than objects', so it is no surprise that her first choice is a book.

"I was recently a guest on Desert Island Discs and the book I chose to take to the island was *To Kill a Mocking Bird* by Harper Lee. I first read it when I was about 12 years-old and it had a profound effect on me. Since then I have met so many campaigners for fair trials and human rights who have also been inspired by it. Because I chose this book and Nina Simone's song *I Wish I Knew How It Would Feel To Be Free*, a columnist in a national paper described me as 'The most dull woman in Britain'.

"Fortunately not everyone reacted in that way. I received a touching letter from a listener who offered to share her *To Kill a Mocking Bird* story. While working with children in Alabama, she helped with a stage adaptation of the book. "She wrote: 'During a rehearsal, an old lady came in and asked 'What is going on here? What are you doing?' The teacher in charge replied 'Well ma'am we have been reading the book in class and thought it would be good to stage it too. Why are you interested?'

'Her reply was "My name is Harper Lee and I wrote that story." Stunned, we told her 'How wonderful. We so admire your writing but do you mind us asking why you did not go on to write other books?' Harper Lee's explanation was 'Because I had said everything I really wanted to say in my entire life in that one book!'

"This lovely correspondent endeared herself even more to me because she enclosed a cheque to Liberty!" Shami added.

"Stories have so much more power than articles or speeches. I love the scene in the film of Harper Lee's book, where Gregory Peck, playing Atticus Finch, tells his daughter: 'You have to know what it is like to walk around in someone else's shoes.'

"The idea, of treating other people as you would like to be treated yourself, is universal; it is in most religions and underpins human ethics. I think that book led me to choose to study law.

"The first image that really impressed itself on my psyche, I saw in France about 20 years ago. While I was a law student, I worked for a while as a short order cook in a café in Central London.

"One of the waitresses was a French student and she was not enjoying the hard work. When

Delacroix's La Liberté Guidant le Peuple

she suggested I leave with her and stay at her mother's house in the South of France, I jumped at the chance.

"I spent a delightful summer there including July 14, Bastille Day. Every village had its open celebrations and it was then that I saw Delacroix's *La Liberté Guidant le Peuple*. A woman personifying Liberty leads the people forward over the bodies of the fallen, holding the tricoleur. The actual painting is in the Louvre, but I bought a poster back with me and it hangs on the wall in my windowless 'dungeon' office.

"While working in the 'black tower' that is the Home Office, I bought another poster to remind me why I wanted to become a lawyer. When at the Museum of Modern Art in New York, I saw *Brown v. the Board of Education*. It concerns the case that helped bring equal rights to education in the States. Alongside that and my Delacroix poster I now have lots

of drawings by my son who is a keen artist," Shami said.

"They all remind me of the instant impact images can have. That is why on the few occasions we commission advertisements we are careful with the design. Recently we had one made for Liberty to celebrate our 75th anniversary.

"We used another to oppose the extension of the period of detention without trial to 42 days. I think it really helped to win the case because the simple bar chart compares the time a suspect can be held in custody without charge in all advanced counties. The number '42' next to '3' or '4' stood out starkly."

There is one object at Oxford Brookes University that now has significance for her. Brookes is named after John Henry Brookes, the education campaigner and there is a bust of him in the University Campus.

"As a 19 year-old undergraduate, I heard Helena Kennedy give an inspiring talk about following your heart into the law. I decided she was my kind of lawyer and she was also the first chancellor of Brookes. When I received a call from John Snow asking if I would like to become chancellor I checked my diary to make sure it wasn't All Fools Day! Surprisingly, it wasn't a practical joke.

"I think I prefer to regard myself as Brookes' mascot! I am really happy to be here. Brookes is not only a fine academic institution, it also has its roots in the local community. It is not an ivory tower for its courses are so varied, they can take you onto the factory floor, the hospital ward and into the classroom. I really enjoy my visits here because, once among the students, I almost feel like a teenager again."

When Shami came to chose her lone item for the desert island she went for Delacroix's *La Liberté Guidant le Peuple (above)*.

"Liberty the organisation has loomed so large in my life that looking at her on the desert island would evoke so many memories," she said.

18

Andrew McLellan

Education officer, Pitt Rivers Museum, Oxford

Andrew McLellan spends his days working with children, opening their eyes and imagination to other cultures, just as his were when, as a boy, he spent many happy hours among the strange artefacts housed in Oxford's Pitt Rivers Museum, where he is now the education officer.

But which of the museum's 80,000 exhibits would Andrew choose to take with him to our desert island?

Andrew has some prior experience of selecting useful items. To engage and inspire young visitors, he asks them what they would take with them if they had to survive alone on a remote island.

"I ask children who visit the museum on family activity days to complete this sentence: 'Help, I am stuck on desert island and I've only got a...'

"We do get the odd child who wants to take a Gameboy, but many of the suggestions are thoughtful and charming. One I particularly like was 'A compass, a bottle of water and a book of poems.' Unfortunately the author didn't put a name to his suggestion.

"But Elizabeth O'Connor chose a blanket and three toys while another suggestion, signed by 'Rita', was 'A bone knife, a machéte and a ukelele'," Andrew revealed.

"The Pitt Rivers shows children that what is most needed is the imagination to use what is around you," he added.

"This museum does not organise objects like other museums, grouping things from one country together. It arranges them by their function. There is not just one way of making a light or a fish trap.

"Visitors can see that the natural and manufactured things around us can have multiple uses. A frisbee can be used to play games — or as a bowl or a scoop.

"Things can be beautifully-crafted, nostalgic and practical at the same time."

"The Pitt Rivers gives an idea of how rich the world is — and how adaptable human beings are. We encourage children to develop craft skills. With the family activities we try to make things from scrap materials. These are skills you can apply in any environment.

"On a desert island a coconut shell can be used as a water carrier. One popular family activity is making musical instruments

and coconut shells can make music and be decorated. Art and music are also common to people everywhere."

But what item from the museum's collection would he want to find on our desert island?

"Marooned on a desert island, I would need food, water, fire and shelter. I would consider taking with me a machéte. I think of it as an equivalent to the Swiss army knife," Andrew said.

"With a machéte and a credit card I could provide all I need to live. What I can't make with a machéte, I could buy with a credit card, but most airlines frown on people with machétes! So, I would want to find on the beach the late 19th-century machéte from the Congo, which is part of the teaching collection here.

"I could use it to chop trees to make a shelter and chop firewood. With it I could make a bow drill to make fire more easily than rubbing sticks together. I could even use it to make a boat.

"But if I was allowed to take anything from the museum, I would take the boat with outriggers and sail that hangs in the centre of the museum. Outriggers act as stabilisers, so the boat doesn't need a keel and can be sailed in shallow water. A boat with a keel would have its bottom ripped apart on coral reefs. This boat, from Zanzibar, is stable in rough ocean waters too.

"The museum is so rich in examples of humankind's flexible thinking, and I think the outrigger is one of the great designs. It would give me some freedom to island hop and go fishing."

The outrigger is old and beautiful but I wondered whether we should allow our castaway to escape quite so easily!

The Pitt Rivers has a fine collection of textiles and Andrew showed me some he particular admired.

"I taught for five years in South East Asia and have spent a lot of time travelling in that part of the world. One craft I saw being applied and particularly admired that is also beautiful to look at, is Batik.

"One of its uses was made famous in this country by footballer David Beckham — the sarong.

"There is an attractive sarong from Java in the collection. The dyes used are natural and this one was dipped 30 times to build up the depth of the colour. As well as being an attractive piece of fabric, it is adaptable. It is a comfortable garment, which can be used as a rug or blanket and could shade me from the sun.

"But I shall have to opt for the machéte, because it would be the most useful tool for using local materials to make other tools and objects. I think I could use it to make anything I would need including a boat."

Andrew was also very particular about the kind of island he wanted to be abandoned on.

"Most volcanic islands don't have metals, but volcanic glass makes great knives."

It appears that Andrew will have no problems surviving on our desert island.

19

Charles & Cecille Swaisland

Former district officer in the Colonial Service

When some people reach retirement age, they put their feet up, watch TV and potter in the garden. Others save up for a luxury cruise around the world.

But that is not adventurous enough for Charles and Cecillie Swaisland, who are just about to celebrate their 60th wedding anniversary. In their 80s, the couple, who live in Kennington, were happy to discover Alaska, even if it meant sleeping in cabin bunk beds.

Charles, in his 90s, is honorary curator of the Pendon Museum at Long Wittenham near Abingdon, and also works as a volunteer two days a week at Oxford's Bodleian Library, sorting colonial records.

It is hard to imagine anyone in Kennington who has not come across the couple on village committees, organising litter picks or the library festival, or pounding the streets for the annual Kennington Overseas Aid (KOA) house-to-house collection.

Cecillie has been known to bake 40 cakes at a time for KOA fundraising. Most locals however, will be unaware that the couple lived for more than 30 eventful years in Africa and Asia.

Their connection with South Africa deepened when Charles and Cecillie were approached to be peace monitors in the run up to the first democratic election in South Africa in 1994. when Nelson Mandela became president.

During the Second World War, Charles, a Quaker and pacifist, served in a Quaker surgical and medical transport brigade — but his posting was unusual. His unit was sent by the International Red Cross and the Foreign Office to help the Chinese in their prolonged resistance against the Japanese occupation.

After two years, Charles was invalided out of China and, on the difficult journey home, his boat was bombed and sunk.

When he complained about losing his cap during the dramatic incident, a Welsh sailor

who hauled him aboard the rescuing corvette, said: "You are bloody lucky you did not loose your life!'"

Back in England in 1945, Charles was stationed at the Middlesex Hospital and, with responsibilities for demobilisation, worked with Brian Bone, who introduced him to his sister, Cecillie, then a young student studying sociology at the London School of Economics, who was also a Quaker. Charles and Cecillie quickly discovered they had much in common and were soon married.

After studying sociology and law at Birmingham University, Charles applied to join the colonial service, was accepted and was posted to Nigeria. Their first daughter, Ruth, was born in Port Harcourt in 1951, and their second, Alison, in 1954 in Gloucester, on their first home leave.

As a district officer in Nigeria from 1949–1963, Charles was in charge of the local police force, as well as being a magistrate and

prison governor.

From Nigeria, Charles and Cecillie and their two daughters moved to Mauritius, where, after studying for his D Phil in Public Administration at Oxford, Charles taught at Birmingham University, but was often seconded to different parts of the world, with support from the Foreign Office. One such posting was to train district officers in Southern Sudan.

Cecillie researched for her MSocSci at Birmingham and then lectured in social science.

It is hard to imagine there is any part of the world where they have not visited or worked.

So maybe this intrepid couple will not be daunted by the prospect of being marooned on our desert island. But what work of art, antique or antiquarian book would they like to find washed up on the beach?

They showed me an oil painting of a charming thatched bungalow. Charles explained: "This is a painting of the district officer's residence which became our home in eastern Nigeria. I took over the Nsukka District, which is about the size of Oxfordshire.

The previous district officer had removed the thick traditional thatch and replaced it with 'fashionable' corrugated iron.

"So Cecillie and I had the thatch restored, putting it on top of the corrugated iron."

Cecillie said this was a very comfortable home. "The walls were made from mud, stone and cow dung and were three feet thick. They kept the house cool, even in the noonday sun."

Charles and Cecillie stayed on in Nigeria after the country after it became independent in 1960, remaining there until 1963. "We were invited to stay by the newly-independent government," Charles explained.

"Most British district officers returned to the UK, but we chose to remain in Nsukka and never regretted the decision."

Cecillie showed me another possible desert island choice which would remind them of their time in Nigeria. It is a photograph of a couple, getting married.

"This would be rather nostalgic. It is the second wedding of our chief servant James."

Charles added: "At that time in Nigeria, a couple's first marriage came when they were very young with the groom's family giving a 'bride price' or dowry.

"Often, when couples were older and richer and their family complete, they wanted a second wedding.

"As district officer, I had to conduct many of these marriages and, this may sound surprising, but I hated doing it. The reason is that there was nothing about love and commitment in the ceremony. It was simply about avoiding bigamy, which was common because of child marriages which were not dissolved."

Cecillie added: 'The Ibo people also like the idea of a second burial. Because of the climate, funerals have to take place very quickly. Sometime later there is a second 'burial' which is more a kind of memorial feast.

"When James died in 2000, my daughter Ruth received the phone call. She burst into tears on hearing the news. She grew up in that bungalow and James and Ruth adored each other.

Soon after that phone call, a Nigerian bishop contacted us and felt that, as James's former employers, we should send £500 to help pay for the feast, which we did."

Charles showed me another nostalgic choice for the island, the district officer's ceremonial sword. He said it would remind him of a particular day.

"For formal occasions I had to wear a white uniform," he said. "Our head servant James was very particular that the sword should gleam.

"What I did not realise until too late, when I noticed the zebra stripes on my uniform, is that he had cleaned it with Cherry Blossom boot polish!"

"When we finally left Nigeria, I was presented with the robes of an Ibo tribal chief. That is another possibility for the desert island, although ten years ago, we gave them to the Pitt Rivers Museum.

In 1983 they both took early retirement.

"We wanted to spend less time on administration and more on research," said Cecille. We decided to move from Selly Oak to Oxford because the best material on Southern Africa was in the Bodleian Library.

"While house hunting we were shown around a bungalow in Kennington. Seeing its spacious kitchen, I immediately said 'this is the one' and we have lived here ever since."

After retiring she read for her M.Litt (Oxon) and embarked on a writing career, publishing three books on South Africa, including *Servants and Gentlewomen to the Golden Land — the emigration of single women from Britain to Southern Africa 1820-1939* (Berg, ISBN 0 85496 870 9) and *A Lincolnshire Volunteer* (Literatim ISBN 0 9539754 0 1) based on the Boer War letters of her great uncle are set there.

Cecillie's connection with South Africa began when her father sold his business in Scunthorpe and took his family to live in Camps Bay, on the outskirts of Cape Town. He hoped the climate would help his son Brian, recover from TB.

"Seven years later, when my brother was fit and healthy, we returned to England," Cecillie said.

"My father had decided to study at Manchester College, Oxford, which was then a Unitarian College. Once he became the Rev Walter Bone, we moved to Gloucester."

The connection with South Africa deepened in 1994 when Charles and Cecillie were approached to be peace monitors in the run up to the first democratic election in South Africa, when Nelson Mandela became president.

Charles described the official aim of the mission as the "prevention of violence in public gatherings".

"The local clergy were worn out trying to mediate between factions and trying to prevent physical conflict so they sought the help of the World Council of Churches.

"We were among 16 volunteers sent in response and we represented the Quakers. One of the reasons we were chosen was because we are fellows of Rhodes University in Eastern Cape."

Cecillie was posted to Durban and Charles spent his two months in Pietermaritzburg. Cecillie showed steadfast courage when she stood in the firing line between two opposing groups.

Back home in Kennington, Charles enjoys rather less dramatic pursuits.

"I am honorary curator at the Pendon Museum and work there one day a week. Pendon is a Model of the Vale of White Horse as it was in the 1930s.

"If we took the model to the island we could have hours of fun, but I think if we can only take one thing, it must be the painting. I had such freedom of action in Nigeria and that is not possible in the UK today."

20

John Lloyd
Journalist and author

John Lloyd has witnessed monumental
upheavals as a foreign correspondent
in the former Soviet Union. His book,
Birth of a Nation: an Anatomy of Russia,
records one of them. John, now director
of Journalism at the Reuters Institute for
the Study of Journalism in Oxford, spent
ten years reporting for the *Financial Times*
in Eastern Europe and was there as the iron
curtain was ripped asunder.

He also witnessed dramatic events in this
country, resulting in a book on the miner's
strike of 1984-85, titled *Loss without Limit: the
British Miners' Strike* (with Martin Adeney)

As well as editing the *New Statesman*, he
was the founding editor of the *Financial Times
Weekend* magazine. John has collected many
awards, including the British Press Award for
Specialist Reporter of the Year, the Granada
Award for Journalist of the Year and the David
Watt Prize for outstanding journalism.

The Reuters Institute for the Study
of Journalism in Norham Gardens was
established in 2006, and is part of the
Department of Politics and International
Relations at the University of Oxford.

At the heart of the institute is the long-
standing Thomson Reuters Fellowship
Programme for visiting journalists from all
parts of the world.

John's international credentials include
writing for *La Repubblica* of Rome. He has
worked for Weekend World, the London
Programme (LWT) and for Independent
Radio News.

As well as working behind the scenes, he has
often appeared in front of the camera on late
night political discussions. Considering how
well read in many languages and extensively
travelled he is, I wondered which antique,
work of art or book would John want to find
washed up on the beach of our desert island?

Like the world events he has witnessed,
storm and tempest is a theme running through
John Lloyd's choices for our desert island.

His first suggestion was a Turner painting
- Joseph Mallord William Turner (1775-1851)
not his contemporary William Turner of
Oxford.

John said: "Turner is the one artist that I like
most consistently. *Peace: Burial at Sea of the*

Body of Sir David Wilkie would be my choice
of painting. The title may seem rather morbid
but in this case the turbulent sky looming over
a calm sea would remind me of the place I
grew up, Anstruther in East Fife not far from
St Andrews.

"It is a fishing village and my grandfather
who brought me up, was in the merchant navy
and my mother worked for the Royal Navy.
Turner's inspiration was sea, storm, cloud and
rain and growing up by the sea those images
stayed with me.

"I admire the swirls of energy and colour in
his pictures: the way he painted was way ahead
of his time. But while I should derive great
pleasure from this painting, I would also have
the real thing in front of me," John added.

I wondered if there was something that had
particular relevance to his work and the future
of the eager and the talented students from a
round the world who attend his seminars.

"A painting which has echoes in my life
today is one by El Greco, called *Allegory* which
shows a boy blowing an ember till it gives a
light - showing his face, and that of a monkey
and of a fool.

"No-one seems to know what was in El
Greco's mind. But the speculation is that
it shows a (literal) enlightenment. At the
same time, however, the illumination is not
of wise men - but of a boy, a man of limited
intelligence and a monkey."

"To load another meaning on this
mysterious work, that is what journalism is. At
its best, it is an attempt at illumination, which
gives a small, partial and often biased view of a
huge surrounding darkness," John explained.

"It is, or should be, an illumination —and it
is a precious source. It is limited but, like the
glowing ember, it does, for a while, cast a light
so that those who wish to understand, who
themselves will be limited, can see something."

If he can take just one thing would it be the
El Greco? The Scottish National Gallery may
have a problem with this work disappearing to
our desert island but John's final choice turned
out to be a much simpler option.

"I would like to take something to remind
me of home and family but it would also need
to stimulate me and keep my mind active. So,
as I can only take one thing, I shall choose my

well thumbed Oxford Edition of *The Complete Works of Shakespeare*.

"Much of my life has been taken up with reading. Shakespeare's poems and plays are capable of being re-read and releasing endless new insights. It is rich enough and compact enough to engage thoughts about the human condition. With time on my hands, if I also had a supply of pencils and paper, it could even re-ignite an unresolved ambition.

"At university I wanted to write novels and plays and to act in them. I did have one of my dramas performed in Edinburgh but then I turned to the dark side and went into journalism," John said.

"Writing creatively is a solitary occupation but it has a social aspect; it needs an audience. I think it could be easy to lose heart if there was no-one to read it or see it performed.

"If I manage to keep alive the idea of rescue or escape then maybe I could produce my dreamed of masterpiece or at least imagine directing one of Shakespeare's plays.

My son Jacob who is a student here in Oxford wants to be a Shakespearean actor. He has played the part of Prospero in *The Tempest*. So the choice would make me feel close to him."

21

Sister Francis Dominica

Founder of the Helen House Hospice

The founder of the world's first children's hospice, Helen House and of Douglas House for young people, Sister Frances Dominica is the first person I have interviewed who has made a public vow of poverty, so I was intrigued as to how she would tackle the challenge of choosing items for our desert island.

She is not new to the castaway experience having already appeared on the well known Radio 4's programme. Having chosen her luxury, she already has a chaise longue, complete with a mosquito net waiting for her on the desert island. Ingeniously sumptuous but practical at the same time! The book she chose, The Earth from Above, should help maintain her vision of the world as one — a vision echoed in her choices for this feature.

So, stretched out on her chaise longue listening to *The Skye Boat Song,* which antique or work of art would she like to be washed up on the beach?'

"My first thought was a watercolour painting of *The Kyles of Bute* by Thomas Fairbairn which hangs in my office. It belonged to my grandfather and he was a very special person to me." Sister Frances said.

"I was born in Inverness, in December 1942. My father was away in the war and so my mother took me to live with my grandparents, in Greenock. When I was just three weeks old my grandmother died.

"My grandfather was bereft, but focusing on this new baby brought life into his home and we built up a very special relationship which lasted until he died aged 96. I was named Frances and that had added significance for him.

"My grandparents had two children close together in age, the eldest being my mother. Then ten years later, another little girl was born, and they called her Frances. My mother told me how she lit up everyone's life bringing such joy, but tragically she died suddenly of a virus aged only three.

"My grandfather struggled to overcome his grief. Every Sunday from 1925, he would visit her grave, until in 1942 when I arrived and was named after Frances, he finally stopped going there. So this painting is special, resonant not only of Scotland but of this strong attachment between my grandfather and me. Looking at it reminds me of him."

Sister Frances lived in Greenock with her grandfather until she was almost four.

"When my father came out of the army, he took us to live in Petersham, in Surrey where I attended primary school." Sister Frances said "My secondary education was at Cheltenham Ladies' College but I wasn't a success at school and so I left, aged 17, and did voluntary work, in Bethnal Green.

"I had always wanted to nurse sick children and in 1961, started to train as a nurse at the Hospital for Sick Children Great Ormond Street. I loved every moment of it, so when, in 1966, I announced that I was going to join the Society of all Saints, an Anglican religious community, my shocked and horrified family and friends did everything they could to dissuade me.'

Soon afterwards Sister Frances met the little girl who was to change the direction of her life

"I am of the opinion that sometimes a person is blessed to be in the right place at the right moment in time-- and that happened to me," she said "I met Helen's parents at the Radcliffe Infirmary. Their much- loved daughter was only two when she underwent surgery to remove a brain tumour, after which she needed 24-hour care. Looking after a very sick child day and night is exhausting. On occasion, I looked after Helen in my room at All Saints Convent to give her parents a break.

"This experience brought home to me the need for respite care and support for children with life-shortening conditions and their families! "

When, in 1982, Sister Frances founded the world's first children's hospice she named it after Helen, and it was set up to help families like hers cope by providing personalised respite care modelled on that provided in the family home.

Helen House has just eight children's bedrooms. The vibrant building with its small scale provides flexibility and fun, as well as affording the children and families who stay there sensitivity and dignity.

For this groundbreaking work, Sister Frances was awarded an OBE in 2006 and received a Woman of the Year Award in 2007.

Sister Frances explained: "The idea behind the hospice is an extension of the relationship with Helen's family — offering friendship, support and practical help. The emphasis

is on making the most of life, whatever the circumstances. So my second choice to take on the island would symbolise Helen House and remind me of a little girl who gave us so much joy.

"In my office, hangs a colourful collage by ten year old Susie, who made it for me while staying here. She was such a delightful little girl but tragically both she and her mother died of cancer. At that time the Duchess of Kent was our Patron. When she was due to visit, Susan was always waiting for her. She was not in the least shy and asked the duchess questions like 'Do you wear a crown at home? '

"They often swapped earrings, so for a little while, Susan wore the Duchess' precious stones and the Duchess wore Susan's paste. Susan always hoped the Duchess would forget to swap back at the end of the day!

"My third choice cost me £2.50 from a market stall in Ghana. In 1996, while on my second trip to West Africa, I bought a pair of individually made hand crafted batiks and they now hang in the Sister's refectory.

"I love Africa and was overwhelmed by how many people have so little yet are willing to share whatever they have. The batiks would also have a personal resonance, because on my first trip to Ghana, I met a baby badly in need of a home and family and I brought him home and eventually adopted him. The batiks will connect me with him and with Africa but they would also remind me of a completely different part of my life, that of a single parent.

"That has opened doors for me to meet people I would never otherwise have met, and to experiences and insights into aspects of life which were new to me. My son developed a passion for Moto-X racing.

For six years, most of my weekends were spent covered in either mud or dust as 35-40 bikes roared around the track at breakneck speed, and I stood in the middle of the field with my eyes shut! " Sister Francis recalled.

Sister Frances showed me another

To Frances who is a Very Special Person to me. I love her So. And From Susan

possibility, a print of a Picasso painting titled La Ronde. She was able to recite in French the nursery rhyme of the same name. It is a lively sketch of people of every colour holding hands and dancing in a circle around a dove of peace each holding an olive branch.

She said "To me it represents the circle of human fellowship. I came across it for the first time in 1975, when some friends used it on their wedding invitations. The idea has grown on me. It has a feeling of joy because no one is excluded from the circle."

"When I joined the order, I thought I might never nurse a sick child again. I was 23 and in those days we wore the full habit.

"During those early years, I did little that people on the outside would understand, given my training. I cleaned, cooked and, gardened but was not using my nursing skills.

"But I now recognise the value of those years. It was a time of contemplation, delving deep within myself in the search for God. So despite the personal resonances of the other suggestions, if I can only take one thing to the island then it must be this."

Sister Frances lovingly unwrapped a bronze crucifix. "It was hidden for so long but to hold it is to hold history in my hands, the history of Christianity, through good times and bad," she said.

It has the symbols of the four evangelists on the four corners. They kept the message of love alive and I feel I would be nothing without my Christian conviction. It comes with a story attached - and I love it."

"A daughter devoted herself to the care of her father after he suffered a debilitating stroke and lost the ability to speak clearly. She acted as his interpreter, every day for many years, in running his estate.

"The Reverend George Congreve of the Society of St John the Evangelist visited them and she showed him an object sacred to her- this 13th century bronze crucifix was given to her by her uncle who found it in an old manor house, Ufton Court, near Reading," Sister Francis explained.

"It had hung in a secret chapel in a roof top at a time when celebrating the Catholic Mass was a dangerous occupation. It was left to Father George Congreve who gave it to us. It now stands in our convent chapel."

22

Colin Dexter

Author

When reviewing 'My Ashmolean /My Museum', for *The Oxford Times*, I was struck by Theo Chalmers' stern portrait of Colin Dexter.

Colin explained that the photographer's instructions had been to look grim "as if about to be consumed by fire". So some acting was required to resonate with the story, implicit in the portrait, one of the cruellest events this city has witnessed, when Bishops Latimer and Ridley were burned in what is now Broad Street in 1555. Archbishop Cranmer watched his great friends on their way to their death from the window of his cell above The North Gate. Five months later, on a cold wet morning in March 1556, Cranmer also died a martyr's death at the stake near Balliol College.

Who could be more fitting to represent the darker side of Oxford's history than this writer whose novels contain no fewer than ninety one dead bodies?

Theo Chalmers photographed Colin wearing an iron manacle, as worn by Cranmer during his incarceration in the Bocado prison, which was located on Cornmarket, above the city's North Gate. This portrait was one of three connected images based around the Oxford Martyrs, captured by Chalmers for the Ashmolean exhibition.

Actor Kevin Whately, best known for his role as Lewis in the *Inspector Morse* television series based on Colin's novels, was photographed holding the key to the Bocardo, prison, while Laurence Fox (who plays Lewis's sidekick in the spin-off series) is shown holding the iron band which the executioners used to bind the Archbishop to the stake.

All these objects are, of course, part of the Ashmolean's collection. The author's acting ability, in front of Theo's camera, is perhaps not surprising because, like Alfred Hitchcock, he always takes a cameo role in Inspector Morse and the *Lewis* series.

Endeavour Morse, the opera-loving enthusiast of cryptic crosswords and cask ale, was in fact so popular that 18 million people watched the final three of the 33 episodes that were screened.

That description of Morse could just as easily apply to Colin himself. There is surely a double meaning in the title of one of Colin's short stories *The Double Crossing* for, as a crossword champion, he has twice chaired a series of crossword programmes on BBC Radio4.

When Colin agreed to be our castaway, I wondered whether the chosen object would be found in The Pitt Rivers or The Ashmolean as both museums have featured in his books and TV adaptations. But would he want to leave Morse buried and be inspired by the other enigmatic aspects of his own life?

"Education has dominated my life." Colin said. "Indeed, my first books as a co-author were educational textbooks, not crime fiction. My first publisher was Robert Maxwell. Pergamon Press published our three books on liberal studies.

"This followed CP Snow and other intellectuals publicising their concern about the great divide between arts and sciences. They wanted scientists to appreciate Goethe and Shakespeare, and artists to know something about Galileo and Keppler. Liberal Studies in the Sixth Form were intended to add balance and breadth to the curriculum," Colin said.

"I was Senior Classics Master at Corby Grammar School when serious deafness struck thereafter blighting my life. So, I came here, in 1966, to work as senior assistant secretary at the University of Oxford Delegacy, in Ewert House, where I continued to work until I retired in 1988."

Realising that meant his first seven novels were written in his spare time, I wondered how he did it.

"One day, after supper and *The Archers* — and a pint (or two) of real ale at my local — I realised that if I were to write a page a day, by the end of the year I would have written a book," Colin revealed.

"Readers may find my choices surprisingly academic but they reflect a lifetime involved in education. I am best known for my crime fiction, and Morse's favourite artist (and mine) is Vermeer. Morse had a Vermeer reproduction over his mantelpiece and I would have no hesitation in choosing *The Milkmaid*, which hangs in the Rijksmuseum in Amsterdam.

"It is a superb example of an artist at the top of his form. Good art or music for me is that which can be progressively enjoyed more and more," Colin said.

"There is nothing wrong with popular art yet after a while one may become tired of much of it. But who could ever tire of this picture? Was there ever a stream of milk so beautifully painted?"

Vermeer lived and worked in Delft and in one corner of *The Milkmaid* is a solitary Delft tile — on that tile is a tiny cupid. In view of Colin's next suggestion, I wondered if that was significant.

Colin showed me a book on Ancient Greek Pottery by Professor Michael Vickers, the curator of Greek and Roman Antiquities at the Ashmolean.

He pointed to a picture of a fourth century red-figure bell crater, (a bowl for mixing wine) which is in the Ashmolean collection.

"The Greeks were soberly sensible," Colin said. "Professor Michael Vickers told me they used to dilute their wine in a ratio of one wine to four or five of water, so guests could enjoy it without getting mildly tipsy too quickly.

"I suppose this large jar could even be useful for collecting rain water on the island; but

my reason for choosing it is the sophisticated representation of *The Judgement of Paris*.

"Zeus possessed a golden apple 'for the fairest' but he was reluctant to choose between Hera, Athena, and Aphrodite, and therefore, asked Paris, a mere mortal, to do it for him.

"All three goddesses were beautiful but in addition Hera offered him riches and power, Athena wisdom and Aphrodite sexual love.

"Paris chose Aphrodite so you would expect him to be in the middle on this pot, but it is Hermes, whom we recognise as he holds his customary wand, the caduceus."

With the bell crater on the island, Colin joked that he would be in the company of the three most beautiful goddesses in the world. I asked him if the Greek myths had played a role in his novels. Colin said,

'The Oedipus story by Sophocles inspired *The Dead of Jericho*. That was also the first to be televised. The screenplay was written by Antony Mingella and his early death in 2008 was tragic," he added.

"Sophocles was a prolific writer, but we have only seven of his plays. I think the biggest tragedy of all was the burning of the great library at Alexandria. We can only imagine the books that were lost.'

I asked Colin which, of his 13 Morse books, would he rescue from destruction if only one could be saved.

"That would be *The Dead of Jericho*," he said. "But, if I can only have one thing on the island it would have to be a book and not one of mine. The one I would choose is a selection of Latin translations of Thomas Gray's *Elegy written in a Country Churchyard*. It is edited by Donald Gibson, Peter Wilkinson, and Stephen Freeth, and published by subscription.

"It would give me countless hours of pleasure. I could never tire of the brilliance of these versions. There is a personal resonance in that my brother John and I were subscribers to this publication. I feel fairly sure that my greatest literary hero, the scholar — poet, A E Housman would have enjoyed them enormously"

Housman was Colin's choice, on the BBC Radio 4 programme *Great Lives* in May 2008 and the pair have a good deal in common. They are both classicists who found a popular audience in another genre.

In the end, the classics are still the first choice of this great mind.

23

Sir Christopher Ball

Former Warden of Keble College, Oxford, and marathon runner

In 1987, Sir Christopher Ball found himself at the centre of a student protest. At the time, Sir Christopher, then warden of Keble College, Oxford, was Chair of the Board of the National Advisory Body (NAB), which advised the government on the Polytechnics and Colleges of Further Education.

The students wanted more equal distribution of funds for higher educational – but even Sir Christopher could not persuade the treasury to release more cash, even though he shared the aims of the protestors.

A group of Oxford Polytechnic students threatened to burn an effigy of him at the city's Martyrs Memorial. Typical of Sir Christopher's imaginative approach, he and his wife, Wendy, arrived incognito at the Martyrs' Memorial late in the evening of the students' lonely vigil, bearing gifts of whisky and cake, and listened, as they explained their protest.

The next day, the protestors staged a mock trial and were astounded when Christopher turned up to defend himself. The mood was transformed from hostility to goodwill, although his effigy was still burnt.

Sir Christopher resigned as warden of Keble College, in 1988, and set up his own consultancy business in partnership with his wife. This involved him giving expert advice on educational issues to foreign governments, businesses, schools and colleges. His passion for continuing education permeates his life.

He was on the Founding Forum for Continuing Education (1988-89) was Chairman of the Campaign for Learning, and a founding Fellow of Oxford's Kellogg College. He is involved in The Talent Foundation and chairman of The Global University Alliance and more…

Then, at the age of 68, he took up marathon running. Not content with completing the London Marathon and jogging the length of the Thames, he became the founding member of a rather exclusive band of runners when, in 2007, he was one of seven men to run ten marathons in ten days.

Sir Christopher is also a poet, writing under his middle names, John Elinger. I have included one called Endings at the end of this feature and it will give readers a flavour of the power of his words to conjure an image. It is written in memory of the American poet, Emily Dickinson

Meeting in his Jericho home, I asked him, when marooned on our desert island, which antique, work of art or antiquarian book would he like to be washed up on the beach?

His first choice was the exquisite Alfred Jewel, one of the treasures of the Ashmolean Museum.

"I was an Anglo Saxon scholar and taught Anglo Saxon and the history of the English language." Sir Christopher explained. "So I have thought a lot about it. It is inscribed, Alfred ordered me to be made – not King Alfred although he usually referred to himself as king.

"It was found in the Athelney marshes of Somerset, an area associated with him. It is an astel, or pointer, used to follow the text of a book and then as a bookmark. "

Christopher has a theory about the inscription. He said: "Alfred presented a copy of his translation of Pope Gregory's *Pastoral Care* to every bishop together with a pointer, insisting that they should not be separated. Since the preface began with the words 'King Alfred', I think the title was not needed on the accompanying pointer. On the island, the treat of actually handling this treasure would connect me to a place and time I know well in my imagination and of course, to my life in Oxford and to the Ashmolean."

He has another story connecting him to the

museum. "As a curious student at Merton, I liked to wander the Ashmolean to soak myself in other disciplines," he said. "One day, I noticed a ring with an unusual inscription. I asked the curator if I could look at it.

"He took it out and I saw that it was etched with Viking runes. The curator expressed surprise, saying they had not noticed, so could I write a report on it? I was flattered, being a mere student, but in the course of the research, I discovered there was already a museum account of it published in the 1930s.

"Ten years later, I received a telephone call from the curator, saying: 'You know your runic ring (I enjoyed thinking of it as mine) 'a visiting German art historian says it is a fake, a late 19th century German copy, so we are going to take it out of display.' I asked: 'If it is a fake, can I buy it from you?'

"Although they don't sell things from their collections, even fakes, they did not mind me using it as a visual aid when visiting primary schools. When I described a magic Viking ring that told stories, the children asked me where it was and were duly impressed, when I said, "I am wearing it." So the fake runic ring or the Alfred Jewel would be good to have with me," Sir Christopher said.

"But if I took a painting, I think it would be *The Fall of Icarus* by Pieter Brueghel. I often asked students why it makes sense to study language as well as literature. It is important to understand the medium in which we choose to express ourselves, like an artist knowing his palette. I would point to this painting where Icarus can't be both in the sky and in the sea. But language is designed for storytelling. A picture can show a room at a glance but a description of a room in words has to be sequential, like telling a story. So this painting would remind me of the real pleasure of my Oxford teaching days, arousing the interest of students.

"It would also remind me of W H Auden, the poet, who referred to the painting in his poem *Musee des Beaux Arts*. I would so like to write a poem as good as that one!'

Sir Christopher picked up a poetry book, an obviously much-loved 1940s edition of *The Oxford Book of English Verse* saying: "My parents gave me three books when I was 15, *The Complete Works of Shakespeare* , *The Golden Treasury* , and this one.

"No one told me you should read one play at a time, so I read the Shakespeare from cover to cover. Then I studied this book (and *Palgrave's Anthology*), they inspired me to become a poet. This book would remind me of my parents and my school days. Unusually, for those days, I was sent to a co-educational school, St George' School in Harpenden.

Sir Christopher asked if the running shoes with red laces - one of the two pairs he used for the ten marathons in ten days - would count as an antique? I didn't think they were quite vintage fashion, but as we were unlikely to send him unshod to the island, I thought he could go there wearing them.

He had another idea.

"One of my granddaughters, greeted me at the end of marathon number ten and asked if I would be presented with anything. I said 'I think so' and she offered to take a sneak look. When she returned, Juliet said: "Grandpa, you are going to be very disappointed. It is just a lump of old rock."

"This 'lump of old rock' is a fine piece of granite inscribed to mark our achievement of being the first men to run ten consecutive marathons. Maybe it constitutes a work of art - certainly all rock is old! However, I think if I can take only one thing, it has to be this."

Sir Christopher showed me the smallest object any castaway has so far chosen, a blue marble.

"This blue marble was dug up in the garden. All my life, I have been a poet, writer and, above all, a story teller. I told stories as a child, and to my six children, and now tell stories to my eight grandchildren. If I take out the marble, the children know a story is on the way," he said.

"Every year, my extended family gathers in Wales for a holiday; after meals around the camp fire, the children ask for a blue marble story and woe betide me, if I forget to take it. The magic marble allows children to do magical things. It would remind me of our wonderful family holidays in Wales. This little ball of glass represents, for me, the power of the human imagination."

I thought we could be generous and let Sir Christopher travel to the island in his running shoes with the marble in the pocket of his trousers. That way his book of verse, having magically acquired a bookmark could be swept up on the beach.

If there happens to be some paper inside, maybe he will have time to write those poems in honour of W H Auden?

Endings

by John Elinger

Gone – the bright Sun –
Remain some rose-red streaks
across the sky – which fade – and
slowly, light – warmth –
colours die –
The day is done.

A Candle spent –
The bent black wick still smoulders
– glows – and wanes –
Thin smoke uncoils –
vanishes – what remains?
A fading scent.

When our lives cease –
Expect no immortality – in hell
Or heaven – nor lasting fame for
things done well –
Or ill – just Peace.

24

Bettany Hughes
Historian and broadcaster

When she was five, Bettany Hughes was one of the 1,694,117 people who saw Tutankhamen's golden mask while it was on display at the landmark British Museum exhibition in 1972.

Move on 37 years and Bettany is now an acclaimed presenter of history documentaries and enjoys the respect of the academic community for the quality of her research.

Bettany says that her visit to the British Museum was a revelation. The boy king was not a character from a fairytale — this golden youth had actually lived and breathed.

"I still remember the frisson, the heart-in-the-mouth moment when I realised that the stories I had heard of boy-kings dripping in gold, of hidden burial chambers and court intrigue could, sometimes, be true.

"It inspired me, to watch the BBC documentary on Tutankhamen and to write my first illustrated book!" Bettany spoke of her love of the museum at a special reception held to mark the completion of the building's £61m refurburbishment project.

She told a VIP audience that she spent a lot of time at the Ashmolean when she was a student in Oxford. So it is not surprising that she selected an item from the museum as her 'desert island' choice.

"When I was a student at St Hilda's, I worked in the Ashmolean Library. I visited a different gallery in the Ashmolean almost every day, feeling privileged to be so close to other worlds and cultures.

"A friend told me about a dog-eared notice on a noticeboard in the museum, publicising a travelling scholarship.

"I immediately dashed to the museum on my bicycle, forgetting I was wearing a long skirt. I was in such a hurry, it became tangled in the wheels. But I did find that wonderful little piece of paper. l applied and won the scholarship," she recalled.

"It allowed me to travel to Turkey and into Iran to study Hellenistic and Bronze Age Asia Minor. Seeing the remains of these civilisations in the landscape made me feel that it is arrogant to think that I could sit in Oxford writing about these societies and really understand their lives.

"That trip not only taught me a respect for the past and for the importance of the landscape in history, but also to value friendship. If my friend had not made the effort to tell me about the notice, I would never have had that opportunity. It also makes me feel very loyal to the Ashmolean.

"If I wanted to take something to remind me of that special time, in the flush of youth and enthusiasm, seeing places few have the chance to see, I think I would choose something from Hattusa in North Central Anatolia, which was the centre of Hittite Civilisation(1400-1200BC).

"The Egypto-Hittite Peace Treaty (c. 1258 BC) between Hattusili III and Ramesses II is probably the earliest written peace treaty. If I took that and some other diplomatic tablets to the island, they could occupy my mind.

"Reading Hittite cuneiform is a challenge and there are not enough scholars in the world to translate the 7,000 fragments of tablets, which remain un-translated," she said. Bettany acquired the travel bug and, during 1986, embarked on an Inter-Rail tour of Europe.

"I wanted to study figurative sculpture from the prehistoric to modern times," she said. "My aim was to record and understand the importance of the human body in art. I took a sketch book with me on my travels through Greece and Italy and my drawings were my journal. If I took my sketchbook to the island, it would be nostalgic and I could look back to those carefree days."

I wondered whether those memories might make her feel particularly homesick for Europe while on our island. Bettany agreed it might provoke a sentimental interlude.

She recalled a particular location on her 'grand tour'.

'My particular academic interest is in Helen of Troy and Spartan women. The Hill of Therapne, above the Eurotas Valley, is a hauntingly beautiful place. From the river bluff you can look up into the mountains.

"Standing there, I knew that this exquisite location was special and could have been chosen to worship Zeus or any number of Greek heroes but, they chose to make a shrine in honour of 'OREA ELENI' Helen of Troy.

"I knew there must be more to this woman that the boring placid blonde of mythology. I began to study her in depth and discovered that in 2,700 years, there has never been a time when she was not talked about but the opinions are nearly always prejudiced and misogynistic. Following those images is like holding up a mirror to the world, reflecting the idea of what woman should be.

"If I took the painting of *The Abduction of Helen* (c. 1450) by Zanobi Strozzi, which hangs in the National Gallery, it would not only remind me of Helen and the years I have spent studying her, wondering why the idea of her is so potent — but there is a detail in the framing that would make me feel close to my family.

"Scenes from Helen's life were used as decoration on objects in the home in Renaissance Italy. This painting was in fact a decorated tray and its purpose was to carry

treats and a first drink to women after giving birth. Like any mother I can remember that first cup of tea after labour, Bettany explained.

"At the moment, my mind and imagination is focused on a philosopher and mathematician called Hypatia. I used her story to unpick the world of Alexandria, where she lived, for a Channel 4 series.

"She even ran her own school of philosophy but a faction dominated by Bishop Cyril encouraged a mob to flay her alive. Rachel Weiss is going to play the role of Hypatia in the new blockbuster film based on the story of her life.

"Raphael's portrait of Hypatia would be an inspiration, but I think if I can only take one thing, it has to be from the Ashmolean — one of those iconic objects that connected me with the ancient world, when I was a student in Oxford.

"This particular artefact is just under two inches long. As soon as I saw it, I wanted to cradle it in my hand — because it is a tiny, beautifully made representation of a crawling baby, she said.

"The baby has a wonderfully pudgy bottom and is lifting its head up enquiringly – you can imagine it just having made those first, vital moves to start to explore the world around about.

"This was probably a votive offering — it is 3,500 years-old and was discovered by Arthur Evans in the Psychro Cave near Lasithi in Crete. The sad truth is that, in real life, the baby may well have been sick, and its parents were desperately pleading to the gods for help. Modern Greeks still leave these gifts for sublime powers — 'tamata' — when they are ill.

"There is a happier interpretation, that the parents were giving thanks for the successful survival of their precious child through birth and infancy — a flesh and blood token of the future," Bettany said.

"Either way, that little child, short-circuits me back into the lives of men and women from the very distant past, and has always reminded me that, as Wordsworth said, although humanity has many faces, across time as well as space, we all share one human heart."

25

Michael Stanley

Director of Modern Art Oxford

Michael Stanley, the director of Modern Art Oxford, studied art at the city's Ruskin School of Drawing and Fine Art and returned to the city in January last year to take up this exciting and challenging post.

As a boy growing up in a small terraced house in the industrial town of Widnes, Michael, 34, admits it was unusual for a young lad to have a burning passion for art — football and rugby league were more common enthusiams.

Instead of spending his Saturday afternoons on the terraces, Michael headed for the Walker Art Gallery or Tate Liverpool.

"I had two formative experiences and they both involved the journey between two great northern cities, Liverpool and Manchester." Michael said. "I was inspired by the legacy of Victorian philanthropy in the many municipal galleries that exisit in the northwest — and, with the beauty of the Lake District on my doorstep, I was turned into some kind of post-industrial romantic."

One of Michael's early dramatic encounters was with the work of Pre-Raphaelite artist Holman Hunt in the Lady Lever Art Gallery, Port Sunlight — built in 1922 as Lord Lever's remarkable 'gift' to the memory of his wife.

"I saw Holman Hunt's *Scapegoat*. It was one of those incredible encounters with a work of art that I felt I already knew, having poured over so many reproductions of it. Millais and Gerrard Brockhurst's *Jeunesse Doree* also stayed with me.' "It was the perfect accompaniment to a youthful imagination taken up by Victorian artists, The Smiths, Oscar Wilde, and a love of TS Eliot."

Michael is an advocate of contemporary performance art and installations, which seem a world away from the work of Victorian artists. However, he believes that art is a journey which leads each generation to new encounters.

Another formative experience for the new director of Modern Art Oxford was ecclesiastical art.

"I was brought up in a strong Roman Catholic family, so seeing art in churches was inevitable, though in most services I'd be distracted and draw a detail of the Station of the Cross or something on the back of the hymn sheet.

"On a school trip to Tuscany, when I was 14, I had my first sight of the 15th century artist, Piero della Francesca's incredible painting of the Resurrection in Borgo San Sepolcro. Soon after, in a tiny chapel on a hillside in Arrezo, I saw his pregnant Madonna.

"They were such powerful experiences, as vital now as at the time they were made.

"Art is inescapable from the context within which you experience it — the thoughts, memories and emotions that you bring to a work.

"Seeing these remarkable works and the 'encounter' with them has really stayed with me. Still, in my work today, I consider myself choreographing a journey of encounters with works of art — a journey that continues with Susan Phillipsz audio installation at the Observatory at Green College.'"

Michael first encountered contemporary art at an exhibition of the work of German artist, Joseph Beuys, at Tate Liverpool.

"The sight of basalt rocks scattered over the floor of the gallery evoked an immediate response — strong, primitive and yet magical," he said. "Beuys was using materials not usually regarded as art materials to symbolically transcend everyday realities and to build his own mythology."

"During my Easter break, I made a nostalgic trip back to Widnes to photograph the relics of the town's Victorian marketplace that was due for demolition," Michael recalled.

"In a small back room, I came across the old municipal Christmas lights, about to be trashed. I spent three days rewiring them and with the help of a generator, found by my uncle, I managed to get them to function for all of 40 seconds and was able to snap a couple of photographs, before they faded — and with them, in many respects, my career as an artist!

"I was frustrated by not being able to share moments like this with other people and with other artists and, from that point, became more interested in making opportunities to make work for others other than myself." Michael has bought all these formative influences to bear on his new job in Oxford.

"For me Modern Art Oxford is more than just a building, it is an 'idea'— an idea about contemporary life that many different audiences can engage with in many different situations," he said.

"I want to create a bridge, especially for young people, who may be intimidated about crossing our threshold. I want them to have the opportunity to have encounters with art that can challenge horizons and change lives

"I don't like the idea of living with just one work of art but if that is the reality, then it has to be Pierro della Francesca's Resurrection."

— as my visits to the Liverpool and Manchester galleries changed mine.

"Next year, we will be remodelling our entrance on to St Ebbes, literally bringing the street into the gallery and the gallery into the street. We will be looking to extend our evening opening hours and to have a much more dynamic programme that sees the visual arts combining with music, performance, poetry and dance.

"Against the backdrop of the reopening of the fantastic Ashmolean development, now more than ever is a time for the city to embrace the vitality of contemporary culture," he added.

'It is incredible to think that, in 2015, Modern Art Oxford celebrates its 50th anniversary, If there is one thing to take on the desert island, it would be Modern Art Oxford's archive.

"It is amazing to read through the correspondence between Nicolas Serota and Joseph Boeys, for instance."

So would the correspondence be his final choice to take on the island?

"I don't like the idea of living with just one work of art but if that is the reality, then it has to be Pierro della Francesca's *Resurrection*."

26

Helen Rappaport
Historian and author

Historian Helen Rappaport has two great passions, Russia and the Victorians. Her interest in Russia led her in many directions, via a career in TV and films, translating Chekhov and, finally, to writing biographies.

Despite the hard subjects she tackles, at the heart of all her endeavours lies a romantic passion for a country and a language that Helen finds totally beguiling. As a historian, she says she is intrigued by "the incredible Russian capacity for enduring, for suffering. This came through to me very strongly while I was writing *Ekaterinburg*." Helen's bestseller is the poignant story of the last two weeks in the lives of the doomed Romanov family. "Real people and real lives never cease to fascinate me," she said.

I wondered if Russia, or her passion for the Victorian era, rule Helen's choice of item she would most like to find washed up on the beach of our desert island?

"I must have a visual reminder of my roots. Growing up in Kent, my younger twin brothers and I were allowed to wander freely in the haunting landscape of the Medway marshes and along the sea wall to a place called Sharp's Green. At every prospect, there was something to remind me of Dickens, my favourite author, then and now.

"My brother Peter is a photographer and graphic artist, so one of his pictures of that evocative view would bring back memories of my childhood, of Victorian life and literature and of a world, now lost, but which was once safe for children to play in," she said.

"My love of Russia and all things Russian springs from a rather corny but true first-love experience when I made my first serious book purchase as a teenager, using five shillings pocket money. It was The Penguin Classics' edition of Chekhov's short stories, which included the exquisite *The Lady with the Little Dog*. You could say that reading that story was a transformative experience. I still have that now very dog-eared copy. I treasure it and cannot imagine being without it," Helen said. "It is part of who I am, because my love of Russia began with Chekhov. I graduated to *Doctor Zhivago*, a wonderfully poetic and moving work of literature, but not an easy read aged 15! Thereafter, I read and consumed everything and anything I could find by Russians and about Russia.

"When my head teacher at Chatham Grammar School for Girls asked if anyone in the fifth form was interested in studying Russian in the lower sixth, I was an eager volunteer. I just fell in love with the language. I shall be eternally grateful to my school for setting up a class of one, especially for me.

"I consider myself hugely lucky to be able to

speak such a melodic and beautiful language. The wonderful liberal education I received provided me with opportunities that are vanishing from schools today," Helen said.

"Russian Special Studies was an obvious choice at university. My love of Russian drama led me onto the stage in a student performance of Chekhov's *The Seagull*. And, unfortunately, I was bitten by the bug. For the next 20 years I was diverted into a career as an actress.

"Fortunately, I always kept my Russian alive and built up a reputation as a literary translator in the theatre which, over the years, brought the opportunity to translate all seven of Chekhov's plays."

In 2005, Helen was historical consultant on a Channel 4 documentary *The Real Angel of the Crimea* about the little-known 19th century Jamaican nurse, Mary Seacole, a contemporary of Florence Nightingale, whose portrait she had discovered.

"The story begins with a dealer buying what he thought was an undistinguished Victorian print at a boot sale in Burford," Helen explained. "He noticed the signature 'A C Challen' on the back and thought

it rather odd. After removing the backing board, he discovered the painting of Mary Seacole hidden inside.

"The painting was put up for sale at a small auction at Shipston-on-Stour, in 2002, where it was purchased by a dealer in prints and paintings. He had no idea who the subject was but, because Mary was depicted wearing medals, he contacted a friend of a friend in the Order and Medals Research Society who, in turn, knowing of my specialist interest in Mary Seacole, e-mailed me and asked if I could authenticate the sitter. He sent me a copy of the portrait — and as soon as I saw it, I knew it was Mary."

Helen did not want the painting to disappear abroad or into a private collection, so she took a risk and decided to purchase it. "After a long and nail-biting period of six months, I finally got the dealer to agree to sell the painting to

me, but had to borrow the money from the bank.

"Within a couple of weeks of acquiring the painting, I took it to the National Portrait Gallery for tests and authentication — they could tell me nothing about the artist, who was unknown to them, but they did confirm, from pigment tests, that the portrait was indeed painted in 1869 and, therefore, contemporaneous and not posthumous.

"I never brought the painting back home — it remained on loan to the National Portrait Gallery for three years until I sold it to them, ensuring it will remain in the national collection."

The sale provided her with the financial security she needed to continue her career as a writer.

Helen said: "If I could take the portrait to the desert island, it would remind me of Mary Seacole's humanity, compassion and indomitable spirit. I will need some inspiration alone on the island. And here was a woman who crossed all the classic divides of her time — race, gender and social class and never ever let anyone put her down. I love the way she bucked the system and did it her own way. I admire feisty women. There is one in my own family whom I would also like to celebrate."

Helen showed me a photograph of her aunt, Lily Irvine, in an early aeroplane that looked as if it was made from paper and matchsticks!

"Aunt Lily was probably the first woman to fly an aircraft, according to her obituary," Helen said. "This photograph was taken at Hendon in 1909, when she was just 18. Unfortunately, she did not apply to the Royal Aero Club of the United Kingdom for her pilot's licence, so there is no official record.

"The first British woman who flew, in the records, was Edith Maud Cook, in the Pyrenees in 1910 The first two American women to fly also did so that year, but my aunt was clearly flying before this date. Either way,

Born in Bromley, south London, Helen studied Russian at Leeds University, but rejected suggestions of a career in the Foreign Office and opted for the acting profession.

After appearing on British TV and in films until the late 1980's she abandoned acting and embraced her second love — history — and with it the insecurities of a writer's life. She began by contributing to biographical and historical reference works for publishers such as Cassell, Reader's Digest, and Oxford University Press.

In 2002 she was Russian consultant to the National Theatre's Tom Stoppard trilogy, *The Coast of Utopia*.

Between 1999 and 2003 she wrote three books back-to-back for a leading US reference publisher: *Joseph Stalin: A Biographical Companion*, the award-winning *An Encyclopedia of Women Social Reformers* and *Queen Victoria: A Biographical Companion*. Her first trade title was *No Place for Ladies: The Untold Story of Women in the Crimean War* (Aurum Press, 2007).

In 2003, she discovered the lost and now iconic portrait of Mary Seacole that hangs in the National Portrait Gallery.

In 2008, she published *Ekaterinburg: The Last Days of the Romanovs* (Hutchinson), which has become a best-seller in the USA.

Beautiful for Ever: Madame Rachel of Bond Street, Cosmetician, Con-Artist and Blackmailer, is published by Long Barn Books.

Helen lives in north Oxford. She has two daughters and three grandchildren

Lily Irvine was certainly the youngest of the first women to fly," Helen added.

"She married the American aviator James Martin who taught her to fly at Hendon. Her 1959 obituary read: *'To the horror of her mother, grease-smeared Lily spent her youth wandering about Hendon aerodrome in overalls, learning the intricacies of aircraft construction.'*

"Her husband James was an aircraft designer and Lily later flew his flying boats in Canada and the USA. The obituary says that she even gave 'stunt exhibitions,'" Helen added.

It seemed to me that Helen's literary interests are fired by feisty women and cruel men. After Stalin and Lenin, I wondered about her latest protagonist, Madame Rachel.

Helen said: "If I was not a historian, I think I would have made a good detective. I am passionate about winkling out the truth and love the thrill of the chase.

Helen recently published *Beautiful For Ever,* a book which reveals the career of Madame Rachel of New Bond Street — a notorious Victorian con artist and blackmailer.

"Madame Rachel's is a compelling story — which is why I love writing history," Helen said. "Tracking her down has taken me almost entirely to untouched primary sources. Mind you her legend must have persisted into the 1940s, because Sir John Gielgud once considered staging a play about her. He thought Margaret Rutherford would be ideal for the role! That

would have been terrible casting — Madame Rachel was far more sinister!

"As a passionate Victorianist I love the Pre-Raphaelites, the Arts and Crafts Movement, and the Gothic Revival.

"If I had to pick one example local to me here in Oxford, I think it would be the wonderful Burne Jones windows in Christ Church Cathedral. They could even be rather practical when constructing a shelter, the most sophisticated hut imaginable."

Unfortunately, Helen can take only one of her items onto the desert island, so will it be the Burne Jones window, the nostalgic photographs, the portrait of Mary Seacole, or the book of Chekhov's short stories.

"I have two collecting habits, Victorian and Russian books. It all began with that first collection of Chekhov's incredibly

observant and poignant stories about life's little tragedies," she said.

"But the Christ Church window features a real woman, Alice Liddell. Perhaps I could take the Victorian windows to light up the Russian book? But if it has to be one or the other, I suppose it must be the book."

27

Diana Sanders
Counselling psychologist

Those marooned on our island have included the great and the good, such as the Bishop of Oxford, the Vice Chancellor of Oxford Brookes University, Shami Chakrabarti, and Sister Francis Dominica. This month's castaway is not likely to be so familiar to most readers.

But Diana Sanders, a counselling psychologist at the John Radcliffe and Churchill hospitals in Oxford, is extraordinary in her own way.

Diana was born, in 1956, with a congenital heart condition. By the age of 46, she could hardly walk across a room, was on oxygen all day and night, used a wheelchair and was facing the end of her life. Today, she is fit and well, walks miles and is back working in the health service. Diana made a life or death choice and lived to tell the tale, which she has done poignantly in a book entitled, *Will I Still Be Me; Life after a heart / lung transplant* a record of the major operation which saved her life.

She tells her story from the point of view of a health professional used to hearing about other people's pain and vulnerability, having to face up to her own.

She said: "Part of my work is with cardiac patients. The men among them who, having survived a heart attack and focused their attention on what is important in their lives, often express shock at their conclusion.

"They are surprised at how much less their work figures in the scale and how much more relationships and the family. Going through the transplant, I shared that experience.

"My husband and parents were at the heart of my life. I have always been close to my mother, who had the responsibility for bringing up a sickly child. I have grown much closer to my husband, Malcolm as a result of what we have been through together." she said.

So what will someone, who has had to face the ultimate choice, value enough to take on our desert island?

But first I discovered that my subject wanted to change our rules slightly.

"Rather than a desert island, can you arrange a wild Scottish one, where I could be enthralled by the powerful waves breaking on a bleak windswept coast, a kind of Fingle's Cave adventure?" Diana asked.

"In the 1980s, I spent some time in Canada and a friend took me to a remote cabin. When it was time to leave, I asked if I could stay on. So there I was alone with just a dog for company. I loved the solitude, but was also nervous when disturbed by the noise of mice in the roof and something far more frightening prowling outside.

"Once the dog got scared and ran away. I was freaked out. He eventually returned but, by that time, I decided to leave and made my way to the road to be rescued by hitching a lift," Diana said. "In fact, I think I will need to be rescued from the island if there are any dangerous animals on it." she added.

"My father loved plants and was a keen supporter of the Botanical Gardens. In our huge garden, he grew a multitude of flowers and nearly all our vegetables. During the 18 months I waited for a new heart and lungs, I was wheelchair bound and on oxygen, so spent a great deal of time talking with my father. We talked more in those 18 months than in the rest of my life put together. When he died in 2005, I was so grateful that we had that time together.

"Later that year, the Ashmolean mounted a wonderful exhibition on 1,000 years of Botanical Art. He would have loved it. I particularly admired *Plantae Selectae*, one of the books on display, and a painting called *Apple Blossom and Insects* by Jan Van Kessel the Elder. The book and the painting would remind me of my father-and are important to me symbolically."

The intricate line drawings from the early publications categorising plants and insects, fascinate Diana.

"It made you stop and look, and pay close attention to the detail. Having survived against the odds- I was not expected to live beyond my teens-I have learned to focus on the moment. The detail of life, from moment to moment, is the concept of living that is most important to me. Those drawings would symbolise that.

"There are other things in the Ashmolean, that would also remind me of the calmness and quietness that fits in with having lived through difficult times and survived. I find that meditation helps me attain that feeling and there is a tiny gold Buddha which embodies that sense of living in the moment."

"Meditation helps but, if I am going to be alone on the island, I would need some kind of companion, even if only in my mind. People are so important to me. I have memories of them, enough not to be lonely but maybe the painting *A Village Festival* by Jan Breughel, the Elder could help?

"His pictures are allegorical and full of detail, both of which you will gather are important to me. I could look at each figure and work out stories around them-imagine what they might be saying or doing."

Diana was born and grew up in Oxford but her childhood was dominated by her heart condition.

"My life was circumscribed by everything I was not allowed to do. I couldn't run upstairs or play energetically, like a normal child. As well as the heart condition, one of my kidneys wasn't functioning properly. My mother always said, 'You were cheerful little girl – once your kidney was removed.' I began to think that the solution to some problems was having an organ removed! "

"When I was growing up children were not given so many toys. The one advantage, from a child's viewpoint, of my times in hospital, were the gifts people brought. I still have some of them and my teddy bear, Fifi, would help me recapture those memories – and the love behind the gifts."

In her twenties, Diana was able to develop a career and live an active life as her Canadian adventure indicates but then, in her forties, her health deteriorated rapidly.

"At 46, I was suddenly given a new life, but it is a different life," Diana explained "It is not a normal life. It is more like running a vintage car--I require lots of fine tuning and maintenance!"

"I have to take a lot of medication to prevent my organs being rejected, which in turn causes side effects, the kind of life anyone with a chronic condition faces.

"For a few months after the operation, all I wanted was to have my old organs back and do what was always expected - die young. But I know an Indian fable that helped me through this time.

"Swami Kriyanda tells the story of a famous sculptor who was asked by an admirer how he was able to create such a magnificent shape of an elephant out of a piece of stone. The sculptor replied, 'It is easy. I simply cut away all the bits that are not elephant.'

"I have found that story significant both in my life, work and relationships, I feel the way to make a good life is to 'take away all the bits that aren't elephant .'

"Knowing this, my husband, Malcolm, who has supported me throughout, gave me a little elephant- that would be another possibility for the island.

"There is a bronze elephant from Tamil Nadu or Andra Prdesh (AD900-1000) in the South Indian section of the Ashmolean. It is exquisite but of course, Malcolm's gift has more personal resonance."

On the island Diana would have plenty of time to indulge in her joint passion for walking and singing, which she has been able to do since her transplant and which gives her enormous pleasure.

"I can now enjoy the freedom to breathe in the fresh air and experience the landscape.

And now that I can breathe properly, my voice is much louder and I have joined the Summertown Choral Society. But I only plan or think short term.

"Although some people are living up to twenty years, after heart-lung transplants, survival isn't guaranteed. I am always at risk of either infections or rejection, and only 35 per cent of us survive beyond ten years. I have to make the most of every day."

Any readers who face life threatening situations, for themselves, family members or friends, may find help and inspiration from Diana's book.

Before I left her, I reminded her that she can only take one thing to the island.

'I would love to have one of the original sketches but, I think I could settle for the catalogue of *The 1,000 years of Botanical Art* as that will provide me with good memories and infinite moments to savour one by one."

28

Dr Steven Parissien

Director, Compton Verney art gallery

Visiting Compton Verney, the award winning art gallery just over the border in Warwickshire, is a magical experience. This Georgian mansion, once the home of landed gentry is set in idyllic grounds designed by the legendary Capability Brown. But walk inside this perfectly proportioned 18th-century country house and you find yourself transported to the 21st century.

Could it be disorientating to be in a setting so up-to the minute and yet so grounded in the past? One man who knows the answer is Compton Verney's director, Oxford resident, Dr Steven Parissien.

"I was delighted to be head-hunted for the post at Compton Verney, not only because it brings together all my interests and is an institution close to my heart but also because it means I can live in Oxford." said Steven.

"I love this city for many things. I still have lots of friends here and more seem to gravitate here every year. The population is, I think, unusually active and has wonderful organisations like the Oxford Preservation Trust."

Would his castaway choices be from Compton Verney's permanent collections, or would he be influenced by his love of Oxford or his French background? Dr Parissien's ancestors were Huguenot silk weavers who came to England as refugees.

"Although I was born in London, in 1959, I was brought up in Buckinghamshire. I was fortunate in getting a place at the superb Dr Challenor's Grammar School in Amersham and it was there I acquired my love of history and architecture. After studying the Tudors and Stuarts at A level, I knew I wanted to read history at university."

Dr Parissien did not have a privileged background, and won a scholarship to University College, Oxford. He said: " I once brought an incredulous professor from Yale University to Oxford and showed him around boasting 'I came here for free' and watched his mouth drop in disbelief. Sadly, it is not the case today, but it set me off on my career and it feels like it is my home."

Dr Parissien's student studies prompted his first castaway choice.

"Compton Verney has a bust of Charles I made by John Bushnell, in 1675. It is, however, a copy of a work by a much more famous artist, Bernini, who was commissioned by Henrietta Maria, the Queen consort, to make the bust. He based it upon Van Dyck's famous triptych of the king," Dr Parissien said.

" The original bust was destroyed in the

Whitehall Palace fire, in 1698, so this copy by Bushnell, who trained in Italy before returning to England in 1668/69, has become very significant."

"Apparently, King Charles was as arrogant as he was unprepossessing in stature (5ft) and the bust, showing his haughty demeanor takes you right back to the turbulent times of the English Civil War. It also shows the fascinating difference between image and reality. PR spin is nothing new. And as that period triggered my academic career, it would be significant for me personally, too."

Dr Parissien went on to study the Georgians for his honours degree and has written books on the period including *The Georgian House*, and a biography of George lV. He has also worked for the Georgian Group, the national charity dedicated to preserving Georgian buildings and gardens.

But, Dr Parissien' revealed: "It is the Regency era that really caught my imagination. I suddenly understood just how isolated and friendless we were in 1809, after Napoleon had conquered so much of Europe.

"On first seeing the portrait by William Beechey of the Persian Ambassador, Mirza Khan, painted in that year, I realised its significance. Mirza was courted and generally made the centre of attention, hence the portrait. This was a time when attitudes were beginning to change and become more eclectic and experimental. So this portrait would remind me of my time engrossed in the early 19th century."

After leaving Oxford, it looked like Dr Parissien's future lay in a very different world — that of up-to-the-minute advertising.

"In many ways my two years working for D'Arcy-MacManus & Masius were invaluable; I learned about marketing but my passion for Architectural History lured me back to Oxford to work for my doctorate," he said.

After his PhD, Dr Parissien worked in the USA for a couple of years before returning to work for the Georgian Group and English Heritage.

"I also spent six years in London as Assistant Director in British Art at The Paul Mellon Centre (part of Yale University)." he said.

"While I was there, I built up contacts in the world of museums and galleries and during that time developed a passion for 20th century design. I loved the work of Ravillious and Bawden but discovered an artist less well known but equally admirable who was also trained by John Nash. Her name was Enid Marx."

Dr Parissien explained that the successful textile designer, also worked as a painter, printmaker, children's book author and illustrator, designer of book jackets, trademarks and postage stamps. He said

"She was commissioned, in 1937, to design seating fabric for underground trains and made wonderful posters for London Transport. In 1944, Enid was the first woman engraver to be appointed a Royal Designer for Industry and was elected a Fellow of the Society of Industrial Artists.

"Compton Verney has a charming engraving by her called *Tiger Tiger*, set in a garden at night, I think inspired by Blake's poem. I adore cats and want to mount an exhibition on Enid Marx so that would be a good choice. I do not know why she has been forgotten maybe because she is female artist?"

Dr Parissien's next suggestion arose from another interest.

"I love travel and who better to whet ones appetite than Canaletto. Compton Verney owns a painting by him called *Ranelagh*

Gardens, Chelsea. (1740) What I love about this painting is how it portrays not just the rich and powerful but everyday people dressed to enjoy themselves.

"I would like Compton Verney to be accessible and enjoyable to people from all backgrounds. I have been involved with The Prince's Foundation and am now a fellow of Kellogg College and both are about providing opportunities for people from all social backgrounds," Dr Parissien said.

"As well as its Canalettos and busts of kings, Compton Verney has a good collection of Folk Art. One exhibit I am particularly fond of is a mid-19th century wooden model of a butcher's shop, the sort that was placed in the shop window when it was closed.

"My favourite place in Oxford is the Covered Market. I would love to loan our butcher's shop to Feller's Organic Butchers Shop, whose shop window would suit it," Dr Parissien said.

"I love good food and beer and was a judge on the National Pub Design Award and one I enjoy particularly is The Anchor in Hayfield Road. It serves food cooked on the premises and locally sourced.

"I belong to CAMRA and so do regret that there is no longer a brewery in Oxford."

In many ways Dr Parissien has taken us on a journey through time and is obviously at ease with many periods in the history of our country so I think he has answered the query raised in my introduction. But out of all these objects taken from four centuries which will be his final choice?

"I think it will have to be the Canaletto. It is a beautiful painting – it will remind me of Compton Verney and the 18th century and of the time I have spent writing and teaching about life in Georgian England. It plays to my love of architecture and the pleasures of life. Although it will probably mean I shall be nostalgic and want rescuing quickly."

Postscript
Since this feature appeared in April 2010, Steven has been the consultant on a television series based on the era that intrigued him, The Age of the Regency. Elegance and Decadence is the latest in his TV work which includes The Home since 1700 (Laurence King, 2008). His television appearances include stints as presenter of Kings in Waiting: George IV (BBC, 2001) and of the 2006 series Buildings that Shaped Britain (Talkback Thames).

Professor Jim Kennedy

Former director of the Oxford University Museum of Natural History

Professor Jim Kennedy, the director of Oxford University Museum of Natural History, is ideally suited to our desert island. For several months he lived on Aldabra atoll in the Indian Ocean.

Professor Kennedy is also in a unique position when choosing his desert island object because of his profound understanding of the effects of the passage of time.

I talked to him in his magnificent office against the backdrop of Pre-Raphaelite frescoes, by Richard St John Tyrwhitt, and surrounded by ammonites and other fossils.

Professor Kennedy, who arrived at the museum in 1967, was appointed Curator of the Geological Collections in 1976, and in 2003 became museum director. Since then he has overseen a complete transformation of the museum's displays.

In 2005, the museum was voted one of the most family friendly in a nationwide competition staged by the *Guardian* newspaper. Children are invited to touch many exhibits and, on weekend afternoons, the museum echoes to the sound of enthusiastic young people engaged in activities that both stimulate their imagination and curiosity.

Professor Kennedy's interest in natural history was inspired by weekend trips to museums when he was a schoolboy.

"I was born in North London during the war, so my father was away during most of my pre-school years and I grew up in a matriarchal society. When it comes to the fair sex, I do as I am told!" Professor Kennedy joked.

"I passed my 11-plus, enabling me to be the first in my family to have the benefit of higher education. I helped my parents fill in the form for choice of school and we opted for The Quintin School, founded by Lord Hailsham's father. Getting there entailed taking a bus down the Edgware Road to Oxford Circus, and then on to Lower Regent Street, and walking through Soho to the lower school, which was in a former workhouse.

"Every Monday we gathered in the upper school for a joint assembly in the Cameo Poly Cinema on Upper Regent Street. With classes in two different places a 20 minute walk apart, the awkward 25 minute slot left was occupied by seemingly endless half periods of religious instruction. Because of that experience, I can go into any art gallery and work out the iconography of some pretty unlikely paintings," Professor Kennedy said.

"If I took the painting of *St George and the Dragon* by Paolo Ucello, in The National Gallery, it would remind me of that time, and of stolen visits to the gallery."

At weekends, Jim said he often took the bus to South Kensington and explored the nooks and crannies of the Natural History Museum and the Science Museum.

"My mother worried because, if my head was not, in a book it was likely to be in a ditch hunting for bugs on Hampstead Heath. I think I was always interested in creepy-crawlies. She felt I needed a social activity and enlisted me in the local swimming club. I broke my first national record at the age of 15 and so became a serious swimmer.

"In order to pursue my swimming career, I chose to study geology at Kings College, London. Kings is an Anglican foundation, and had a service every morning, so classes did not begin until 10am and by then I had spent several hours in the pool. When the 1964 Olympics coincided with my finals, I had to make a difficult choice — and geology won," he said.

"Maybe my choice was something to do with Michael, better known as Jake Hancock, my PhD supervisor. He had the most outrageous personality and was much loved.

"An ammonite from the chalk at Dover would remind me of him and of field trips on the south coast."

Professor Kennedy arrived in Oxford on his Lambretta, in 1967, but his two-wheeler could have taken him on a different career path.

"Jake pointed out an advertisement for a post in Sunderland. I filled in an application but before I mailed it, a friend told me about a similar post in Oxford. I did not think I stood a chance but it was the right moment," Professor Kennedy recalled.

"The department was worried about the age structure and needed someone young and inexpensive so, on January 1, 1967, I came to Oxford and rented a room in Thorncliffe Road, with a hot bath on Sundays for three pounds ten shillings a week!"

I asked Professor Kennedy about the new life that awaited him in Oxford.

"My research interests lie in the geology and

palaeontology of the Cretaceous Period, and range from chalk sedimentation and diagenesis to integrating stable isotope, geochemical and biostratigraphic schemes," he explained.

"Research in the field means I have travelled and worked everywhere from southern England, to most of Europe, Georgia, Algeria, Tunisia, Israel, Egypt, Zululand in South Africa and throughout the USA, from Mexico to Canada.

"Just as we have visiting scholars from all over the world, I have visited the greatest natural history museums elsewhere. The best are, unsurprisingly, in the old Imperial capitals, London, Paris, Berlin and Vienna. I have been able to combine research with exploring the cultural delights of these cities.

"My wife, Ellen Rice, is an archaeologist and ancient historian, and together we have travelled to the sights of the ancient world in Greece, Italy, Turkey, Egypt, and even the Sudan.

"As a child I had read about these places in books borrowed from the local public library but never dreamed I would have the chance to actually visit them," Professor Kennedy said.

"At home, we have a cast of a head of Alexander the Great — the one in the Acropolis Museum in Athens — supposedly by the sculptor Leochares, and this, or better still the original, would be a source of fond memories.

"In this room are ammonites from around the world, some that I have collected, others sent to me by colleagues to work on. They come from places as far apart as Kazakhstan, Nigeria, South Africa, Greenland, Madagascar, and Yorkshire."

I wondered if it was possible to have a favourite among such a large collection?

"Yes I do have a particularly beautiful mother of pearl ammonite which comes with memories of a rainy day wading around Lake St Lucia in KwaZulu Natal, South Africa, followed by a large, but fortunately well-fed crocodile," Professor Kennedy said.

Looking at a fascinating map in the museum library, the professor said: "One could say this began it all. It was made by William Smith in the early decades of the 19th century. He was an Oxfordshire man from a humble background but we call him the father of English Geology.

"As a self-taught engineer he examined rock exposures in mines, quarries and cuttings and produced the first, and most beautiful, geological map of the country—in fact of any country. A framed sheet of the southeast of England would be a reminder of a land and landscape that has occupied much of my time as a geologist."

Next on Jim's list of possible castaway objects was a bust of William Buckland, another giant in the development of geology.

"He was Oxford's Reader in Geology, Reader in Mineralogy, sometime Canon of Christ Church and Dean of Westminster. He was hugely influential and persuaded the Prince Regent to create a readership in geology.

"He married Mary Moreland of Abingdon who shared his passion," Professor Kennedy said.

"With the deanship came the position of Rector of Islip, and the Rectory. So if I took the bust — it will remind me of my life's work, this museum and my home. So that has to be a real possibility.

"But I need things to satisfy all the senses," Professor Kennedy said. "There will be beautiful sunsets to inspire me but I shall also want sounds and words.

"I could take *A Dance to the Music of Time* by Anthony Powell. It is a comic examination of political, military and cultural life in 20th century England. I like the way he brings characters back in as they get older — they have changed and yet they are unchanged.

"My dog-eared copies are testament to the fact that they are infinitely re-readable."

A Dance to the Music of Time is actually one of the longest works of fiction ever written and appears in a 12-volume cycle so it could indeed occupy a great deal of time on the island!"

But would the set of books be his final choice?

"In the end, it will have to be a replica of something that belonged to my grandmother — a wind-up gramophone," he said.

"If that could come with a tin of needles and in the cupboard underneath a selection of the 78s that went with it — Caruso, Lehmann, Melchior, and the rest, with lots of Wagner, that will provide the music to lighten my time on the island. Could the books be in the cupboard, too?

"Nothing could stop me fossil hunting on the island and hopefully the scenery is a work of art, so the music and books would satisfy my other needs."

Can you locate the art, objects and books chosen by our castaways?

ELEGIA DI
TOMMASO GRAY
POETA INGLESE

THE
Encyclopædia
of OXFORD

What would you take to the desert island?

30

Maria Guadalupe
Author and scientist

It seems unkind to celebrate a skiing accident, but without being immobilised for 12 weeks after just such an event, Maria Guadalupe, alias MG Harris, would not have written her first book *The Joshua Files: Invisible City* which has entertained young readers worldwide.

When *The Joshua Files* contract was signed, in 2008, it was the biggest book deal of the year for a first-time children's author.

The first title in the series, Invisible City, featuring MG's fictional teenage protagonist, Josh Garcia (who lives in Oxford) was the fastest-selling children's fiction debut. Two others in the series have followed, *Ice Shock* and *Zero Moment* and the fourth and fifth books in the series are on the way.

They say there is a little autobiography in all novels. This is true for MG. Her sometimes dark but always exciting adventure stories are partly set in Oxford and part in Mexico, where she was born.

MG said: "My parents failed miserably to get along, resulting in divorce — scandalous for both families who belonged to the strictly Roman Catholic, Mexican middle-class. My mother (also named 'Maria Guadalupe', about 58- times better looking and more fascinating than I could hope to be even on a good day) threw caution to the wind and took off for Germany to work as a stewardess for Lufthansa with me (aged four) and my baby sister, Pili."

Her mother married again, a cellist with the Halle Orchestra, which is how MG came to live in England.

In 1984, MG came to Oxford to study biochemistry at St Catherine's College. Here she met her husband David Harris and she has lived in the city ever since.

So will it be Mexico, Germany or Oxford that will determine her choice of art, antique or antiquarian book which she would like to find washed up on the beach of our desert island?

"Biochemistry bought me to Oxford and St Catherine's College. As a female scientist, Rosalind Franklin was a great inspiration.

Crick and Watson's hypothesis regarding the structure of DNA was built using her data," MG said.

"The colourful model of the double helix in Oxford's Natural History Museum would remind me of life on earth and journeys in science.

"The architect of St Catherine's was the renowned Arne Jakobsen. He even designed the furniture and I remember sitting on his iconic Egg Chair in the library. I used to work there to make some extra cash!," MG recalled.

"One of these chairs would be a comfortable addition to the desert island as well as an example of fine 20th century design."

I wondered where her degree took her?

"I went into IT. It was an exciting time, so many developments we now take for granted were just beginning. Together with our friend, physicist Mark Salisbury, my husband David and I started The Oxford Knowledge Company in an innovation centre in Mill Street, in 1997," MG said.

"Companies around us were being created and destroyed all the time. We survived and expanded but now my writing career has taken off, I have a non-executive role. I remember that time was like living in a dizzying new world."

"I began writing seriously in January 2005, after a ski accident in Gstaad forced me to spend many weeks recuperating. With a ten-inch operation wound and five long pins in my shin bone, merely getting out of bed was a challenge," MG said.

"My husband arranged a laptop on a chair by the bed and for the next 12 weeks, I wrote my first novel — a techno-thriller which combined my two intellectual loves: molecular biology and archaeology.

"Suddenly, I was no longer spending all my free time transporting the children, doing laundry, cooking and the 101 demands that motherhood makes on you. David took care of everything and I was free.

"Like most first novels it was rejected by every agent who saw it. It was not the first time it had occurred to me to write. I had tried my hand at screenwriting from the age of 11, once winning a runner-up prize in a *Blue Peter* competition for *Grange Hill*. I returned to screenwriting in 2004, just failing to shortlist in a BBC New Talent contest to write a sitcom.

"If not for the hugely encouraging letter which the BBC New Talent team sent me, it is likely that I would have given up any hope of being a writer. But after those 12 weeks I had got the bug."

After reading about the 'decoding' of Mayan writing in the book *Breaking the Maya Code* by Michael Coe, I had an idea for another story — that of a young boy who made an outstanding discovery about the origins of Mayan civilization.

"I tried some out on my daughters and they liked it. So encouraged, I started working on *Invisible City*. This time, the response was immediate. By the end of 2006 I had several publishers keen. I have not looked back," MG said.

It is easy to see why the science and technological background in *The Joshua Files* series has such authenticity. But where does the fascination with Mayan culture come from?

MG revealed that it stems from when, aged 15, she visited the Yucatan region of Mexico for the first time, methodically visiting Mayan ruins in sweltering heat.

"In a Cancun hotel bookshop I bought *Mysteries of the Ancients* by Eric and Craig Umland —a non-fiction book positing the theory that the ancient Mayan civilisation was a remnant of Atlantis. I was hooked," MG said.

Her father's choice of reading matter also helped.

"My father had a beautiful leather-bound collection of comics by Carl Barks, the creator of Uncle Scrooge McDuck," she said.

Barks was an illustrator for Disney and invented Duckburg and many of its inhabitants. He surrounded Donald Duck and his nephews with a cast of eccentric and colorful characters, such as Scrooge McDuck, the wealthiest duck in the world.

Despite the fact that Barks was not himself well travelled, his adventure stories often had the duck clan globetrotting to the most remote or spectacular of locations — which Barks imagined with the help of *National Geographic* magazine.

"I had such fun reading his stories to my half-sisters in Mexico," MG said. "One favourite was *Crown of the Mayas*. The comics big collectors' items on the other side of the Atlantic. It would be fun to revisit and could provide a nostalgic link to my parents."

Mayan dates play an important role in *The Joshua Files* series. December 12, 2012 is the end-date in the Mayan Long Count calendar — something that has spawned many doom-laden predictions.

In *Invisible City*, MG's hero Josh discovers his Mayan ancestry and is concerned that 2012 may mark the end of the world — something that he is, of course, keen to prevent.

The date came up when MG spent the night in the British Museum along with some of her young fans.

"That night in the museum was a special Moctezuma-themed event, featuring storytelling about the Mexican Day of the Dead. In my session we spent time looking at the Yaxchilan lintel," MG explained.

"The inscription dates it precisely as January 14, 537 AD. It also mentions Yaxchilan's rival city-state of Calakmul — the Snake Kingdom. A king of ancient Calakmul features as a character in the fourth in the *The Joshua Files* series.

"It was such a good experience. If I took the lintel it would remind me of *The Joshua Files* and all the children I have had the good fortune to meet because of the series."

MG will have a lot of time to herself on our island so what, I wondered, would she do with it?

"Actually, I think I will have to reject my other suggestions and ask for a fortepiano," she said. "It was the instrument Mozart composed on and sounds something between a harpsichord and a piano. Wouldn't it be great to have the actual one? I don't know if it still exists.

"Mozart's was made in Vienna by Anton Walter. I love how originally the keys were the reverse of the modern piano.

"If my desert island had a nice dry cave nearby I could learn how to play it. If it came with a piano stool full of music, I could learn works by my favourite composer, JS Bach.

"You don't hear a lot of Bach played on a fortepiano, I'd love to know how it would have sounded when Mozart was playing music by Bach. I tend to throw myself into things almost obsessively. I think it would keep me sane on the island. So maybe that is what I should settle for."

Photograph:
Jess Hughes
(St Catherine's
College, Oxford)

31

Ray Foulk

Architect and co-founder of the Isle of Wight Festival

T he 1970 Isle of Wight Festival was the most famous of the early rock festivals. At the time, it was said to be one of the largest human gatherings in the world, with estimates of more than 600,000 people, surpassing the attendance at Woodstock USA.

The 1970, line-up of more than 50 performers included The Who, Jimi Hendrix, Miles Davis, The Doors, Ten Years After, Emerson, Lake & Palmer, Joni Mitchell, The Moody Blues, Melanie, Donovan, Free, Chicago, Richie Havens, John Sebastian, Leonard Cohen, Jethro Tull, Taste and Tiny Tim.

But its success was also its undoing-alarmed by the high attendance Parliament passed the 'Isle of Wight Act' preventing gatherings of more than five thousand people on the island, without a special license. Why you must wonder, am I writing about this fortieth anniversary in Limited Edition, which is after all the magazine of Oxfordshire and not of the Isle of Wight?

Wander through the streets of Jericho and you could find yourself admiring a corner block of multi-coloured modernist houses that blend seamlessly into their surroundings. Ray Foulk is the architect who designed them and lives in one and he was also the impresario who invited Bob Dylan and all those legendary acts to England.

Ray was 23 when, with his brothers Ron and Bill, he founded Fiery Creations to promote the 1968 Isle of Wight festival. He was later head-hunted by the developers of the new town of Milton Keynes, but that was only the second of his careers and each has been successful.

I met Ray on a screenwriting course and through our shared admiration of the designer Keith Murray and, with my brash curiosity, I uncovered his amazingly varied life. Watch your cinema screens –he may have yet another career on the way. His home contains elements from all his various lives but which will predominate in his choice of art, antiques and books to be swept up on the beach of our desert island?

"I worked for a while at the *Isle of Wight Press* before my life was turned upside down by the success of the festival I organised with my brothers."

I asked Ray what it felt like to pick up the telephone and invite Bob Dylan to play?

"At the time we were young, brave and ambitious, and the result has been that I sometimes have a tendency to overreachmyself," he said.

It must have been awe-inspiring to look

out over that sea of people and know Fiery Creations had made it happen.

Ray showed me a photographic panorama of the festival and the trendiest of photographs with Dylan *et al*.

"I have become quite a film collector and we commissioned Murray Lerner to film the 1970 festival. He distilled his recordings into *A Message to Love:The Isle of Wight Rock Festival* and released it in 1996. It would be quite nostalgic to take some memorabilia of me with Bob Dylan and other legendary figures to the island but more important would be pictures of my children and grandchildren," he said.

I asked Ray what happened after that act of parliament was passed?

"Fiery Creations continued. We organised the first rock concert at the Wembley Empire Pool with Led Zeppelin (1971) and we even got Prince Charles' permission to bring The Who to The Oval.(owned by the Duchy of Cornwall) That concert was in aid of famine relief in Bangladesh," Ray told me.

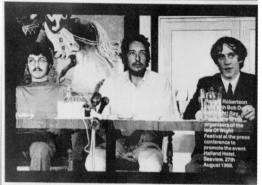

Robertson
th Bob Dy
nd) Ray
ganisers of the
Isle Of Wight
Festival at the press
conference to
promote the event.
Halland Hotel,
Seaview, 27th
August 1969.

"The following year, we staged the first rock event in Wembley stadium with Chuck Berry, Little Richard and Jerry Lee Lewis.

"My life at that time looked glamorous – the Bentley, high powered lunches in Mayfair and so on but that was just a product of a hectic life style"

Then Ray was head-hunted by Milton Keynes to develop their leisure complex.

"During my research, I became aware of one of the greatest visionary thinkers of the twentieth century, Richard Buckminster Fuller. In the 1920s he was raising environmental issues that are only now being addressed," Ray said.

"His solution to the exploitation and waste of resources was not a hair shirt; he wanted to build more with less. His solution was 'design efficiency'. Even then, he argued that we could provide energy for the world with renewables.

"Buckminster Fuller said 'nature never builds in rectangles' and invented the geodesic dome, and designed a mass produced round house that still looks modern today. I am proud of persuading him to come to Milton Keynes when it was just 150 green fields, to lecture to their 120 architects. But the developers did not take his advice: I wasn't able to get a single domed building."

Ray's next suggestion for the island was one of Buckminster Fuller's Dymaxion world maps – his idea being the creation of a global system to power Spaceship Earth.

"He was so much in advance of his time but most of his ideas were achievable. I could take the map and maybe you could attach it to the model hotel I designed, inspired by his geodesic dome, which was my project when I studied architecture."

"After Milton Keynes, I sought a less hectic life and, in 1977, with my partner Jenny Lewis I rented a five storey building, in the Fulham Road, and turned it into a gallery. I had been a collector since my teens but it was at this time that I developed a passion for Art Deco."

Ray was being pretty avant guard for the time, as in those days even Victoriana was looked down upon by mainstream antiques dealers.

"We were lucky. Had we started later we could not have raised the money needed to purchase the things we did. We began to buy furniture and objects by the top French designers, such as Emile Jacques Ruhlmann and Sue et Marr (Louis Sue and Andre Mare).

"Even then, I needed the equivalent of a small mortgage to buy their best pieces but ten years later the prices would have been prohibitive.

"Other Deco dealers in London had smaller premises in more expensive locations. Because we took on these run down premises and turned them into a palace, we had the space for furniture."

Ray showed me photographs and lavish exhibition catalogues of some of the iconic pieces he exhibited which are now in some of the great museums of the world. I asked how he found them?

"In 1977, a friend took me on my first trip to

Paris. We scoured the city, from the fleamarket to the posh galleries until in Gallery de Luxembourg , we spotted a fantastic Ruhlman bed. The price seemed beyond us and the time to leave grew closer but we had bought nothing. I resolved that it had to be the bed, just the bed. We could only put a deposit on it and needed to borrow the rest when we got back to London."

I admired the evocative picture of him and Jenny Lewis laying on that bed like John Lennon and Yoko Ono in Montreal. It was the start of the Foulk /Lewis Collection. They had the feature exhibition at Olympia 1978, and a year later the landmark Ruhlmann Centenary Exhibition, with pieces once bought for The Elysee Palace.

One of their dressing tables was hired for the filming of *Death on the Nile*. Ray said: "I also promoted, on television, a phenomenal cabinet by Sue et Marr which is now principle Art Deco exhibit in the Richmond museum, Virginia."

So which pieces from that time would Ray like to furnish his island?

"It would have to be either the Ruhlmann grand piano which I could enjoy playing or the bed. At least that would be a comfortable place to read and I could hide my copies of Proust's *A la recherché du Temps Perdu* under the mattress?

"I might be tempted to choose one of our surrealist pictures bought by Jack Nicholson— Raphael Delorme's *Cleopatre* – it might be my last chance to get it back."

So Ray sold his collections, closed the gallery and started on career number4.

'I did continue collecting smaller pieces such as ceramics by Keith Murray, the architect and ex-First World War pilot, who designed for Wedgwood.

"But I decided that I should make up for my lack of education by taking an Open University mixed arts degree and then secured a place to read architecture at Cambridge. Once qualified, I set up my own practice in design and build. I read more about Buckminister

Fuller's ideas, his science, philosophy and about his technological and environmental solutions," Ray said.

"With my daughter, Caroline I established The Millennium Debate NGO to promote these ideas. We organised Blue Planet Days based on Fuller's *Operating Manual for Spaceship Earth*, which is all about valuing and not wasting our natural resources, especially not burning fossil fuels.

"Fuller accused mankind of not examining earth's plumbing- the weather, the water systems and our supply of clean free energy from our mothership ,the sun." said Ray

"We organised one hundred exciting all day events in schools across Oxfordshire. Caroline wrote the multi -media play *Destination Spaceship Earth*, which our team performed at the start of each day. Later students presented their work *Environmental Showtime*.

"We made a film and mounted two performances at The Pegasus Theatre. It was hard work but, without doubt, the most satisfying time of my life. We reached 20,000 children before we hit funding problems, when the landfill tax policy changed and funding for environmental education dried up."

Ray practices what he preaches. He thinks his house is the most energy-efficient in Oxford .

"It is triple-glazed with under-floor heating and the solar panels on the roof and walls provide much of the energy. But the solution is not the solar panels. Once you have heat, the secret is not to loose it. Good insulation is the answer."

Ray is unlikely to cease being an environmental designer but screenwriting with Caroline, is his current obsession. He has two other daughters, Jacqueline and Cordelia and eight grandchildren.

I asked him 'If you can take only one of the things we have talked about, which will it be?

"Buckminster Fuller's Dymaxion map. I will just have to memorise the collected lyrics of Bob Dylan and make my own furniture."

Michael Smith

Journalist and author

Writer and journalist Michael Smith's latest book *Six — a History of Britain's Secret Intelligence Service:Murder and Mayhem 1909-1939* is the first comprehensive account of the successes and failures of Britain's secret service during the First World War — and the critical period between the two world wars, when British and Russian spies pitted their wits against one-another.

Michael Smith, now defence correspondent of *The Sunday Times*, writes about his subject with some authenticity as he was once a spook himself.

After a career in military intelligence, he turned to journalism and has a track-record of breaking stories that the establishment has attempted to keep under wraps. This was demonstrated graphically when, in 2004, he broke the story of the Downing Street memos which showed how US president George W Bush and then prime minister Tony Blair agreed to use military force to bring about regime change in Iraq more than six months before votes in the Congress or the United Nations were deemed to have authorised the allied invasion.

Michael, who lives near Henley-on-Thames, with his wife Hayley and their two children, explained: "Managing sources in journalism has much in common with managing agents. You must treat them as you would want to be treated and develop trust, often becoming good friends."

Born in 1952 in Lambeth, London, Michael attended Borden Grammar School in Sittingbourne, Kent, but left aged 15 "just because I wanted to get away from school". He joined the Army, training as a surveyor with the Royal Artillery.

"I didn't find the work satisfying because I often ended up surveying Forestry Commission land or cleaning Land-Rovers," he recalled. "I had a facility for learning languages and transferred to the Intelligence Corps, who taught me Arabic and, later, German."

Michael worked in the Middle-East for three years, collecting intelligence on terrorists operating in Syria, Iraq and the Lebanon. He admits he had a romantic image of intelligence work in the Middle East, inspired by T E Lawrence's *Seven Pillars of Wisdom*.

"I have a copy of the Oxford edition of Lawrence's *Seven Pillars*, given to me as a gift for a lecture I gave," Michael said. "That is probably the book I would like to find on my desert island because I would finally have the opportunity to actually read it!

"But my job at the time was more Bletchley Park than T E Lawrence! I was listening in to Arab terrorists in the Middle East — and later East Germans in Europe.

"I spent a lot of time writing reports and thought I could transfer that skill straight into journalism, but it wasn't that simple.

"In 1982, I began working for the BBC monitoring service, the British equivalent of the CIA's Foreign Broadcast Information Service, hoping to move into a reporters post.

"I was soon disabused of my ambitions because they only wanted native German speakers or graduates," Michael recalled.

"While in that post at the BBC, a Persian monitor listening in to Tehran Radio told me that a Fatwa against Salman Rushdie had been announced.

"At the time, I did not know the meaning of the word. My Persian colleague explained that a Fatwa was a sentence of death — allowing a 'true believer' to kill the subject of the Fatwa. I realised this was an important story and, to the concern of a nervous editor, released it."

In 1990, he became a newspaper journalist writing on Eastern Europe for the *Financial Times* and the *Sunday Times* before joining the *Daily Telegraph* where he became defence correspondent.

"This was a time of dramatic foreign events — the Berlin Wall was coming down — and because of my knowledge of Eastern Europe and foreign affairs generally, I was recruited by the *Telegraph* and reported on the 'second' Gulf War — the 'first' being between Iran and Iraq, Michael said.

"Working in the field fired my enthusiasm. That was when I started writing my own copy rather than working on other people's reports. I spent ten years as a *Telegraph* reporter. It was a fantastic job. But I have seen a lot of dark, awful things.

"I covered the Dunblane shootings and that

was obviously horrific, not just because of the deaths of the children, but in the way someone turned from normal humanity into a maniacal killer.

"But he was such a nice man', is what you hear said so often of killers, and I don't doubt they were. Something turned them, like someone flicking a switch in their brain. We have seen that again in Cumbria. The horrifically dark side of human nature is something you see a lot of as a news reporter."

Michael also reported on various conflicts in the Balkans — twice going into Kosovo under fire to meet the Kosovo Liberation Army during the 1999 war. More recently, he has reported on the wars in Afghanistan and Iraq.

"In the Balkans murder and brutality became almost institutionalised, just another part of society. I cannot forget the stench of dead and the sight of a Serb paramilitary camp where a young girl had been raped and murdered. One of her shoes still lying there on the ground — truly awful.

"I saw people struggle to hold on to hope and, despite all that dark stuff, you do come away at times with an admiration for the resilience of the human spirit."

Becoming defence correspondent for the *Telegraph* was Michael's dream job. "I only left to have more time to write books," he said. "But it often kept me desk bound so I sometimes broke free and went to Iraq and Afghanistan!" he said.

Michael started to write books after stumbling across an amazing story in the newsroom. "A guy called Peter Elphick came to the foreign desk with an amazing story about a New Zealand man who was recruited as a spy by the Japanese.

"This became my first book, published in 1993, called *Odd Man Out: The Story of the Singapore Traitor*. I wrote the book with Peter, who had come to me with the story of Patrick Heenan, an Indian Army officer stationed in Malaya at the start of the war in the Far East.

"Heenan was a sad character who failed to fit into the class-ridden officer society. He passed secrets to the Japanese that led to the destruction of the RAF's forces in Malaya, ensuring that Singapore fell to the Japanese.

"He was stationed at an airbase in Malaya and notified the Japanese when planes were about to take off or land. So they were easily destroyed — and once air cover was gone so were our ships. That was why the Japanese

were able to move in so quickly.

"Writing this book made me think I could write more. And because I knew the intelligence services, I understood how they worked, and realised a lot written about them was, frankly, rubbish."

"Then, in 1996, while working on my history of British Intelligence Services, I interviewed a former MI6 officer and said 'Is there anything I haven't asked that I should have? '

"He replied that there are a couple of guys who have never been properly recognised, Sydney Cotton — a maverick Aussie pilot who pioneered air photography, and Frank Foley, described as 'The Pimpernel of the Jews'.

"The ex-MI6 man told me: 'One of the interesting things about Foley was that normally, to be a good case officer, you have to be a bit of a shit'. But Foley managed to be a brilliant case officer and a near saint. Schindler pales into insignificance alongside his work on getting Jews out of Germany.

"I wondered why Foley's story was not better known and contacted Yad Vashem (the Israeli Holocaust Martyrs and Heroes' Remembrance Authority) and they said there was no evidence to back up Foley's case," Michael said.

"But I requested some information from Yad Vashem archives and, in it, I read a report of a Jewish aid worker, Hubert Pollack, describing how Foley had saved 'tens of thousands' of Jews.'

"Yad Vashem had been under the misapprehension that Foley was protected by diplomatic immunity, but that was not the case. He risked his life every day, going into camps and harbouring Jews in his own home almost every night.

"He could have been arrested at any time, indeed, one of Foley's colleagues in Vienna was arrested because the Nazis wanted to send warning to MI6 about what they knew."

As a result of Michael's research, in 1999 Frank Foley was recognised as Righteous Among Nations, the award also granted to Oskar Schindler.

"I flew to Israel with the foreign secretary, the late Robin Cook, and met many people rescued by Foley," said Michael. "One of them wrote: 'I myself have five children and 18 grandchildren — none of whom would ever have seen the light of day had I not lived. May God bless his memory.'

"It was a moving experience and if I took a copy of that certificate to the desert island it would remind me of a great human being," Michael added.

"Before my book *Foley: The Spy who Saved Ten Thousand Jews* was published, Channel 4 approached me. They were doing series on Bletchley Park called Station X and asked me to write the book to accompany it. The book became a best-seller.

"Behind that story was the success of the Enigma machine. Maybe I could have one on the desert island, and see if I could use it!"

Michael has recently edited Mavis Batey's *Dilly — The Man Who Broke Enigmas*. Alfred Dillwyn Knox was born in Oxford and went to Summer Fields School.

Bletchley recruited many academics like Dillwyn, especially those with experience of deciphering and reading ancient scripts. So Michael considered the Linear B tablet from Knossos as his desert island treasure. This tablet was deciphered in 1952 and is now in the writing gallery at the Ashmolean Museum.

Michael Smith with Lawrence's robes in the Ashmolean Museum, Oxford

After the success of Foley and Station X, Michael wanted to write a history of MI6, but the announcement of an official history looked like it had stymied the idea.

"But I realised that an official history would not be able to name agents or talk about them — but I could," he said. "I have two good researchers in the UK searching the National Archive and a couple abroad. Once I began writing I found I had too much material for one book. So it will end up as a two part history. The first part covers the years 1909-1939. At that time, agents did swagger around with a licence to kill like James Bond,

so the subtitle is *Murder and Mayhem*.

"I think if I had the cover of my book on the desert island it would remind me of the flamboyant characters I have met and written about. But if I had to pick a photograph of just one to represent them all it would be of Sir John Norton Griffiths.

"He led a group of British secret agents who rampaged across Romania ahead of the invading Germans, destroying the oilfields so the Germans could not get them.

"His entry in the Oxford Dictionary of National Biography talks about his engineering triumphs building railways around the world, but does not mention that he was working for the secret service in Romania."

33

Dr Helena Whall

Campaign manager, Campaign to Protect Rural England

Doctor Helena Whall took up her post with the Oxfordshire branch of the Campaign to Protect Rural England in 2008. She has been actively involved in several successful campaigns, saving both the Radley Lakes and Warneford Meadow and was involved in the creation of the Oxford Green Belt Way.

Dr Whall and the Oxfordshire branch are currently campaigning for Green Corridors to make it assessable on foot from every part of the city. But, before 2008, her life journey involved difficult and dangerous situations.

Dr Whall's career path was not what her family expected. Instead of following in her father's footsteps into the art world – or her mother's into literature – she chose instead to read sociology and politics.

After completing an MA at the School of Oriental and African Studies (SOAS), and gaining her Doctorate in International Relations, she had a research fellowship at the Institute of Commonwealth Studies, University of London.

She also acted as consultant for the Commonwealth Secretariat, Commonwealth Foundation, Commonwealth Policy Studies Unit, the Centre for Human Rights and Development, Sri Lanka, the National Integration Policy Unit, Sri Lanka, and the Berghof Foundation for Conflict Studies, Sri Lanka

Her work took has taken her to all parts of our global village, so what aspects of her well-travelled life would determine her choices for our desert island? What objects, works of art or antiquarian books would she consider?

Helena began by selecting a treasured book given her as a child – *The Little House* by Virginia Lee Burton to hold clues to her current career and passions-in a way bringing

her life full circle. Although she was born in Cardiff, the family moved into a house in what she remembers as an idyllic rural village in Monmouthshire, where she lived until she was five.

"We lived the good life. As children we were able to run free in a rural setting rather like that of the house in the book." Dr Whall said.

"So I empathised as the house wondered about the lights of the city, which grew ever closer. Eventually a road is built in front of the house. This is followed by roadside stands, petrol stations, and more little houses. These are replaced by tenements and apartments. Streetcars, an elevated railroad, and a subway appear to surround the house.

"Finally, two gigantic skyscrapers are built – one on each side. Then one day the great-great-granddaughter of the builder sees the house and remembers stories that her grandmother told about living in just such a house, albeit far out in the country," Dr Whall added.

"When the great-great-granddaughter discovers that it is the same house, she arranges to have it moved to a hill in the country where she can once again watch the passing seasons.

"I loved the ending with the little house wheeled to its new location -- but as an adult, I am more cynical since I now realise that the little house could be engulfed by urban sprawl all over again. Indeed, our own little house in Monmouthshire met the same fate."

When her artist father took up a post in the Fine Art Department at Coventry University, Dr Whall, like the little house, found herself unwillingly in an urban setting, in a modern house in Leamington Spa.

Dr Whall explained that an inspiring tutor at Bristol University opened her eyes to the ethnic politics of South Asia and, in particular, to the conflict in Sri Lanka.

She said: "This led to a lifelong fascination with South Asia so, if I take a book, it will have to be EM Forster's *A Passage to India*. It paints a vivid picture of colonialism, class, caste and gender and would remind me of my first visit to India where I travelled for six wonderful months with just £750 spending money, in 1991. I learned from this trip the impact of poverty and marginalisation of vulnerable peoples, a concern which would go on to inform much of my career."

Dr Whall's PhD thesis was entitled *The Peace Process in Sri Lanka* and for many years her energies were immersed in the problems faced by the Tamil minority. She published an impressive array of books, articles, reports and conference papers.

"In 1995, my book, *The Right to Self-Determination: The Sri Lankan Tamil National Question*, was published. It was banned in Sri Lanka and I was declared *persona non grata* by the Sri Lankan government. But, some years later, I was invited back to lecture at Jaffna University and to be involved in the negotiation of a resolution to the conflict," Dr Whall said.

"I was given a painted wood mask of Maura Raksha, the peacock demon. It is a common tourist souvenir but perhaps because of that it would be an image that would symbolise that beautiful and tragic island."

Dr Whall's interest in minority rights fitted her to head up a project, with EU funding at a Commonwealth think tank.

She said: "At that time, the Commonwealth had no policy on the rights of indigenous peoples. My three years lobbying made a real difference and led to the most fantastic job in which I travelled in Australia, Africa, South Asia and the Caribbean and had the privilege to meet wonderful people.

"I treasure a painting by Narnarnyilk Jimmy of the Kunwinjku People of Arnhem Land, Northern Australia. In their language the title is Ngalmanguji (Long –necked Turtle). They are a people who have a spiritual unity with their environment. This would inspire me on a desert island and remind me of those indigenous peoples I met who had few material possessions but who knew who they were and where they belonged, yet whose very existence and homes were being threatened and destroyed."

In 2004, Helena had a life -hanging experience, the birth of her daughter. She was later offered a contract to write a book on the marginalisation of indigenous women, but with a toddler in tow she was prompted to leave her job in London to look for work nearer to home.

She saw the advertisement for the position of CPRE campaign manager here in Oxfordshire and the rest, as they say, is history. Since being offered the post, her sense of home and belonging has taken on a new meaning.

"We are often accused of nimbism but the CPRE is only against development in inappropriate and sensitive environments," she said.

"People want to live and work in Oxford because it is a beautiful city with access to diverse and attractive countryside but urban sprawl destroys the balanced life most of us desire. We want planning which is strategic and which puts the needs of the environment high up the agenda."

Dr Whall and her husband, Rick, rent a house in Dorchester on Thames and she has become attached to the surrounding landscape.

"The Ashmolean has a picture by Paul Nash called *The Wood on the Hill* (Wittenham Clumps) showing the view from my house – so if I took that to the island it would remind me of my family. But I think my final choice would have to be a piece by my father Dick Whall. Both my parents grew up in Norfolk and on retirement they were drawn back to the landscape of their birth, where they have a sense of belonging.

"My father has traced his ancestry back nine generations. I love his marqueterie series because it uses driftwood from the north Norfolk coast and is reminiscent of the coastal scenes I enjoyed during my childhood holidays. I often go there now with my family who have also grown to the love the land and seascapes, so *Marqueterie No 95* by Dick Whall represents home and belonging in all its meanings."

Post Script
In 2010, Helena said of the house in the storybook, "I am more cynical since I now realise that the little house could be engulfed by urban sprawl all over again." Maybe prophetic? She is currently involved in the struggle to prevent urban sprawl engulfing Oxfordshire. To learn more about the campaigns, values and aims of CPRE Oxfordshire visit the website: www.cpreoxon.org.uk

Marqueterie No 95
by Dick Whall

34

Patrick Collins

Playwright and tutor

Patrick Collins is an award-winning writer of 30 stage plays. He founded and directs the Broken Lace Theatre Company, based in Thame, which performs his plays and workshops many others, including plays written by his students on the Diploma and Masters in Creative Writing at Oxford University's Department of Continuing Education.

"I love the ephemeral nature of the theatre," Patrick said "I rarely keep any reminder of productions either seen or directed or written by me. If a production is good, it will be remembered, if bad, it will be forgotten."

Will his choices for our desert island be equally ephemeral?

Patrick was born in West London, and now lives in Thame with his wife Barbara who dabbles in a bit of transformation magic through her quirky joke shop.

Patrick's brother was nine years older than him, so he grew up like an only child and remembers being an avid reader but not the process of learning to read. He showed an early talent for writing, winning a yellow Rupert the Bear annual at nursery school!

"My mother liked musical theatre and, not having a sitter for me, tended to take me with her. The production that had the most impact on me, when I was ten years old, was *Hamlet* at the Old Vic," Patrick recalled.

"It opened with a colourful court scene but my eyes did not focus on the centre of the stage but on a solitary figure dressed completely in black, sitting on the edge of the stage to one side – it was Richard Burton, then in his early twenties playing, the lead role. It was my first experience of charisma. That amazing voice and presence had a profound effect on me."

I asked if he thought ten was a bit early to watch Shakespeare?

"Probably," Patrick said. "My mother had not told me anything about the story in advance and I think that is generally a mistake. I suggest introducing children to Shakespeare with *A Midsummer Night's Dream*. The reason that performance of *Hamlet* worked for me was because it was a great performance. Make sure their first experience is known to be an absorbing production.

"I think Shakespeare would be horrified by the way we teach his plays. The effect of children reading it around the class is enough to persuade any child that Shakespeare is boring. It would be much better to let them talk about their experience of seeing a play performed and answer their questions, then just leave it to make its own mark.

"I have one thing in common with Shakespeare – he couldn't write his own stories; he borrowed them from the likes of Holinshed and mythology," Patrick said.

"I was fortunate in having an exceptional teacher, in junior school, who helped me get a scholarship to Latimer Upper School in Hammersmith, even though it entailed passing three entrance exams which gradually whittled down the applicants. She produced a class performance of *A Midsummer Night's Dream* in which she played Puck and I played Oberon. Now there is the ideal way to get kids interested in the Bard."

Patrick became bored with secondary school and did not want to go into the sixth form, but reluctantly returned to school persuaded by his insistent parents. One month later he left, believing he wanted to be a journalist, and went to work in the cuttings library of the *News Chronicle* in Fleet Street.

"I saw this as a prelude to becoming a reporter. In those days, before the computer, the cuttings library was vast. Anyone famous had an obituary already written. So when George VI died in 1952, we had his obituary in print within two hours."

Patrick was soon disillusioned.

"The reality of a reporter's life in the early 1950s was waiting around to be sent out on a job, possibly working all day on it – only to have the story binned," he said.

"National Service saved me. Although I was not particularly numerate, I was sent into The Army Pay Corps and posted to Winchester for two years.

"We did very little work but although the camp was small it had a library so I taught myself, by reading English and French literature and language, to A-Level standard. I sat the exams at the *Daily Express* office and passed. Then I lazed around for 18 weeks post demobilization until my mother insisted I get a job or leave home.

"After trying one, of mind-destroying dullness, I applied to teacher training college, St Mark and St John in Chelsea – just five minutes walk from the Royal Court Theatre."

Patrick looks back on that time with amazement because of the location and the timing, 1956. British theatre was about to be revolutionised!

"I was there when it all happened. Osborne's *Look Back in Anger*, Miller's *The Crucible*. I saw them all for a pittance – the price of a balcony ticket. Those experiences inspired me to start writing myself. So, if I took a photograph of the Royal Court Theatre, to the island, it would evoke vivid memories," Patrick said.

"I started my 30 year teaching career in London but, in 1962, I moved to Great Missenden in Buckinghamshire and taught at the secondary school opposite Roald Dahl and his wife, Patricia Neal.

"In those days, she was much more famous than him. In fact, when Patricia said to me, 'My husband is going to be the best children's writer ever', I was not convinced. He came to the school and talked to the kids and was charismatic but when he asked for questions, one child put up his hand and said 'Who are you?' "

"When I became head of English at Waddesden, I discovered that the teachers joining the staff had better educational qualifications, so I decided to return to college for further studies. One of my tutors was the poet Thomas Blackburn, who had lived with Dylan Thomas for a while.

"Blackburn turned me on to poetry, which is possibly the oldest art but made me aware of how good writing for the stage takes on the mantle of poetry," Patrick said.

"Another tutor, John Heath Stubbs, spent the whole year teaching us *Paradise Lost*. John was blind but he didn't let it hold him back. He walked everywhere and expected the traffic to stop for him! One day, he stopped me in full flow saying 'Mr Collins, I think you will find there is a comma after inferno. I did not hear it in your rendition.' He knew every word by heart. "

As well as running school productions, Patrick had become involved in adult drama producing his own plays and entering festivals.

"I prefer minimalist sets and for festivals that is ideal. This was the origin of my first theatre company we travelled light, in scenic terms, from festival venue to festival venue,

hence The Suitcase Players." It was his wife, Barbara, who encouraged him to take early retirement so that he could concentrate on writing.

"My last teaching post was at Princes Risborough, where I had stayed for 16 years because the head actually respected and enjoyed being in the company of adolescents. Following that, as well as pursuing my own work, I began to teach creative writing eventually becoming Buckinghamshire Writer in Residence which led to my appointment as tutor on the Diploma for Creative Writing (Oxford) and on the Masters when it was initiated six years ago. It is satisfying to see students suddenly understand what drama is about and some of them go on to have their work performed," Patrick said.

By this time, Patrick had his own group of players and was well established as a playwright.

"I had begun by entering drama festivals. My first prize was, in Luton, in 1965. Once I had won prizes in the 'Best Original Play' category in Buckinghamshire and Oxfordshire, commissions came my way.

"Two of them were large community plays with casts of one hundred. One, in Aylesbury, was about the effect the coming of the railways had on canal people. That was a production with songs. I write lyrics but not music." By 1982, Patrick was living in Long Crendon. He says

"My next group, Fundamental Theatre, based in Princes Risborough, was followed by Oxfordshire based Broken Lace. I suppose, on the desert island, posters from performances would bring them all back but this would be a less ephemeral choice."

Patrick showed me a stunning painting of himself by the Scottish artist, Dorothy Smyth who now lives in Oxford.

"I met Dorothy when she had written a play for a festival at the Old Fire Station, which I directed. It used masks. I could have fun with mask like the ones in the Pitt Rivers—they can be powerful but, on the island, there would be no audience to react to them, so I would rather take her painting of me, which I love. It is like the theatre. It is not me but is more like me than the so-called truth of a photograph."

When we talked about influences on his life and work, Patrick pulled out a book, *The Philosophy of Samuel Beckett* by John Calder.

"Samuel Beckett had total integrity. He tried

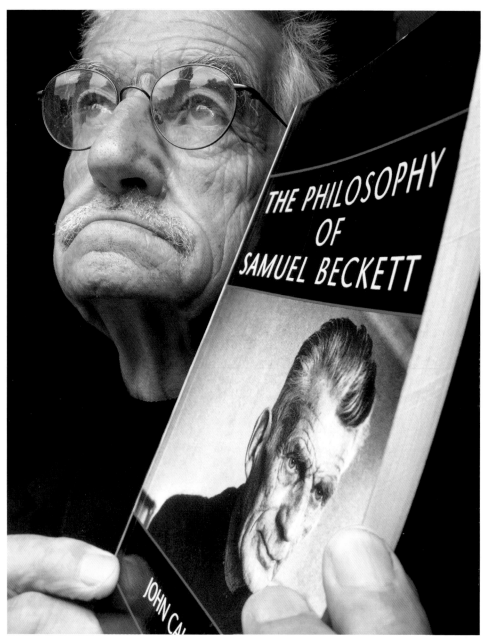

to record the world as he saw it, devoid of sentimentality, utterly honest but with huge compassion.

"My fundamental belief is, like his, that life has no intrinsic meaning and so consequently one has to invent a meaning. It may seem paradoxical because Samuel put his life on the line fighting with the French resistance. He came within minutes of being arrested by the Gestapo.

"His life is testimony to human resilience. I admire him immensely," Patrick said.

"He wrote for years before he was recognised and didn't compromise his belief in speaking the truth. Despite this bleak view, he wrote with heart warming humour. I would want this book on the island. I return to it again and again."

I asked which would be his final choice, the posters, the photograph, the masks, the book or the painting? The unwavering answer was "the book."

John Baugh
Headmaster, Dragon School, Oxford

Life has taught John Baugh, headmaster of Oxford's Dragon School, many lessons – including some hard ones. After a free ranging childhood in Africa, where he was born, he found the restrictions placed on him at prep school back in the UK pretty difficult.

"Creativity was quite literally beaten out of you," John recalled. The indelible impressions of his own schooldays informs his own attitude to education .

Now running what is possibly the most famous preparatory school in the country, John, 54, has the confidence to challenge the current educational system which he suggests is not fit for purpose.

"I think the current system squashes the creativity that enables us to adapt – to learn, unlearn and relearn as we go through our lives. It is this skill that will be so important to the next generation," he said.

"We should be going back to the drawing board. Four-year-olds, entering school this year, will be about 45, in 2050. We haven't a clue what life will be like then and yet must somehow prepare them for it. Fortunately, this school does all it can to encourage individuality and creativity, despite the country's industrial model of education."

John was born in Uganda, and later moved to Botswana, so Africa looms large in the choices of items he would like to see washed up on the beach

"My father was a policeman, when he first moved to Africa in the 1950s and often had to confiscate weapons to stop fights. Most of these would have come from Karamoja in the north and I have a collection of them at home," he told me.

"One of them is a ten foot long spear which separates into three parts; each end is made of metal and the middle is wooden. It would be carried in parts and quickly assembled and used. The cow skin shield is not ceremonial yet it feels like it weighs a ton. I guess if I took the spear, it could be useful on the desert island."

John also showed me a beautifully made swagger stick completely covered with tight patterns of blue and white beads.

"It was made by my ayah, who was like a second mother. When my parents were out in

the evening, she would sit with me, usually on the floor, and spend hours making beadware and sharing her supper of matoke (steamed green banana) and meat."

The swagger stick would have tender personal memories and were part of a free- ranging early life that reminded me of fellow castaway, Korky Paul's childhood in Zimbabwe. But John's idyll was soon to end.

"My parents, like most expats, expected me to be educated in England," he said "So, after primary school in Africa, at the age of eight, I acquired my BOAC Junior Jet Club log book and became a frequent flier.

"My first prep school in Surrey is now a nursing home, so I fantasise that I could also end my days there as well. My recollections of that school are warm but my parents felt it was not sufficiently academic and moved me, aged 11, to another prep school."

John did not want to name it because, although he believes it is now a good school, his memories of it are grim.

One incident stands out in his mind. "I was mad on football and a keen Leeds supporter and remember dressing up in their team colour, white, to go on the games field. When that was reported, I was beaten, for wearing PE and not games kit," he recalled.

"In Africa, I had attended a school that allowed me to be an individual and I was transplanted to an establishment where the aim was to regiment boys into obedience. In Africa, I rarely wore shoes and my habit of taking my shoes off was also punished. Even at the time, I knew there was a better way of doing things."

"In the late 1960s, I moved on to Aldenham School in Hertfordshire and even though it was a good school, like all adolescents at the time we began to rebel against the system. I considered a professional career in football but wasn't sure and talked it over with an inspiring school master at Aldenham," John said.

"His recommendation was to take time out - this was long before the days of the gap year. So I went to work at Heath Mount, a prep school in Hertfordshire, loved it and decided to apply to St Luke's in Exeter to train as a teacher."

But he kept both possibilities open and said "While still a student, I managed to play two seasons with Exeter City football club, as a goalkeeper. The first season I was unpaid but they began to pay me in the second."

John pointed a large print on his wall – *Three Happy Jumbos* by the famous wildlife artist David Shepherd.

"My wife Wendy prefers to have original works at home so this limited edition print hangs here in my office. I have another Shepherd sketch at home of a bull elephant emerging from the swirling dust. It reminds me of scenes in the bush when elephants suddenly appeared as if from nowhere. I bought it with my earnings from Exeter Football Club," John said.

"The first year I played, Exeter were promoted to the then third division. That was thrilling – it was a big deal in Exeter – involving open top bus rides and civic receptions. I managed simultaneously to get my teaching qualification but was then faced with a dilemma." John was faced with making the decision that would affect his whole life and said,

"I was offered a contract by Everton. I clearly remember that moment because I had a broken finger and couldn't play for two months. I had plenty of time to make up my mind but I chose teaching.

"My father, Michael, thought I was mad because, as a child, my dream was to become a professional footballer. Most of the players at Exeter wanted nothing more than to play football. I found 3pm on Saturday thrilling but turning out to train during the rest of the week and having someone shout orders at me, I actually found tedious and I questioned everything.

"I also could not face the thought that much of my week would be idle – remember that this was the world of professional football in the late 1970s. Heath Mount asked me to take up a post there teaching geography and running the sport. They even offered me a little cottage to live in; so, at 21, I thought I was sorted. But I did keep my green goalkeepers' shirt – now an antique – so that could be a useful addition on the island."

In 1980, John took a post at Haileybury College, an independent boarding school in Hertfordshire.

"It was a great experience," he said. "In 1984, Wendy and I were married – having persuaded her back over from New York where she was working as a fashion director at Macy's.

"We were expecting our first child in 1986, and I was just 29, when the headmaster David Summerscale was about to leave to become headmaster of Westminster School. Before he left, I asked his advice about what I should do next. His first suggestion was to aspire to be a housemaster. That did not appeal to me, so he suggested a headship at a prep school.

"I do not think either he or I expected events to move so quickly. Within two weeks I had secured a post as head of Solefield School, a boys' day school in Sevenoaks in Kent," John said.

"It was a lovely school but the previous head had retired after 30 years in the post and it needed refreshing. It was a weird situation. At 29, I was the youngest member of staff but also the headmaster. So my eldest daughter, Isobel, was born in Sevenoaks and not in Hertfordshire.

"There is one antique from that time I could consider taking. Abandoned in a skip, at the school, was a stunning antique iron wine rack. We rescued it and still have it. I guess I would also need it filled with bottles and the ingredients to make wine for it to be of use on the island," he added.

"In 1997, after 11 years at Sevenoaks, I moved to Edge Grove School in Hertfordshire, where I had five very happy years running the school. I found leaving there, in 2002, very

difficult, but the opportunity to be head of the Dragon School was one I could not turn down."

Understandably since its alumni include Leonard Cheshire, Hugh Gaitskell, Peter Jay, Nicholas Shakespeare, Humphrey Carpenter, David Shukman, Tim Henman and Hugh Laurie, not to mention John Betjeman, John Mortimer, Antonia Fraser, Tom Hollander, Rageh Omaar and Emma Watson.

John describes it as a: "very modern traditional school. When it was founded, Victorian schools were generally places where you were seen and not heard and children at prep schools were expected to behave and be dressed like mini-adults.

"Skipper Lynam, as inspirational headmaster in the school's early years, decided to re-write the book. He chose robust clothes for the children and expected them to have fun while they learned. That philosophy is still deep within our DNA. Thinking about education for life, if I can only take one thing on the island, it has to be this."

John showed me a copy of a 19th century painting that hangs in the Musee d'Orsay. (A framed copy hangs in his dining room.) It is called *Peter and John running to the Tomb*. The artist is Eugene Burnand.

"I saw it first with Wendy when tagging along on one of her trips to Paris when she was working for Macy's," he said.

"This painting just grabbed me; the faces of the two men. We can't see exactly where they are going but their faces are lit up with a mixture of expectation, disbelief, excitement and hope.

"I am an optimist and that is why I teach. I want children to look forward with excitement to their future, whatever it may be. We should educate for the lives they will live, not the ones we have had," John said.

"The British thinker and educationalist, Sir Ken Robinson, puts it well. He believes we should replace the conveyor-belt, industrial model of education with an agricultural model, where we aim to get the climate and the soil right to nurture healthy minds and bodies.

"So I think this picture has to be it; a reminder to look forward with the same hope and expectation as I face the possibility of some long and lonely days on my island."

36

Marios Papadopoulos

Musician and director of Oxford Philomusica

Marios Papadopoulos is the founder and director of Oxford's professional symphony orchestra, Oxford Philomusica. For such a uniquely gifted musician, he is modestly reluctant to talk about himself. His mission is to communicate a passionate love of music.

Marios does not remember learning how to play the piano — but does recall a fascination with sound and a desire to reproduce it.

He recalled an incident when he was about six years-old.

"I used to stare at my father as he shaved and loved the rasping sound the razor made. I was driven to recreate that sound — and so I shaved off one of my eyebrows!"

" Fifty years ago, I was given a small toy piano. I listened to music on the radio and replicated the tunes on its little keys," he said.

"A great uncle, who was a fine violinist, recognised that I had a talent that needed nurturing. So he encouraged my parents to arrange piano lessons for me.

"I still have that toy piano which started my journey in music. I brought it with me to England, and would like to have it with me on the desert island.

"I was born in Limassol, Cyprus, in December 1954, but was brought up in Nicosia. When, at the age of 12, I had reached Grade 8 both piano and music theory, there were no opportunities to take my studies further in Cyprus. So my parents made arrangements for us to come to England.

"My childhood was rooted in music but, occasionally, I needed to escape and freedom took the form of my first bicycle which might be useful on the island," Marios said.

He was not fluent in English when his family

came to the UK, settling in Brent. Apparently, he was offered a scholarship to St Paul's School, but his parents turned it down and sent him instead to Brent Comprehensive.

Marios has vivid memories of his early days in this country. "The warmth of the welcome I received was quite overwhelming. This country has given me so much, so many opportunities and I hope that I have been able to give something back," he said.

"In Cyprus, I had two LPs. One was Liszt's Hungarian Rhapsodies and the other was a recording of Brahm's Piano Concerto No2 by Sviatoslav Richter. I played them over and over again. When I arrived in London, I had an amazing experience. I was able to buy the scores of those two pieces and saw how that experience of sound was formed, how it had all come together.

"I shall never forget making that connection between the audio experience and the visual one. So I should consider taking those LPs, together with the scores."

By the age of 14, he had obtained a Performers' Diploma (ARCM) the Royal College of Music and, at 16, was the soloist with the Royal Philharmonic Orchestra at the Royal Festival Hall. But most memorable was his introduction to the Bath Festival in 1972.

"I met the composer, Michael Tippett, and he conducted me in *Fantasia on a theme by Handel*. I also met William Walton in Bath," Marios said.

"Aged 18, I won the Young Musician of the Year Award and my concerts were broadcast on Radio 3. I played all the Beethoven concertos. And, by my late teens, I had already begun to conduct.

"When I hear music I see shapes in it. My PhD thesis was based on that theme of shape in music. That was why I went into conducting. I can see the patterns going up and down in an almost mathematical manner. The concept is not tangible, but the baton represents that thought process in my mind, so I would like my baton on the island. I buy my batons at Guiviet of Mortimer Street in London and like them to be light, elegant and to have good balance," he said.

"Away from the concert hall, Marios is a family man. "I like to be rooted," he said. "When I married Anthi, in 1986, we moved into a house just up the road from my parents in Brent. We still live there with my two children, Michael and Stella. Family is very important to me." Not surprisingly, Marios's family is a musical one.

"Anthi teaches music and is a director of Oxford Philomusica and Michael is reading music at Trinity College, where he has an organ scholarship. Stella plays the violin but wants to read chemistry at university."

In Oxford, we have a very particular reason to be grateful that Marios and his parents made this country their home.

"I first visited Oxford in 1973 and loved it immediately. Oxford has given me opportunities to better myself and I am constantly learning and in awe of the people I meet who inspire and educate me. It has given me a new opportunity to be creative, too," he said.

"Some people have described me as a maverick because I also enjoy being an entrepreneur. I loved founding Oxford Philomusica, even though I was warned against it, since the musical world is fraught with difficulties and the financial obstacles huge. But I actually enjoy the challenge of the fund raising, administrative and management side of the business."

"Oxford has provided me with a stable environment. The idea of travelling from one concert hall to another around the world does not appeal to me. I have conducted more than 200 concerts in Oxford. I feel so privileged to conduct at the Sheldonian. I love the intimacy of the space. I feel able to stretch out a hand and almost touch the audience. The Sheldonian, to me, is like a spiritual home — with a special but intangible atmosphere, so I would like to have it rebuilt on the desert island!"

However, our castaways can only have one object on the island, and rebuilding Oxford's iconic concert hall doesn't come within our budget. So what would our maestro's ultimate choice be?

"Can I have my piano?" he said. " For me, playing is not only about the sound, it is also a tactile experience. When I play, I am always motivated when someone is moved by the music. That touches me. That is why I perform.

"I remember my first exposure to opera, in my teens — it was The Marriage of Figaro — and how I marvelled at the human voice. From then on, I wanted to make the piano sing. That has remained my aim and it is what I teach my students. At least on the island I can do that, if I take my piano.

"But it will be hard leaving my home and family and Oxford and the Sheldonian."

37

Professor James Leonard
Paediatrician

We have all probably watched one of those television dramas in which an air stewardess rushes into the aircraft's passenger cabin urgently asking: "Is there a doctor on board?"

Professor James Leonard and his wife Halycon, also a doctor, have actually answered that call for real — and on more than one occasion.

The most dramatic was when a Kenyan lady unexpectedly gave birth to twins on a flight to the Gulf. That incident received international publicity, but Professor Leonard believes that the circumstances were far from unusual.

"The chance of a doctor being on board is actually very high because medics involved in research travel a lot," he said.

Professor Leonard has visited more than 40 countries to attend conferences and consultations. But despite all this international travel, he has worked in this country throughout his distinguished career.

His first post, in 1972, was at London's Great Ormond Street Children's Hospital, where he remained until his retirement in 2004. By then he was Professor of Paediatric Metabolic Disease at the University of London and honorary consultant physician at GOSH.

He met his wife Halcyon at Cambridge, in 1963. They married three years later, while they were both medical students.

Professor Leonard said: "We embarked on our in-house training — I was at St Thomas's and Halcyon at Middlesex Hospital. Those early years were really tough, as we were working so hard and mostly passing each other like ships in the night."

The couple moved to Oxfordshire in 2004, as Professor Leonard wanted to be near his father, Graham, the former Bishop of London, who was then living in Witney. And they ended up in Kennington, with a little help from his brother, Mark.

Mark, a musician with an interest in early music, was playing for friends at a house in Kennington, when the owners mentioned that they needed to sell the property.

"We have not regretted for one moment buying it and moving to Kennington,"

Professor Leonard said. "It is such an active village and so convenient."

But why did Professor Leonard decide to go into medicine and not the church, like his father? The question revealed more fascinating family links.

"My grandfather was a qualified doctor," Professor Leonard said. "But my grandmother said he was not sure whether to choose pathology or paediatrics. He chose pathology, but unfortunately died, aged only 32, of septicaemia, after he cut himself during a post mortem.

"This was in 1925, before penicillin, when my mother was just three. So, I never met him because I was born in December, 1944," Professor Leonard said.

"My uncle, Michael Meredith Swann, was a celebrated biologist and my mother, Priscilla Swann, went into science. My mother graduated here at Oxford in 1943, when women graduates were few in number.

"She was, against the general guidelines, allowed to marry my father while still an undergraduate because he had enlisted in the army," Professor Leonard added. "My grandmother was delighted when I followed grandfather into medicine.

"As part of the Natural Science Tripos, at Cambridge, I opted to study bio-chemistry and enjoyed it. Paediatrics and bio-chemistry came together nicely to inform my career."

Modestly, Professor Leonard failed to mention the scholarships and prizes he won at Cambridge, nor any of the awards and honours he has been given since.

A list of his more than 300 publications includes books, peer-reviewed papers, international named lectures which, with his editorial positions, could easily fill these pages.

But on meeting him, you quickly become aware of his real passion for paediatrics.

He showed me a print of one of the wards at Great Ormond Street in 1856, made soon after it was founded in 1852. GOSH was the first hospital in the English speaking world to provide in-patient beds specifically for children.

"What I love about this picture is the detail," Professor Leonard said. "There were no appropriately trained nurses, so the figures by the bedsides are probably mothers.

"On the left are Charles West, the founder and William Jenner, who became the Queen's physician. For years, they were the only two doctors at the hospital, and gave their time for free.

"The space walker is amazing — with its spikes — it may not have been just for fun, even though there are toys in evidence. Like the trapeze, in the background, it was probably designed to exercise the child," Professor Leonard said.

"The hospital was in the middle of the most appalling slums, a devastatingly poor area. The Thomas Coram Foundation (Foundlings Hospital) was close by. The hospital was in a private house with open fires. Initially, the poor were quite suspicious of the hospital. But once it was trusted, the demands on it escalated to crisis point.

"Charles Dickens came to the rescue and gave public readings of *A Christmas Carol* in aid of the Hospital for Sick Children (as it was then named) at St. Martin's church hall in Long Acre in 1858 to launch an appeal.

GOSH has benefited from many writers. The royalties from JM Barrie's *Peter Pan* go the hospital, and Oscar Wilde was another supporter," Professor Leonard added.

"Once the risk of cross infection was recognised, they banished the parents! Access to the children was only allowed for one-and-a-half hours on a Sunday afternoon.

"That began to change in the 1950s and, by the time I retired, parents were also given a bed. So things have gone full circle," Professor Leonard said.

"When I started, it was still quite a small hospital. Although the number of staff has increased enormously, the number of beds has shrunk. The reason for that is that work has transferred from in-patients to out-patients. Most of the hospitals around the world, that I have visited, failed to see this change coming."

"When I was training most of us were general paediatricians, but it became clear that there was a need for specialists for GOSH to maintain its position at the forefront of world studies in the field.

"Sir Archibald Garrod founded my speciality, which he described as chemical variants — inborn errors of metabolism. But he was not convinced they were important," Professor Leonard explained.

"My tutor, Professor Wolf, looked at every problem in meticulous detail revealing effects that could be devastating. He died recently, aged 90, and I gave the tribute at his memorial service. Things are again going full circle for now there is a shortage of generalists."

"My patients are born with a change to their chemistry which can affect any part of their body. These genetic conditions are relatively rare and they appear early in life. So many of my patients were babies.

"Part of the reason I have never shaved my winged eyebrows, is that if I wiggled them, I could take a crying toddler by surprise and have a short interlude to examine him or her.

You have to enjoy looking after children even when they are sick over you!

"As we discovered more, we detected an increasing number of conditions caused in this way and, with time, the treatments became more sophisticated. Pinpointing the problems became easier with advances in imaging, CT and MRI scans, spectroscopy and the understanding of the human genome," Professor Leonard said.

"Cousin marriages increase the risks of these birth conditions and are more common in the Islamic world. I have probably visited every Middle Eastern state and grateful patients have given me an amazing variety of gifts. If I took

One of the wards at Great Ormond Street in 1858, made soon after it was founded in 1852. GOSH was the first hospital in the English speaking world to provide in-patient beds specifically for children

some of those to the island, it could be quite nostalgic."

James showed me a selection, including a mug decorated by child with a 'thank-you' message, an elaborate Persian miniature, a Khangar ceremonial dagger and stylised models of animals.

"If I wanted to remember some interesting trips, I could take my tray of Solidarity badges given to me in 1987, during the turbulent days before the Iron Curtain came down in Poland.

"A more recent trip saw us visiting the twins we delivered in the aircraft. The photographs from that trip could be interesting. The mother was abandoned by her husband, so we have supported the twins.

"Also, on that trip, we visited the HDRA project that we helped raise funds for through Kennington Overseas Aid," said Professor Leonard.

"KOA's £20,000 was used to show Kenyan villagers how to use the prosopis tree for animal and human food, as well as for wood products. This project has really taken off, and governments in neighbouring countries are showing an interest in copying it.

But what about his desert island choices?

Professor Leonard showed me a coin tray, made by his uncle Hugh Swann, former cabinet-maker to the Queen.

"His cabinets were both beautiful and functional, inspired by Barnsley and Gimson. William Morris would have admired them."

James' uncle supplied the Royal Mint with cabinets to house its complete collection. He began working for the Queen in 1975 and was involved in a complete reorganisation of the coin collection at Windsor Castle.

Hugh, who died in 2007, also made the crosier and pectoral cross for James's father, who used these pieces when he officiated at the wedding of Prince Charles and Lady Diana Spencer.

"When it comes to antiques I ought to consider this to take with me to the island. If I wanted to take a family heirloom, I could take a piece made by him," Professor Leonard said.

"Another possibility, that would remind me of my home, of Halcyon, my children Peter and Sarah, and even of my early attempts at observation, would be a mosaic by the Oxford artist Becky Paton.

"We saw her work at an exhibition in the Oxford University Museum of Natural History and loved it. So, for my retirement present, we commissioned her to make a piece which now hangs on our garden wall."

The mosaic, Professor Leonard explained, was inspired by the hoverflies he collected as a youngster.

What would his final choice be — the mosaic, the family heirloom, or the gifts from grateful patients?

"None of those," he said. "In the end, it has to be the print of the ward in Great Ormond Street in its early days."

Brian Aldiss

Author

Brian Aldiss began his writing career in 1928, at the age of three. His mother, May, lovingly bound those early stories with pieces of left-over wallpaper and placed them alongside Dickens and HG Wells on the family's bookshelves.

Now aged 85, Brian's prodigious talent has been celebrated by the greatest writers of the age — his writing has been compared with that of Isaac Asimov and Aldous Huxley.

In 1977, he was elected chairman of The Society of Authors' Committee of Management and, in 2000, was made Grand Master of Science Fiction by the Writers of America. His books have been a source of inspiration for many readers around the globe.

Brian was born in East Dereham, Norfolk, in 1925.

His father, Stanley, expected the young Aldiss to join the family business — in particular the gentleman's outfitters which was a part of the extensive enterprise founded by his grandfather, Harry Hildyard Aldiss.

Just before the outbreak of the Second World War, Brian's family moved to North Devon, eventually settling in Barnstable where, in 1939, Brian became a student at West Buckland School. In 1943 he enlisted and was sent with the Royal Signals to the Far East.

After being demobbed and having experienced the world beyond Devon, Brian decided Barnstable was not for him. He had heard that Oxford was full of libraries and bookshops and so purchased a train ticket to our city.

Wandering down the The High, he came across Sanders, which is now well known as the UK's largest seller of fine prints, maps and engravings. In those days it also sold books.

Brian went inside and asked for a job and after questioning him, the owner asked when he could start work.

Brian's confident reply was: "Now".

"Coming to Oxford was the best decision I ever made," Brian said. Here he wrote his 61 books and novellas and, with C S Lewis, founded the Oxford University Speculative Fiction Group, in 1955. He also became the literary editor of the *Oxford Mail*.

While working at Sanders he wrote a number of short pieces for a booksellers trade journal about life in a fictitious bookshop, and this attracted the attention of Charles Monteith, an editor at Faber and Faber. The result was Brian's first published book, *The Brightfount Diaries* (1955), a collection of his bookshop pieces.

"After life in the army, I did not adapt easily to a nine-to-five job but the experience was lightened by the characters who walked through the door of Sanders. I began writing sketches about them. Sanders subscribed to *The Bookseller* and I wrote to its editor suggesting he could enliven the magazine with a humorous column written by me.

"He suggested I write six of them for him to study — six without a guarantee of publication! But I did it and he published them all, week by week for two years. Faber and Faber contacted me saying they were fans. Would I like to make a book out of the series? I agreed 'and could it be illustrated?'."

To be approached by a publisher must be every writer's dream — and Brian got his illustrator too.

The Brightfount Diaries came out with Pearl Falconer's sketches in November, 1955. That same year he won his first literary prize for a short story competition in *The Observer*.

No surprise then that a copy of his first book would be first choice to accompnay him to our island.

"My copy of *The Brightfount Diaries* with the letters and reviews would be a bit of nostalgia on the island," he said.

"There was still some way to go before I could become a full-time writer. The manuscript of my first attempt at a novel is somewhere in a box, possibly in the Bodleian. I called it *Shouting down a Cliff*. It was 80,000 words long but I knew it was no good — too amateurish. I never looked at it again but I learned from that experience."

His experiences in the forces are also reflected in his writing. Brian showed me a copy of his 1962 novel, *Hothouse*.

It is set in a far future where the earth has stopped rotating and plants are engaged in a constant frenzy of growth and decay. Small groups of elvish humans live beneath a giant banyan tree that covers the day side of the Earth.

"Penguin have just reprinted this as a Penguin Classic. When I was stationed in the Far East, I spent some time in Calcutta. I took a ferry across the Houghli to the botanical gardens. There stood this huge banyan tree, which they claimed was the biggest tree in the world. It was not tall like a giant redwood but wide-spreading, branch after branch — as if it could eventually stretch around the world.

"The gardeners used forked posts to support each section because goats climbed into it. It was so surreal, it looked like a creation of Salvador Dali. Julian Huxley had written about that very tree. The idea for *Hothouse* was also born in those venerable branches."

While in the Royal Signals regiment in 1944, Brian was sent into a real hothouse, fighting the Japanese.

"Burma is a beautiful country but it is difficult to talk about war. The Battle of Kohima was fought from either side of a tennis court," he recalled.

"When we were trying to take back Mandalay, at times, I was dropped with my radio set in the jungle, to pass messages from brigade ahead and division behind. But you did not know which was 'front' or 'behind'.

"After Kohima, the Japanese army was breaking up, but that meant small groups could be anywhere. I tried to sleep with my rifle beside me but there were so many animal noises, mostly birds and rats in the undergrowth; but that same noise could be made by a Japanese soldier," Brian said.

"After we had taken Mandalay and were back in Calcutta, I remember marching in uniform with my steel tipped army boots, sten-gun over shoulder, passing by half-starved, half-naked barefoot people. I looked at their faces and was struck by their serenity. I thought, 'We must be doing something wrong.'

"Eventually, we were shipped home. Our troop ship moored in Liverpool docks, in a deserted dockyard – absolutely no one to welcome us. Not so much as a sergeant-major!

"I took the train to Aldershot to sign off. People appeared weary and unfriendly. England seemed a miserable place after India.

"I made my way to Barnstable, but did not feel it was the place for me. The army experience, although disciplined, had given me a sense of independence. I guess that is how I was able to leave home and come to Oxford."

Brian's 1964 novel, *Greybeard*, is set in Oxford, decades after the Earth's population has been sterilised as a result of nuclear bomb tests. The book shows an emptying world, occupied by an ageing, childless population.

"When my first wife left me to live in The Isle of Wight, I was devastated. I knew I couldn't earn my living there — I felt that I had lost my children, Clive and Wendy, so precious! That intense emotion led me to imagine a whole world without children. That marriage was a flop. My second marriage to Margaret was different altogether," Brian said.

"Margaret died in 1998, after a long illness. My daughter Charlotte and I went to Palaeohora, in Southern Crete.

"I was feeling shocked but we made the most of things. Wandering, I found myself in a forest of ancient, scabby, olive trees. In the middle of the forest was an abandoned private chapel. On the wall, in a state of decay, was a mural which I took to be of Mary with Jesus in her arms. I was intrigued.

I asked the local priest about it. He said 'Oh no, that is not Mary, it is St Anna, Jesus's grandmother.' In the Near East there is a legend that, when Mary ran out of milk, Anna suckled the baby. I returned and took a photograph of the mural.

"Later my daughter and I were in a café by the seafront. The daughter of the owner was pressed into service as the waitress but we found her in a cramped space behind the door.

"When she was not waiting at table, she practiced painting in the Byzantine manner. I asked her to make a copy of the mural. I paid her enough for her to leave the café and go to Athens, where she probably paints pictures for tourists."

Brian explained that the story does not

really end there.

"A publishing company called Stratus had recently brought out *Moreau's Other Island* and *Last Orders* and some other out-of-print books of mine. They had come up with an idea called print-on-demand, which avoided paying expensive warehousing. But the general public were not ready for this idea and Stratus was struggling to survive. So I offered them the novel I had been working on. Its opening line was: 'What a bugger', I said to myself in my old-fashioned way. 'What an absolute bugger.'

"I guess that was how I felt at the time and I called that book *The Cretan Teat*. Charlotte and I had travelled inland from Palaeohora and discovered an unhappy town.

"Here the priest said, 'You know there is a curse on this town'. Wherever we went, people told us about what had happened there in the Second World War," Brian explained.

"Because it was mountainous country, the Germans parachuted their troops in and the partisans were able to shoot them down as they fell. In revenge the Germans rounded up the women and children, locked them in the church and set fire to it.

"After the war Willy Brandt, then Chancellor of the Federal Republic of Germany, went to this little town to attempt to make amends. He had a bridge and road built, and a monument to the victims. When he finished rebuilding the church, a band played and the Germans marched away. But no one in that town clapped.

"I thought 'I must write about this'. That novel gradually changed into my imagined story, one of history, of blame, corruption, sex and the novelist growing old disgracefully. Stratus accepted the novel but the company was collapsing.

The editor, Edna Grey had been given her notice but she doggedly worked on my novel and it was eventually published."

Brian showed me a copy of *The Cretan Teat* and there on the cover was a reproduction of the picture of St Anna.

"I think this picture must have been painted by a celibate priest who had never seen a woman's breasts!" he laughed.

If I can only take one thing to the island, it has to be the portrait of St Anna because it has so many connections. "

39

Brigit Hegarty

Designer

Brigit Hegarty's interest in design began at a tender age. Her mother, Kerstin, enjoyed walking the boards in her local amateur dramatic productions.

While sitting through rehearsals, four year-old Brigit liked to play with the props. By the age of six she had moved on to helping make them and painting scenery.

So it is hardly surprising that for her first work experience, aged 14, she chose the Pegasus Theatre and worked on Steven Berkoff's adaptation of *The Fall of the House of Usher*.

Her family moved to Warborough in Oxfordshire when she was three. She attended the European School in Culham and was expected to do well in her Baccalaureate but Brigit's strong will and self belief led her on an exploration of other possibilities before she established her design company.

She was determined to leave school at 15 and transferred to the Oxford College of Further Education to study graphic design, French and Italian. From there she went to Banbury and entered the Foundation Art/Design Course and established a good grounding in art, craft and design.

Brigit continues her story:"I then went to Chelsea School of Art to study interior design, but left shortly after, as I wanted a more hands on craft based approach to design. Following a gap-year working in Italy I went to Plymouth University graduating with my degree in 3D design."

Brigit showed me a tray of striking silver rings.

She said: "My grandfather, Bertie, made these. He was a barrister, but in his spare time he was a passionate silversmith. He was influenced by Scandinavian design as my grandmother, Klares, was Swedish."

Brigit pointed out one ring that holds

particular significance for her.

"This Zircon stone fell out of my mother's engagement ring on to gravel but was later unexpectedly retrieved. The Zircon came from my paternal grandmother. Bertie (my maternal grandfather) reset it in this robust yet elegant half spherical setting," Brigit said.

"For my first business venture I designed a set of playful acrylic rings inspired by my grandfather's imaginative silver-smithing designs. I managed to persuade a Maidenhead firm, who usually only worked with industrial enterprises, to manufacture them for me and secured a large order from the Octopus company."

That was how her grandfather inspired her first commercial success but he was also an inspiration for her in other ways.

"Towards the end of the war, when the Allied forces entered Berlin my grandfather found this in the rubble of a bombed out building"

Brigit showed me a well-crafted wood carving of the Madonna and child.

"My mother passed it on to me and I love it. I would have to consider taking it on the island along with the rings, as my family has always supported me.

"It meant I could become self-employed and, after producing the rings, I started at the bottom of the ladder in a film production company in Soho, called Rogue Films.

"I soon developed networking skills that led to projects in art departments in film and TV," Brigit said.

"A slightly different assignment was for *Top of the Pops* designing costumes for a troop of dancers. Although that was fun, I preferred the art department work. I have not abandoned costume design and have since worked on outfits for fashion shoots.

"I worked with Bill Bailey on a short film but was then lured to a job on *The Face* (the music, fashion and culture monthly magazine) when it was selling at its best. I secured a lot of photography and advertising work," she added.

"By then I was living in Hackney and also took up the opportunity to work on an urban regeneration project for The Freeform Arts Trust.

"My first large installation was a nine metre wood, metal and glass sculpture for the Touchwood Shopping Centre in Solihull.

"I was on tenterhooks when it got transported to the Midlands because it was so fragile. I had visions of a lorry full of broken pieces, if it had to brake suddenly.

"I love sculpture and have worked with special needs children for Freeform, running workshops encouraging them to make three- dimensional work.

"An inspirational figure for me is Barbara Hepworth. I also admire Henry Moore, the Bauhaus movement, Kandinsky, Mondrian and Picasso, especially for his humour. It would be great to have work by all of them on the island but if that is not possible then *Pelagos* (1946) by Barbara Hepworth, please."

Brigit is fascinated by the natural world, in particular the healing properties of plants. The University of Oxford Botanic Gardens is a favourite place for her in Oxford — as is Port Meadow, where she likes to run.

She said: "I love gardening and plants as they provide nutrition, ingredients for medicine and above all natural beauty.

"The Oxford University Botanic Gardens are used for research as well as for our pleasure.

"The oldest tree in the garden, the English yew, is a species from which taxotere is made, used for the treatment of breast cancer. Aloe Vera is one of my favourite medicinal plants and is a basis of so many remedies."

Brigit said: "I have a design philosophy. I am conscious of the psychological impact. Shape, form, colour, composition and lighting all have a conscious and sub-conscious effect. I have them in mind when designing magazine covers and advertisements."

I wondered what is the job of a set designer?

"Sometimes I interpret or co-ordinate a brief from a client. I have to create the environment so that the product sells well. It involves designing a set, sourcing and making props and creating a subtle image that will appeal to the consumer. I have to be a problem solver, working with the art director. My job is to set the scene. My aim is to make their vision a reality."

Her design company can list clients such as Harrods, Adidas, Marks and Spencer, Miss Selfridge and Top Man.

Now that her business has achieved such success, I wondered what plans she has for the future.

"Last year I initiated a design collective aimed at helping and encouraging young talent. It is called On the Road.

"Saatchi & Saatchi Advertising agency profiled the work of seven young designers in their Soho window.

"I art directed the photo-shoot which featured each of the designers products with a mirror reflecting a road in the background. The reflection of the road was symbolic of their journey. Following this Saatchi & Saatchi have scheduled continuing exhibitions for young designers."

As well as her mother and grandfather, her aunt Karin Ann Tesdorf has also had a strong influence on Brigit.

"Karin Ann is an interior designer. She gave me this beautiful copy of *Alice in Wonderland* which has been in the family since 1911, (Macmillian edition)," she said.

"If I take this to the island it will remind me of Oxford. It is also a book that can be read and interpreted on many levels.

"I can identify with Alice's experiences: She is on a journey of mental and physical progression through life's adventures. She makes her own choices which for me symbolise learning from experiences and finding personal identity."

I wondered if the book would be her final choice?

"To remind me of my mother, I could take this watercolour painted by her in Norfolk. She is an artist who paints purely for pleasure and this is one I particularly like. I find it a peaceful and serene picture."

"But the book and my mother's painting might not last on the island, and I could perhaps make a sculpture or carving.

"I would take the ring as it represents both sides of my family and I hope would endure the island's climate."

40

Weimin He

Artist in Residence, Radcliffe Observatory Quarter, Oxford

Passing by the Radcliffe Infirmary during the recent demolition work, part of the development of the new Radcliffe Observatory Quarter for Oxford University, you may have seen a solitary figure in a hard hat and carrying a clipboard, eyes focused intently on the scene and hand busy with a pencil.

You may have idly wondered if this was the architect, an engineer or project manager? You may have been surprised to discover that the tall figure was Chinese artist Weimin He, artist in residence at the Radcliffe Observatory Quarter.

This is not the first building site in Oxford that Weimin has recorded. He was artist in residence during the building of the new Ashmolean. A copy of his book, *Building the New Ashmolean* was presented to the Queen when she opened the new building.

Weimin was born in Manchuria in 1964, just two years before the Cultural Revolution.

"My father, He Jixing, was born in Jiangxi province, once the centre of the Imperial porcelain industry in the warm south," Weimin said. "Leaving the army at the end of the Korean War, he wanted to return there, but was given no choice but to stay in the cold climes of Manchuria and teach Chinese literature in Mudanjiang," Weimin explained.

"He quickly became head teacher in the secondary school where he met and married my mother, Lu Lilian, who taught mathematics. My older sister, He Haiyan, was born in 1962 and I have a younger sister, He Yinyan.

"At the time I was growing up, Maoist propaganda was ubiquitous. My name means 'To serve the people' in a Maoist sense. When I was 17, I tried to change it to 'Blue Sky'. Written Chinese is hieroglyphic. The characters for blue sky and 'to serve the people' are different but they sound the same. Bureaucratic problems made it almost impossible to do officially but I signed my early adult pictures Blue Sky."

During the Cultural Revolution in 1966, Mao closed the schools and urged the youth to destroy 'the four olds' — old customs, old ideas, old culture and old habits.

Since teachers passed on those old ideas they were among the first targets.

I asked Weimin what happened to his

family. "My father was tortured and sent to the countryside for re-education as a peasant.

"My great-grandfather on my mother's side had worked in the Imperial court, so my mother was labelled landlord. The ostracism was painful for her for decades," Weimin said.

"In 1970, when the situation was becoming more normal, we were allowed to join father in a village 70 miles from Mudanjiang. There had been no secondary school in the area and my parents, with help from villagers, built a school calling it 'new dawn'.

"Despite all that had happened, people were eager to learn. I was lucky because my mother had taught me maths and taught me to read. So when I went to primary school, I was bored and sometimes played truant.

"My parents' life was tough, but as a six-year-old, I enjoyed much more freedom than the Chinese children of today.

"I explored the countryside, caught fish, picked water melons and was close to nature. We all had to work hard on the land if we wanted to eat," Weimin said.

"From my earliest memories, I loved to draw. By the age of five, some of my sketches of people were recognisable. Of course, my father was not pleased by my truanting nor by my habit of compulsively sketching in the margins of my school books, but those experiences have affected me.

"Daoism is an important Chinese philosophy that is close to nature. In Daoist art, the empty spaces are important. I often make use of that concept in my work."

Weimin showed me some of his sketches from the Cultural Revolution. In one there is a smiling benevolent looking Mao Zedung and an idyllic village scene with Maoist slogans.

"After Mao's death, I erased the characters 'Long Live' from Long Live Chairman Mao. Some people keep a written diary. I have

sketched every day of my life — that is my visual diary," he said.

In 1975, the year before the death of Mao, his family was able to move back to the city. I wondered whether his formal art education began then, at age 11?

"Yes and informally, too. A colleague of my mother had been able to hide a book of Western art from the Red Guards," Weimin explained.

During the Cultural Revolution, Red Guards raided homes destroying 'poisonous books'. It was not just Western art that was attacked but traditional Chinese landscape painting was banned. Socialist Realism, featuring workers and peasants, was the only acceptable form of art to the authorities.

"The book was my first sight of Western art and especially of Renaissance art," Weimin revealed. "I was fascinated by the sketches of Michelangelo and Leonardo.

"The art teacher in my mother's school taught me western techniques of light and shade and, from then on, I used it. I even went over some of my old drawings adding shade. I joined a youth art club. The most inspiring thing I could have on your desert island would be Michelangelo's *David*."

In 1982, Weimin became an undergraduate student at the Harbin College of Art.

"Father would have preferred me to become an official, but I am lucky that my family have always been supportive and respected my choice of career. It is a passion, a way of life for me really," he explained.

"At college, I studied oil painting and traditional Chinese ink painting. In 1982, I was still occasionally subversive. I took a piece of wood from a classroom chair so that I could make my first wood block print.

"I saw my work published for the first time when still at school, aged 17. I was really surprised because I received letters from all parts of China about it everyday in the post for months — sometimes 20 per day."

Weimin taught art in a teacher training college for one year before attending a famous art school in Luxun Academy of Fine Arts as a post graduate.

"I was still in Luxun, in 1989, when the Democracy Movement took to the streets," he said. "Like most young people, at the time, I was excited by it. It was not just happening in Beijing.

"After the demonstrations were suppressed, security bureau officials were sent everywhere to investigate. I had painted posters to mourn the dead and was in a difficult position, but was fortunate in that the official who investigated me turned a blind eye to them. So in 1991, I was able to work as a professional artist at the Heilongjiang Artists' Association."

How did Weimin come to leave China?

"Christer von der Burg and the late Verena Bolinder-Müller (founders of the Muban Foundation) came to China to collect prints. They liked my work and introduced me to Professor David Barker from Ulster University.

"They also agreed to support me financially so I could go to Belfast to study for my PhD. I arrived, in September 1999, two days before my birthday," Weimin said.

"Although I had learned some English in school, I had only studied it seriously for six months in 1997. So my English was not good —and I was floored by the local accent. I felt completely lost and unable to communicate.

"I lived in a dirty shared flat with a Kosovan refugee and a local man living on benefits. Professor Barker was supportive and I moved into better accommodation in the city centre. I was adapting so well I even came to enjoy Guinness, which at first I though was like drinking Soy sauce!" Weimin laughed.

"One morning I was woken by the police saying 'Bomb get out' and, in pyjamas, I found myself on the street. A pipe bomb had been thrown though the next door's window. Up until then I had felt safe in Belfast, but after that experience, I decided to move out of the centre.

"One day I was in the park and I started to sketch. I realised that the people lazing there enjoying the sun were Catholic and Protestant, Unionists and Nationalists, enjoying a shared experience. I called my picture *In the Sunshine* (see page 153)."

Meanwhile, the Ashmolean Museum had advertised a post for a research fellow and Professor Barker encouraged Weimin to apply. He arrived in the city in 2005, with an accent part Chinese part Northern Irish!

The first exhibition he curated was entitled *The Mystery of Empty Space*. It was well received and reported in the national press.

Weimin said, "In Daoist art, the void is the place where life originates; being comes out of nothing. I would like to take on the desert island something that symbolises that idea. I think a folder of absolutely blank Chinese album leaves ready for creation would do that."

Weimin went on to curate the stunning exhibition of Chinese prints at the Ashmolean with Shelagh Vainker.

"Shelagh was such an encouraging person to work with," Weimin said. "She trusted my judgement to go to China and select prints. It was interesting seeing the changes taking place as an outside observer. Prints throughout the 20th century reflected every change in Chinese society."

How did he become artist in residence at the Ashmolean?

"It happened suddenly. My contract was about to end. I still sketched anything I could

in my spare time and I had begun drawing the builders demolishing the back of the Ashmolean," Weimin said.

"Christopher Brown, the director of the museum, heard about my sketches and on my last day, invited me to stay on and be artist in residence. I was delighted, because I had come to love Oxford."

Weimin's *Building the New Ashmolean* was the opening exhibition. His parents were able to come and see his exhibition — symbolic of an incredible life journey for the boy from a Manchurian village.

Weimin's curiosity led him to his present post. While the building work on the Ashmolean progressed, his office was in the Gibson Building in the Radcliffe Observatory Quarter and so he couldn't stop himself sketching what was going on.

He explained: "Art doesn't just record like a photograph, but expresses a spirit that touches you. When I saw the university was advertising for an artist in residence for the site, I applied and of course had plenty of work to show them.

"They have been extremely supportive to my project, and offered the prestigious St Luke's Chapel as a place for me to restore a printing press from the 1840's. Block printing is time-consuming, but symbolic."

But what would Weimin like to take with him to our island.

"If I had my printing press on the island, complete with materials, I could carry on working," he said

"I have one little piece of jewellery, a silver mounted claw given me by my grandmother. She was of the generation who had bound feet. This is the only thing I have of hers and I take it with me everywhere; I feel it has some mysterious power and represents my family," he added.

"I would also need an example of the work of my tutor Quan Xianguang. His teaching method was unique and inspiring. He painted one especially for me of Zhongkui ,who desired peace and fought evil spirits."

But I reminded Weimin that, in the end, he would have to choose just one thing.

He said: "In that case, could you assemble in one folio a collection of prints by Rembrant, Durer and Goya and by Ren Bonian Wu Changshuo, Huang Qui Yan and maybe attach a Han dynasty seal from the Ashmolean? That way I would have plenty to inspire me, especially if they came on top of my press."

41

Sir Roger & Moyra Bannister
Neurologist and athlete - Artist and mother

When my brother Michael Harry came from Australia to visit me in 1970, he wanted to make a pilgrimage to the Iffley Road running track where Sir Roger Bannister ran the first sub-four minute mile on May 6, 1954 — with the help of Christopher Chataway and Christopher Brasher.

If, like me, you remember 1954, you will appreciate the morale-boosting effect this event had on the country. Life in post-war Britain was largely grim and grey — illuminated in 1951 by the Festival of Britain, and in 1953, by the conquest of Everest and the coronation of Elizabeth II.

When Sir Roger achieved what many thought impossible, we felt we had entered a new world, filled with possibilities.

1954 was also the year when wartime rationing finally ended.

"All that training was done on a limited diet," Sir Roger recalled. "I cannot understand people who are nostalgic for the 1950s — they were very tough times."

Norris McWhirter (perhaps best known as the publisher of *The Guinness Book of Records*) was the timekeeper on the day. He excited the onlookers by delaying the announcement of the record breaking time as long as possible.

He said: "As a result of event four, the one mile, the winner was R G Bannister of Exeter and Merton Colleges, in a time which, subject to ratification, is a track record, an English native record, a United Kingdom record, a European record, in a time of three minutes . . ."

The roar of the crowd, which drowned out the rest of the announcement, could be heard a mile away.

Later that same year, on August 7 at the British Empire and Commonwealth Games held in Vancouver, Roger Bannister competed against John Landy — the Australian athlete who was the second man to achieve a sub-four minute mile — for the first time in a race billed as 'The Miracle Mile'.

It is said that 100 million people heard the race commentary on the radio, while millions

more watched on television. The outcome of the race will have pleased all true Brits. On the final turn of the last lap, as Landy looked over his left shoulder, Bannister raced past him on the right.

Vancouver commissioned a larger-than-life bronze statue of the two athletes by artist Jack Harman to commemorate the event.

While that day in 1954 stands out for many of us, Sir Roger revealed that he is prouder of other achievements during his career in medicine.

"I was a 25 year-old medical student at St Mary's Medical School when I ran the four minute mile and qualified as a doctor six weeks later," Sir Roger said.

"St Mary's was the hospital where Alexander Fleming isolated crude penicillin, in 1921, although it was synthesised here in Oxford by Florey and Chain, in the 1940s. " said Roger.

In 1958, conscripted as a medical officer

Sir Roger was sent to Aden — now the Yemen, then a British protectorate — to fathom the mysteries of a heat-related illness after troops died of heatstroke.

Sir Roger marched up and down mountains with the soldiers to work out what the problem was and continued the research when he was back in the UK.

Sir Roger's wife, Lady Moyra Bannister, recalled the results of that research.

"Knowing that lives depended on his work, Roger put himself at risk," she explained. "Back in London, he injected himself with pyrogens made from bacteria and exercised in a heat chamber made to simulate conditions in Aden and published the results in a paper in *The Lancet*.

"I just remember, after one experiment I opened the door at home to find him standing there him looking green and ill. It would not be allowed now."

Sir Roger added: "That was how a lot of research was done in those days. You often had to be a guinea-pig."

Sir Roger once said of the four minute mile: "The man who can drive himself further once the effort gets painful is the man who will win." Again and again he has applied that attitude to medical research. Roger said,

"My training and first appointment in neurology was in 1959, at the National Hospital for Nervous Diseases, in Queen Square, which was the first hospital in the world to specialise in neurology. I became a consultant, in 1963, shared between Queen Square and St Mary's Hospital, Paddington."

Sir Roger's desert island choice — a 19th century ceramic head used by Victorian phrenologists — is inspired by his interest in the workings of the brain.

"I am most fortunate in having led a satisfying life as a neurologist with a special interest in research into the autonomic nervous system," he said. "As a neurologist, my choice to take on the desert island is this head," he said. "A Victorian phrenologist would feel the lumps on a patient's head using the ridiculous notion that qualities like ideology, caution and insight were situated in particular regions of the brain."

"Moyra bought it from an antique shop as a joke. But it shows how much my subject of neurology has advanced in the last 100 years.

"I have chosen this as a startling reminder of how spectacular the advances in neurology

have been. The achievements of the early British neurologists at Queen Square should fill us with pride, as their work is carried forward," Sir Roger explained.

"During 30 years practicing as a neurologist and doing research, the new procedures, such as brain scanning, have advanced the scope of neurology rapidly. For instance, with a stroke victim, we are able to use imaging to find where a vessel is blocked. And sometimes we can operate to remove the clot or use drugs to dislodge it.

"The analysis of brain function first with special x-rays and now brain imaging, shows the structure inside the brain. We can even relate the blood supply to each part of the brain," he said.

Sir Roger pioneered research into diseases of the autonomic nervous system, as well as bringing out six editions of a test book of neurology. His definitive book, Disorders of the Autonomic Nervous System is still in print.

In 1985 Sir Roger received a letter that was to change his direction once more.

"To my surprise I was asked to be the next Master of Pembroke College, Oxford," Sir Roger said.

"It was quite a career change, so I discussed it with the family and we decided to accept and this brought us back to Oxford. But I did not lose touch with neurology and research."

Lady Moyra Bannister (nee Jacobsson) came to Oxford in 1945, to study at the Ruskin School of Fine Art and Drawing. From here she went to the Corcoran School of Art in Washington DC.

She was well on her way to a successful career, having exhibited work in major London galleries, including the Royal Academy and the Royal Portrait Society. She met Sir Roger in 1954, just before his record-breaking run..

"I met Roger just before that glorious time. And he became a doctor in that same year. We married a year later in 1955.

"As a young doctor he was absent much of the time, so when we started a family we had four children in six years, — I had to give up ideas of a career in art to concentrate on them. I never stopped painting and drawing, but my art reflected our family life. If I hold a paint brush it makes me enormously happy."

"I was appointed in succession to two Government councils, one on education and one on child health-a fascinating time."

When her father was chairman and

managing director of the International Monetary Fund, she and Sir Roger met many American politicians and enjoyed being at one of the Kennedy's inaugural balls.

She says," Through a combination of my father, Per Jacobsson, and Roger's work and fame, our lives have been enriched by meeting marvellously interesting people— from Churchill to the Clintons, — but what we treasure most is our close friends."

There is a framed letter on the wall of the Bannister's home expressing condolences on her father's death from President Kennedy who wrote 'The world is by far a better place in which to live because of Per Jacobsson's untiring efforts.'

Lady Bannister has kept diaries throughout her life, impressive illustrated and bound volumes.

Tough is the best description of the Bannister's early married life. From Lady Bannister's paintings and sketches of their family, and Sir Roger's appreciation of them, it is easy to see that their four children and fourteen grandchildren are the bedrock, joy and pride of their life together. But those early years were not easy.

Sir Roger took up posts in London and had to live in the hospitals, working all hours.

Lady Bannister said: "We rented a flat in Earls Court, but I had no family around to support me. Christopher Brasher's mother lived nearby and she was like a mother to me. I found a solution by organising an informal nursery with five other mothers so that we could share the child care and cope with the exhaustion of sleepless nights."

"I had to take three little tots on the tube in order for Roger to see his children. The highlight of our children's Christmas was seeing St Mary's students performing Gilbert and Sullivan.

"When the Queen Mother, the medical school patron, was in the audience she laughed and laughed at their antics. The only problem was finding her a suitably regal chair."

"On Christmas Day we followed Roger from ward to ward where he ceremoniously carved the turkey. Red cloaked nurses sang carols, their voices soaring up in the central old St Mary's stairwell."

Lady Bannister has painted her husband

skulling on a significant spot on the Thames.

"Under Roger's aegis as Master of Pembroke College, new accommodation for 100 students was built south of the river. It was difficult raising the money at a time of economic depression, but he did it.

"There were a few comments that the architecture was not cutting-edge, but the students love it," she said

"That painting could be one option for the desert island. Roger's sporting interests have not only been athletics. We enjoyed sailing too and he started an orienteering club near our country cottage in Sussex. Roger believes in sport for all. I feel the same about art."

That brought us to Sir Roger's work as the first chairman of the Executive Sports Council, in 1971.

He said: "With our motto of Sport for All, we meant to improve sports facilities not only for the elite but for everyone. We aimed to spread 400 multi -purpose sports centres across the country."

With the 2012 Olympics looming, we have reason to be grateful for his foresight.

Lady Bannister's sketch of her eldest daughter, Erin

"Another council achievement, in 1972, was the devising of at test to detect anabolic steroids which was a form of cheating that I foresaw would become a major problem. The test is still in use today," Sir Roger said.

During their 56 years together, Lady Bannister has sketched as well as kept the diaries to give to her children.

While Roger was Master of Pembroke she returned to painting with renewed vigour and was rarely seen without a sketchbook and pencil in hand.

She said: "I spent most Sunday afternoons painting and drawing with the children. When Erin was 13, I realised that she had surpassed me as an artist. I should consider taking my family sketches to the island and Erin particularly loves the one of her which I put in my recent retrospective exhibition at The Dragon School."

Erin Townsend, the Bannister's eldest daughter, lives in Oxford and is a successful professional artist.

Their sons Clive and Thurstan went into management and finance. Lady Bannister said: "Clive makes wonderful inlaid woodwork and our other daughter Charlotte Bannister Parker is assistant priest at the University Church of St Mary the Virgin.

"She has developed contacts with Kimberley in South Africa. Twice a year she goes to the township where she has set up a woman's refuge and Aids prevention schemes.

"We are very proud of our children and grandchildren. After taking her degree in French and art history one of our granddaughters started working on the Teach -First scheme in Tower Hamlets."

I wondered what she would take to our island?

She said: "I love English poetry, so if there is only thing I can take on the island it would be the collection I assembled for the children. I have copied and illustrated the ones that inspire me.

"The pictures I use are mostly reproductions of works of art which I admire, from Rembrandt to Renoir.

"I have woven into each volume, pictures of the children to inspire them. I wouldn't want to be without my paints and artists material, but I suppose if I can take only one thing to the island, then it must be this anthology."

42

Dame Jessica Rawson
Former Warden of Merton College, Oxford

Dame Jessica Rawson has been fascinated with China for as long as she can remember. At school, she expressed a wish to study Chinese at Cambridge, but was discouraged. Her teachers said: "Nobody goes to China. Nobody studies Chinese."

Instead she read history at New Hall, but never lost the desire and determination to learn Chinese and somehow get to China.

She managed it in 1975, as a junior member of a distinguished and high-powered delegation following US President Nixon's famous visit, when China opened the door sufficiently for a few to squeeze through.

The Cultural Revolution was on the wane, and Mao Zedong was still in power.

This was not the only groundbreaking event in her life. It is easy to forget that women students were not admitted to the old Oxford colleges until 1974, and even after that, the career path for female academics did not run smoothly.

But, in 1994, Dame Jessica became Warden of Merton College. She retired from that post in 2010, but remains Professor of Chinese Art and Archaeology at the School of Archaeology and is still a phenomenally active researcher.

Dame Jessica's interest in China is not confined to its past. She has helped develop the China Centre in Woodstock Road, Oxford. The centre's activities cover modern as well as historical China. It aims to embrace all aspects of Oxford's interaction with China — from classical literature to modern medicine.

Dame Jessica said: "I do not think we put enough energy into studying and interacting with China. Changing our universities' outlook is rather like turning around an ocean liner. We need to build up knowledge about China, to be prepared for the future.

"China is a difficult part of the world to understand. Many countries are connected, like cousins, by our common heritage of Indo -European languages; the two major exceptions are the Middle East and the Far

East, especially China. The Chinese language is challenging and structures ideas very differently from the ways that are familiar to us. China covers a vast area and has a huge population; our government really should be investing more in studying and connecting with Asia."

During Dame Jessica's career at the British Museum, where she worked for more than 25 years, she handled thousands of amazing objects. But which of them she would want to find washed up on the beach of our desert island.

"Although I grew up in London, I spent every single holiday in the Lake District, and spent some time there as a baby during the war when London was being bombed," she said. "Our flat was in North Kensington. In those days the area was not prosperous and was extensively bombed.

"I went to school in London and was quite a successful student and ended up as head girl, but I was rather solitary, even lonely."

"I still share a house in the Lake District with my sisters. It is the one that my great grandfather bought to retire to as his wife came from there," Dame Jessica explained.

"My maiden name was Quirk, a name originating in the Isle of Man. All my father's relatives are from the North West. I write many of my articles in the Lake District, and we have held a number of family parties in that house, with up to 50 members of our extended families. One sister made a photographic scrap book of such a gathering and I should want to take that with me to the island."

Like many of the brilliant people who have arrived on our desert island, Dame Jessica is modest about her abilities.

Her formidable intelligence is apparent, but she also has what the antiques trade describes as 'an eye'.

It can, indeed, be acquired by training oneself, not just to look but to see. Dame Jessica experienced a 'eureka' moment in Jerusalem which proved she had an 'eye' for antiquities.

"I spent three summers in Jerusalem as a student, excavating there. It was the mid-1960s and we were working in the then Arab half of Jerusalem," Dame Jessica explained. "Kathleen Kenyon, the Principal of St Hughes, was leading the expedition.

"I am a little dyslexic but discovered then that I have a good visual memory. I was able to identify objects, especially pots and pottery fragments relatively easily. Everyone has this talent, but in most people it is hidden and needs bringing out. I realised that, unusually, for me it is on the surface of my intelligence."

It was then that Dame Jessica realised what she wanted to do, namely to explore the world though the buildings and objects that people had made over many centuries.

In 1967 she headed for Afghanistan and felt that she was one step closer to her dream of China, which has a slither of border with Afghanistan.

"I went with friends who had parents working in a development agency. I have some pieces of turquoise pottery from that trip which could represent that time and a hint of what was to come," she said.

But the death of her father put paid to her ambitions at least for a while.

"I had wanted to study for a PhD, but funding was a problem, so I entered the Civil Service fast stream in the Department of Health. I discovered I had some aptitude for administration," Dame Jessica said.

"It is not something that I particularly enjoy; it is however a valuable tool. I like the civil service ethos, dedicated to public service .I learned then to be accurate and not write to a member of the public until I had the facts. That training came in very useful when I became Warden of Merton.'

"While in the then Department of Health, I had begun to learn Chinese at night school, I saw a post advertised at the British Museum in the Oriental Department and applied for it.

"The British Museum employed me, not on account of my early efforts to learn Chinese, but because of the signs of motivation in trying to learn the language and in going digging. It was an extraordinary chance — a stroke of luck that could not happen today," she said. "No-one would be employed on that basis now.

"Concurrently with working at the British Museum, I did a degree in Chinese at the School of Oriental and African Studies situated behind the museum. It was a considerable effort, but because of it here I am now. "

Quite early in her career at the British Museum, Dame Jessica broke with a tradition.

"I realised that you could not study China properly without going to the Far East. In the past it was the norm for academics studying China to remain in the West. Arthur Waley, who was a pioneer in translating

Chinese poetry, never went to the Far East. But I wanted to see archaeological sites and museums — it is such a complicated society — I do not think you can understand China without going there.

"I have been 50-60 times now. I am interested in the edges, away from the enormous polluted cities, where the Yellow River Valley interacts with Inner Asia.

"It is surprisingly difficult to go to these remote rural places, particularly to the ranges of North West China and the Altai mountains, which connect Chinese Central Asia with Russia, eastern Kazakhstan and western Mongolia.

"If you fly from Beijing to England your flight path crosses these enormously high mountains. I have 12 elaborate diaries and a vast photographic record in which I have recorded the changing face of China. They help me jog my memory. I could take those on the island, " Dame Jessica said.

"My career benefitted from China's development. When I was taken on as a junior curator, no one believed that China would become open to the world. Then came 1975 and my first trip to China with a high-powered delegation."

This was the groundbreaking trip to Mao's China. During the Cultural Revolution, the young people had been urged to destroy 'the four olds' and went around smashing art and antiques. It is ironic really that that same generation now wants to recover the past.

Dame Jessica said: "It appears that the world owes a great deal to Zhou Enlai who locked the exhibits away in the Forbidden City."

Recalling her first visit behind the walls of the Forbidden City, Dame Jessica said: "It was an amazing experience. I can still remember being there for the first time.

"I can remember the dress I wore and the swallows flying overhead. Nowadays there are few birds in many parts of China because of the pollution. I remember the feeling that I was a European and that here I was, a stranger in a quite different part of the planet. That was my best insight, and it is still true."

I wondered if there was something from that time she would like to take to our island?

"During my time at the British Museum, I learned a lot about jade. I have written the catalogue for the British Museum on the subject.

"The Chinese discovered jade in Neolithic times and have never stopped using it. Even before I went to work at the British Museum, the spectacular jade terrapin from Mughal India was my favourite object. At first, I didn't realise where it came from. "

This unique Mughal sculpture, dating to the 17th century, was carved from a single piece of green nephrite. It was found at the bottom of a water cistern during engineering excavations, in 1803, at Allahabad in Northern India. Dame Jessica said,

"This wonderful sculpture, created out of a very hard stone may have been installed in the palace of one of the princes of the Mughal Dynasty.

"As a child I admired the terrapin and longed to stroke its smooth shell. Today, even though the creature is not Chinese, it is still my favourite jade."

Dame Jessica curated many exhibitions for the British Museum during her 25 years there. One was the gorgeously named *Chinese Ornament: The Lotus and the Dragon* in 1984.

"I think that my jade book and my book on Chinese ornament are the nicest ones that I have written, although not as well known as my work on bronzes," she said.

"While at the British Museum in the 1980s, I had one of my biggest academic breakthroughs working on a joint project with academics from Harvard and the Sackler Collection in New York.

"This opportunity gave me a foothold in the USA. My work concerned the Western Zhou (1040BC-770BC). I was allocated this period to write about, in part because most of the other researchers were less interested in it as the bronzes are less elegant than the earlier and later pieces.

"There had just been a key find at

Zhuangbai, west of Xi'an- a large hoard of bronze vessels. The Zhou buried their most important bronzes when they were defeated and fled in 771BC," Dame Jessica explained.

"Many of the bronzes were made by generations of the same family, so they could be put in a datable stylistic sequence. This find revolutionised the study of the period.

"I learned from that find and, indeed, from the whole project that it is important to look at all objects in groups, not one by one. In that way, new shapes and designs are made much more conspicuous and, from such observations, it is possible to think about the changes in society that are reflected in the ways in which the objects, in this case bronzes, were developed."

Dame Jessica has advised Sir Peter Moores, the founder of the Compton Verney, the award-winning art gallery in Warwickshire, on the gallery's outstanding collection of Chinese bronzes.

"It came as a surprise when I was elected, in 1994. Three women were chosen as heads of colleges in that week. One national paper reported it as: 'Women Three — Men Glum.'

"Even now Peter Moores is adding a few small bronzes every year," Dame Jessica said. "I particularly like the mirrors with decorative bronze backs that he has recently acquired. Perhaps Compton Verney would let me take one to the island?"

Dame Jessica did not believe she was a serious candidate for the Wardenship at Merton. "It came as a surprise when I was elected, in 1994. Three women were chosen as heads of colleges in that week. One national paper reported it as: 'Women Three — Men Glum.'

"I enjoyed the experience enormously, interacting with fellows and students, getting to know the alumni, helping to improve the college buildings and to create a choir," she said. "For me Merton will always be the most beautiful place in the world. But I treasure its atmosphere, which is intangible, above all. Every new academic year began as I banged the gavel in Hall for the grace on the first Sunday of the Michaelmas Term. With more than 100 students in that huge, dark, candlelit space with its massive wooden beams, I could feel the past, a long long past, join the present.'

Seeing Dame Jessica's portrait on the dining hall wall, the only female among all those illustrious male wardens, is like uncovering a piece of history. She described her workload of administration, teaching and research and I was surprised that she found time to sleep.

"I am married. I met my husband, John, an architect in London, in 1968, while still a student, learning Chinese. While I was Warden of Merton, I lived in the Warden's Lodgings in Merton Street. I was only able to go home to London at the weekends. It was a bit like being a weekly boarder. But perhaps living on the site made it possible for me to focus on the college, concentrate on its needs and to live life as a Warden, as it should be lived, to the full."

I wondered what she would want to take with her to our island from Merton College?

"If I were to take something from Merton, the sixteenth century lectern in the chapel or the sundial on the lawn would be the most memorable objects for me."

But if she could only one thing? "The jade terrapin," she replied, without hesitation.

43

Jenny Lewis
Playwright and poet

Jenny Lewis is a playwright, a prize-winning poet, a children's writer, a teacher and a singer- songwriter who has partied with Monty Python stars and worked for Tony Blair at Downing Street.

Her first book of poetry, *When I Became an Amazon* was published in 1996, and was inspired by a mastectomy she had undergone.

Her work came to the notice of the long-running Radio 4 show *Woman's Hour*. The response to her interview and recorded extracts was immediate and emotional. The BBC received a flood of letters and telephone calls.

The inspiration for the sequence of poems was a card from a friend which read: 'Dear Jenny — now you are a true Amazon." Then, after reading reports of the unearthing of Iron Age woman buried with armour and weapons, she had discovered the dramatic context she needed.

Jenny explained: "*When I Became an Amazon* is not intended to be historically or biographically accurate but to provide a dramatic context in which the power and courage of women is celebrated."

Her latest work, a play called *After Gilgamesh,* was performed at Oxford's Pegasus Theatre during the MESH International Youth Arts Festival, also combines ancient and modern events — and has a strong family connection.

Her father, Thomas Charles Lewis, fought in Mesopotamia in the First World War with the 4th Battalion, South Wales Borderers. He was wounded at Kut al Amara in January, 1917, and invalided out of the army.

While researching these events for a collection of poems called Taking Mesopotamia, Jenny came across the Babylonian Epic of Gilgamesh.

Gilgamesh was king of Uruk, modern day Iraq, circa 2500 BC. In Mesopotamian mythology, Gilgamesh is a demigod of superhuman strength, who built the city walls of Uruk to defend his people from external threats

The modern-day invasion of Iraq threw up historical similarities with this legendary character, and Jenny was again inspired to parallel ancient and modern events, comparing the modern wars in Iraq with the ancient epic in her play.

Jenny collaborated with director Yasmin Sidhwa and Rabab Ghazoul to structure and develop the play, which features music by composer and singer Anita Daulne and choreography by Allan Hutson. It will be performed to launch the youth arts festival on July 21.

Looking back at her early life, Jenny said: "My father died in 1944 aged 48, when I was

about six months old and since my mother had to work, my sister and I were largely brought up by my grandmother.

"I was sent to boarding school aged seven. I hated it. I was incredibly homesick and books were my salvation. At the age of about four, I remember being excited by the discovery that words could rhyme. My early attempts at poems were trite but the interest led, in my teens, to a passion for the poetry of Keats and, especially, Wilfred Owen. Reading Jon Stallworthy's biography of Owen and seeing the number of revisions the poet made gave me an insight into the creative process.

"My granny used to take us up into the gods at the Old Vic where I developed a taste for drama — and my mother's sister, my aunty Joan, was also an inspiration as she was a ballerina and danced, under the name Joan Kent, with the Markova/Dolin Company. The other great influence on my life has been art. *The Story of Art* by E.H. Gombrich is a book that always reminds me of my early, formative years. So that would be nice to find washed up on the beach of my desert island."

It was one of those strange chance occurrences that change lives that brought Jenny to Oxford in 1962.

She wanted to study at Leeds University, following a course that combined English Literature and Art, under Quentin Bell, the art historian and author. As she headed for the interview, carrying her portfolio, the case broke in the rain.

Despite this Jenny was offered a place at Leeds conditional on getting an 'A' grade in A-Level Art. She finished the exam early, but, instead of leaving the exam room, she was tempted to make 'improvements' and accidentally spilt some water, ruining her painting and and her chance of a place at Leeds. Her second choice was the Ruskin School of Fine Art and Drawing in Oxford, which is where she came to study.

Jenny said: "That was a turning point in my life and there is a painting in the Ashmolean Museum that I admire intensely and which reminds me of that time. It is Uccello's *Hunt by Night*. That is a real possibility for the island."

On her first day at the Ruskin, on the steps of the Ashmolean Museum, Jenny bumped into Vashti Bunyan (now hailed as the 'mother of Freak Folk') and they became friends.

Vashti learned to play on Jenny's old guitar, Benji. Later, with Angela Strange, the three Ruskin students founded a group called The Three of Us.

Jenny recalled: "Vashti and I shared a flat at 219 Iffley Road. Sitting on the floor with our hamster, Heap, we wrote a song called *17 Pink Sugar Elephants*, which Vashti later developed into the haunting *Train Song*.

"It reappeared recently as the soundtrack to an award-winning Reebok commercial which was shown on a 30ft plasma screen at Wembley during an American Football game.

"This month our song will be heard again — this time in a Samsung TV and cinema advertisement," Jenny added.

"Vashti met and worked with many other musicians and is famous for setting off for the Isle of Uist in the Outer Hebrides in a horse-drawn caravan looking for a commune supposedly set up by Donovan."

In those heady student days doing gigs and singing at Oxford balls with Vashti and Angy, Jenny was lucky enough to count Michael Palin (Brasenose College) and Terry Jones (St Edmund Hall) among her close friends .

Jenny said: "Terry had digs in Wellington Square and he and Michael acted with the Experimental Theatre Company and performed mock tea ceremonies — it was all very Pythonesque long before the Pythons."

The Three of Us also sang with the Oxford band The Four Beats.

Jenny said: "The Four Beats introduced me to their agent, Mervyn Conn, and thanks to him, a music publisher in Denmark Street published about ten of my songs, three of which were released by Columbia Records and Verve Folkways in the US.

" '*Bring it to Me*' '*You Know*' and '*I've Heard it All Before*' have recently been re-released on *Dreambabes* a compilation albums on the Cherry Red label. Angy and I were on *Ready Steady Go* with the New Seekers, Big D Irwin and The Honeycombs."

After all this, Jenny got herself a 'proper job' at S H Benson, a London advertising agency — at a time when London was buzzing with creativity and TV commercials were being directed by people like Ridley Scott and Alan Parker.

Jenny said: "I started out as an art director but moved into copywriting, developing concepts and writing press ads and TV and cinema commercials. A lot of my friends worked on *Yellow Submarine*, the animated film based on Beatles music.

"It was an exciting time to be living and working in London. In 1970, I married a lawyer who worked in the north east. We first lived in Hampstead, just off Keats Grove, then set up home in Yorkshire."

While living in the wilds of Yorkshire, Jenny, now a mother to two sons, Tom and Edward, wrote children's books under her married name Jenny Hawkesworth. They include *The Lonely Skyscraper*, illustrated by Emmanuel Schongut.

In 1987, Jenny collaborated with illustrator Colin McNaughton and Mark Bramble, the producer of *Barnum* and *42nd Street*, on a musical version of Colin's book *Fat Pig* which, with the title *Fat Pig — the Musical* was performed at the Leicester Haymarket Theatre.

The following year, Jenny's play *Me and My Dinosaur* (for which she also wrote the music) was performed at the Polka Children's Theatre in London.

She divorced in 1989 and returned to Oxford where, initially, she worked as a copywriter. But after the publication of *When*

I Became an Amazon, she threw her energies into poetry. Then an old friend called.

"Terry Jones invited me to a party in London. We stayed up talking until 3am. I told him I had always wanted to do a degree in English. Terry encouraged me to go for it and introduced me to English Fellow, Lucy Newlyn at his old college," Jenny remembered.

"I had just finished the two year English Literature and Language Certificate at the Oxford University Department for Continuing Education and was thrilled to be offered a place at Teddy Hall to study for the remaining two years of my degree.

"As a result I sold my house in Lonsdale Road, giving myself the means to walk into my present life and the ability to teach poetry at Oxford University on the Undergraduate Diploma and the Master of Studies in Creative Writing.

One possible choice for the desert island, therefore, would be the books Lucy and I edited (Synergies: Creative Writing in Academic Practice, volumes one and two) which came out of a two year programme we ran together for undergraduates and graduates, funded by the Institute for the Advancement of University Learning."

In 1996, Jenny was given an Arts Council grant to work with Yasmin Sidhwa from Pegasus Theatre.

Yasmin dramatised *Amazon* and it was performed in Oxford and London with Pegasus' Artistic Director Euton Daley and composer Juliet Russell's choir, Chandalay Quor.

Then, as Writer in Residence for the Oxfordshire Community Arts Theatre Group, Coral Arts, Jenny worked on a site-specific promenade performance — *The Gifts of the Angels*.

Involving 400 people, a huge carnival of puppets, music and multi media, it was performed to great acclaim at Dorchester Abbey, in 1997.

On her second stint for Coral Arts, she worked with a mixed group of adults and children, with the Butoh Dance Group, Café Raison and classical ghazal singer, Jayanta Bose (whose amazing voice can be heard on Nitin Sawhney albums) on *The Forest that Sailed Away* — about the deforestation of Oxfordshire in Tudor times to build ships to fight the Spanish Armada. It was performed at Minster Lovell Hall in 2000.

After completing her degree , Jenny had a stint as a civil servant working in the Strategic Communications Unit at Number 10, preparing briefings for the then prime minister Tony Blair, before spending some time at the Equality and Human Rights Commission.

With so many strands to her career and traumatic life experiences, I wondered what Jenny would want to have with her on the island. ?

"It is difficult because, at the moment, I am caught up with the fantastic young cast performing *After Gilgamesh*, so the book of the script, published by Mulfran Press, which has rehearsal photos in it, would be a possibility; then I will never forget my first sight of *The Hunt by Night*, it is such a wonderful painting.

"The *Synergies* books would remind me of an intensely rewarding time of my life, reading English at Oxford and afterwards, with Lucy's help and encouragement, sharing my love of poetry and creative writing with a new generation.

"But I couldn't be without the book that started it all off and has inspired me for so long, so I will take the poetry of Wilfred Owen to my desert island".

44

Robin Bennett

Musician and founder of Oxfordshire's award-winning Truck festival

Oxfordshire's Truck Festival, held annually on a farm in Steventon, is a unique event. It has a genuine community feel — rather like a village fete but with the addition of 5,000 music fans.

Founder of the festival, Robin Bennett, explains that the name came from a compilation CD called *Ten Trucking Greats*, the soundtrack of the movie *Convoy* — but festival mythology has it that it was adpoted after a flatbed truck was used as a stage for the early events.

Truck, which was first staged in 1988, has has since developed into a real family business. Robin's brother, Joe, has been involved since the outset and the entire Bennett family all help out.

In February 2010, Robin opened The Truck Store in premises on Oxford's Cowley Road.

"Everyone said I was mad opening a record shop at a time when other well-established stores were shutting down. Some people regard the idea as antique, but I see The Truck Store as a community facility," he said.
"I stocked it with music and memorabilia reflecting the icons of music culture that interest me, and which cannot be found anywhere else.

"I love the atmosphere in the shop, which reminds me of a summer festival, whatever the month of the year."

Robin, 33, was born in St Mary's Hospital, London, in 1978.

"I grew up in my grandfather's home in Cambridge surrounded by his books," he said.

Robin's grandfather, New Zealand-born J A W Bennett, Professor of Literature at Cambridge, was a member with Tolkien and CS Lewis of the literary group, The Inklings, who famously met to discuss their work at the Eagle and Child pub in Oxford.

Perhaps because Robin grew up with all that literature he became a precocious reader — and had read *Lord of the Rings* by the age of six.

He said: "As a boy, I thought it normal to read a signed edition of Tolkien. We had a signed first edition of *The Hobbit*, given to my grandfather by his fellow Inkling. I devoured all the CS Lewis books, too."

"My grandfather died when I was four. My parents, moved to Steventon — and used grandfather's library to start an antiquarian book business called Bennett and Kerr."

It is hard to imagine that Robin was destined for a career in music. Books at home mostly reflected his father, Edmund's interest in the medieval and Renaissance periods — although it should be said that Robin's father has a great collection of 1960s vinyl LPs.

Everything changed when, aged 15 and a student at Oxford's St Edwards School, he read On the Road by Jack Kerouac.

Robin said: "That book must be a candidate for the desert island. That and Tom Wolfe's *The Electric Koolaid Acid Test*, which tells the story of a group called The Merry Pranksters, led by author Ken Kesey (best known for his novel *One Flew Over the Cuckoo's Nest*) who drove across the USA in a school bus decorated with psychedelic pictures."

For Robin, these books opened a window on adventure and a more colourful lifestyle — less Oxford medieval, more1960s counter-culture.

"I also watched the movie *Backbeat*, about the Hamburg years of the Beatles and realised they were only 17, impoverished but full of art school glamour. I wasn't into sport and so, instead, I began writing songs and set up my first band called Cresta. We had our first gig in the Wheatsheaf in Oxford, in 1995."

It still looked as if music would be a hobby when, in 1997, Robin was awarded a choral scholarship to Gonville and Caius College, Cambridge, to read English.

He went to Cambridge after a short sojourn in Australia where he sought out and interviewed Richard Neville, former editor of the satirical magazine *OZ*, having read his memoir, *Hippie Hippie Shake*.

"Copies of *OZ* magazines are another possibility for the island — visual, readable and reminders of iconic moments, like the famous 'schoolkids' edition' obscenity trial. Those who wanted *OZ* banned thought16 year-olds would run riot if they read it."

"Back in the UK, I had my first taste of a British festival when Radio One Sound City came to Oxford — just as the Britpop scene

"I had tasted the life I wanted, so by the end of term I had resolved to quit university. Unsurprisingly, most people tried talking me out of it."

was happening. That motivated me to watch the documentary movie about the Woodstock festival — and the idea that I could organise a music festival was well and truly planted.

"So, in the summer of 1998, I though I would like to stage a festival on my birthday. I went to Alan Binning, the farmer who owned the land near where I lived, and told him a few friends and I wanted to have a little party.

"He agreed that we could use the field but said he would sell the burgers for the Rotary Club and he still flips burgers at Truck to this day. He likes to joke that he didn't say 'no' fast enough."

This was just two weeks before his 19th birthday, and Robin had not taken bureaucracy into account when he was directed to the local district council in order to obtain a licence.

"This was the first request of its kind, that the council official had received," Robin remembers. "He said it would take 15 working days to process and, in the meantime, the police were concerned that there would be riot.

"So we postponed the first festival until September 18. The weather was good, the music was good and 5-600 trouble-free people

turned up to hear it. I was living my dream – so returning to Cambridge felt like an anti-climax.

"I had tasted the life I wanted, so by the end of term I had resolved to quit university. Unsurprisingly, most people tried talking me out of it."

Undeterred Robin set about organising the next Truck Festival while also writing songs for his band Whispering Bob. He said

"I worked in the local Spar shop to earn some money to support the music and a certain radio DJ who still lives locally used to drop in. That is how the band got its name," Robin chuckled.

"We had some success. John Peel played our track from a compilation of four Oxford Bands on his Radio One show. Our second release was titled *Wheat is Murder,* which included a song I wrote called *Joy is a High Window.*

"My obsession at the time was for The Band, who accompanied Bob Dylan on his US tour in 1965 and on his world tour, in 1966. We learned to sing and play all their songs. John Niven, an artist and repertoire man, was as obsessed by them as we were . When he heard some of our recordings, he arranged to meet us. I was quite impressed when the venue he chose was The Randolph Hotel in Oxford," Robin explained.

"John said he wanted to sign us up to his label but suggested we should change our name. We shouldn't have the name of a DJ. We decided to call ourselves Goldrush.

"John was slow coming back to us and in the meantime we had other offers. Paul Conroy, then president of Virgin Records, picked up our record in a shop in Wallingford, liked it and signed us up to the label."

Goldrush had their first recording session for Virgin in the iconic Abbey Road studios.

Robin recalls: "That was the day George Harrison died and the studio was mobbed by fans. It felt like a shrine to the Beatles."

When their A&R man was fired, Goldrush's relationship with Virgin soured and they left the label in 2002. But Robin's entrepreneurial spirit came to the rescue.

"We created our own recording studio in a cowshed at Hill Farm and released them on our own label. Our recordings were better because we were less pressured. I guess we have always been into DIY.

"By now we had met other bands who wanted to play at Truck and a lot of them took advantage of the recording studio on the farm."

Then came a new collaboration with Mark Gardner, a former student at Cheney School, and member of the successful alternative rock group, Ride.

Robin said: "Mark came to one of our gigs and liked what he heard. We happened to receive a larger than expected royalty cheque, enough to pay our fares to the USA. So we embarked on our own 'On The Road' adventure in the USA, with Mark, starting out from Boston and moving up the east coast.

"We could not afford flights and used slow Amtrak trains. Dave Fridmann, a well-known record producer and founder-member of the band Mercury Rev, met us in Buffalo, and we filled his car to overflowing with all our gear and from there headed west to California. Then came a great moment, our first visit to Woodstock, home to Dylan and The Band where we recorded a song for our collaborative album, *These Beautiful Ghosts*, at the Bearsville Studio. *The Last Waltz*, the movie documenting The Band's last concert, would be a candidate to take on the island, providing there was a DVD player!"

Between 2003 -2005, Goldrush spent three months each year touring in the USA before returning for the Truck Festival. During that time Robin took up residence in his Grandmother's attic.

By 2005, audiences had risen to 5,000 and the expenditure on artists had risen. The Magic Numbers were booked early and by the time of the 2006 festival they were at the peak of their fame. That year's festival generated a lot of media coverage, including a Channel 4 film.

So with the popularity of the event growing, Robin felt he could contact an old idol and ask him to come to Oxfordshire for Truck 2007.

"I emailed a member of The Band, Garth Hudson, and brazenly invited him to play. His wife Maud replied 'yes'. He and his band, The Brian Jonestown Massacre, were due to arrive on the Friday and Garth was going to celebrate his 70th birthday at the festival," Robin said.

"Then the rain started; just a little to begin with and then a lot and then a lot more. I inspected the site- half the farm was underwater, in some places knee deep. Then a nearby brook swelled and the whole farm flooded, along with our house and many other homes in Steventon. Even some valuable C S Lewis papers were ruined by the floodwater.

"The festival was sold out in advance so we called Radio One to announce that it had to be postponed. In the meantime, what to do with our American guests?

"We quickly organised a concert at Oxford Brookes. Being on stage playing alongside that phenomenal keyboard player and legend, Garth Hudson was magic — one of the best moments in my life," Robin said.

The postponed festival went ahead later that year, but it meant double the costs of marquees and equipment had doubled.

"This was a big financial burden," Robin revealed. "It looked as if Truck was doomed."

At this time Robin was faced with more personal concerns. At the 2006 festival he had met Megan Jones, an old flame. They decided to make up for lost time and marry quickly.

By the time of the 2007 festival, Megan was pregnant, and the baby due in November of that year. But complications arose and Megan was admitted to the John Radcliffe Hospital a few days before the postponed festival was due to take place.

Robin had a call from the hospital. Megan had gone into premature labour.

"Our son, Brynmor, was put into intensive care and I spent the week going back and forth from the hospital to the festival. After it was over, we had to review the situation. We had been wiped out financially and many of the committee, like my parents, had to salvage their homes after the floods.

"Joe and I realised, for Truck to survive, it had to be put on a more commercial footing. So we formed Truck Enterprises and found an investor. We did not want the community atmosphere to change and Truck still generates a lot of money for charities including Mali Development Trust and Rotary supported groups, but the company was able to expand our activities."

That wasn't the only thing that had to change. Fatherhood meant an end to the Jack Kerouac-lifestyle and so Goldrush wound up.

Since then his family has grown, their daughter Marcie was born this year and at one day old attended her first music festival, a new venture called Wood in the lovely setting of Braziers Park in the Chiltern Hills. Robin described it,

"Taking place in May, it feels like a pagan celebration of the end of winter. We are hoping to make Wood the greenest festival ever. The wooden stage is solar powered and the food and the showers are heated by wood-burning stoves.

"It is more than just a music festival. It has lots of ways for people to get involved including arts and crafts workshops. The music was mostly acoustic, Ashley Hutchings, a founder member of Fairport Convention, and Get Cape. We took yurts to the site and had singing around campfires."

After picking up his flute, and playing with and producing the band Danny and the Champions of the World (named in homage to Roald Dahl) for the last three years, he recently formed a new band called The Dreaming Spires.

"I am feeling more settled in the Oxford environment, but there is still a restless side to me, Robin said. "My brother Joe married Claire, a girl from New Jersey, who said 'let's do a festival in Woodstock'. Not the market town in North Oxfordshire, the place in the USA made famous by another big music festival.

"We decided to explore the possibility. Grasshopper, a member of Mercury Rev, said he knew just the venue — the Full Moon Resort on the outskirts of Woodstock near the Catskill mountains. Log cabin country.

"Truck America came to fruition last year. The kind of atmosphere generated by the original Woodstock festival had died in the US, so we felt like we were bringing it home.

"Truck America is not on the scale of the original Woodstock — the site suits just a few thousand but we hope we are true to the spirit of Woodstock," Robin explained.

So we had come to the point where Robin must make his final choice for the island.

"The problem with taking CDs and records is that although the covers are artistic, the point is lost without electricity to hear them. If I could take the shop to the island, I would have them and all the books, t-shirts and magazines?"

I though we could consider it but if that isn't possible what would it be?

Robin replied "My copy of *The Lord of the Rings*. It should keep me going for a while and I haven't read it since I was seven".

45

Dr Christopher Watson
Scientist and musician

As a man who has fitted a great deal into a busy life and career, scientist Dr Christopher Watson, 74, is working as hard as ever as chairman of the British Pugwash Group — the UK arm of the Pugwash Conferences on Science and World Affairs.

This is an international network of scientists and others concerned about the social impact of science on world affairs, with particular emphasis on abolishing weapons of mass destruction and war.

It was founded by Bertrand Russell and Albert Einstein. Dr Watson joined the organisation in 1969 and his membership has involved him in the process of verification of the dismantling of nuclear weapons.

Dr Watson also has a lifelong passion for singing, but in his sixties he decided to change direction and learn to play the cello, and now plays in a string quartet.

His interest in song led to his involvement in the annual Oxford Lieder Festival, and he has acted as chairman of the organising committee for the past seven years.

I wondered whether science, music, family life — he and his wife Anne have been married for 45 years — or his close ties with Russia would influence his choice of art, objects and books to transport to our desert island.

"I was born in Edinburgh in 1937," Dr Watson said. "My parents were both Oxford graduates. My father John was a solicitor and my mother Barbara was a teacher of gifted and disturbed children. They were not scientifically inclined.

"I have my wonderful grandfather, HE Wimperis, to thank for sowing the seeds of my passion for science. He was involved in the early days of flight and became the first director of scientific research for the Air Ministry. In that role, he persuaded the government to fund Watson Watt's research into a system of radio location using a pulse–echo which lead to radar and the setting up of the various wartime radar establishments," Dr Watson explained.

"I was fortunate that we lived in a rambling house and in a room behind the kitchen, I set up my own private lab.

"I was most interested in chemical experiments but for chemistry you need to weigh things accurately. So when I was about 13, my grandfather presented me with this lovely chemical balance with its set of weights and also his gyroscope. They are definite candidates to take to the island."

While the science came from his grandfather, his parents introduced him to music.

Dr Watson showed me their gramophone — a device with the longest horn I have ever seen. Unusually, its needles were made of wood.

He said: "If I take that on the island I shall need my parents' 78s too. I still have their wonderful recordings of Monteverdi made by Nadia Boulanger."

Dr Watson's parents were also interested in religion and his next chosen object was the family Bible. And it is not just any old family Bible.

This is an edition of the Breeches Bible, published in 1599, before the King James version which is celebrating its 400th anniversary this year .

The Bible was passed down from father to son. Dr Watson pointed to some handwritten notes in its margins:

"According to this family member the age of the universe was 5687 years. The note on the next page, dated 19 March ,1722, is, I think, even more interesting.

"It says: 'On this day between 11 and 12 am Dr Willis, my Lord Bishop of Salisbury laid the first stone of the church of St Martins in the Fields."

Dr Watson left Edinburgh in 1955 and spent two years performing National Service, becoming a Second Lieutenant in the Royal Engineers.

"I was sent to lead a troop of sappers working in Germany and made responsible for the operation of a heavy ferry which was specially designed to carry atomic cannons across the Rhine. It was not at all simple to operate," he said.

"It had four enormously powerful engines, operated by four different people stationed at each corner. I had to stand on top of the cannon and signal directions to them.

"The Rhine is a fast flowing river — and on one occasion we made a not very soft landing. Afterwards they presented me with this! "

Dr Watson handed me a piece of thick metal containing robust bolts from the hull of the ferry — a permanent reminder of an embarrassing moment.

Dr Watson explained that this posting was his first introduction to nuclear weapons.

"At that time it was not at all clear how the military could use these weapons — apart from the terrible example of Hiroshima," he said.

"I was asked to write an essay on how I would use the nuclear weapons under my responsibility in the event of a third world war. That made me realise how impossible it would be to use them, and that eventually led to my involvement in Pugwash."

After National Service, he began his academic career, studying chemistry at Corpus Christi College. But after his MA, he abandoned chemistry for a new challenge, theoretical physics! The subject for his DPhil thesis was plasma kinetic theory.

After that, he took part in a Royal Society exchange with the Russian Academy of Sciences.

It was the height of the Cold War, but Dr Watson said he was treated incredibly well, and learned enough Russian to be able to give lectures in the language. He then returned to Oxford and had a junior research fellowship at Merton College.

Dr Watson said: "When that ended, Merton College kindly gave me a Pringle Fellowship which allowed me to continue my association with the college while I was working at the Culham Laboratory.

"I had eight research students under my supervision between1966-1981. It was a wonderfully rewarding period. They were amazingly diverse people, ranging from the son of a hill shepherd to a student from Khartoum who was much the best mathematician I have had the privilege of teaching.

"Merton was a wonderful environment. We knew each other well and dined together several times a week," Dr Watson recalled.

In 1966, Dr Watson married Anne Crace. They met while she was an undergraduate at St Hilda's. They wed at Merton Chapel and now have three daughters.

Dr Watson showed me an elegant set of framed silhouettes of his family.

"We were in Paris in 1978 and, on the steps of The Louvre, a Vietnamese student called Ho Lui was making them. He created each of them in just a few minutes and we had them mounted together. They would remind me of a happy family life, which now includes three grandchildren."

The silhouettes were made soon after Christopher joined the Joint European Torus Project (JET) which created Europe's largest fusion device. Dr Watson was project control officer under Hans Otto Wurster.

"Hans Otto was an amazing character and it was fascinating to witness the prima donna relationships between top scientists from all over Europe," Dr Watson said.

"It was usually down to the Brits to act as mediators of compromise between, for example, a particularly meticulous German and a rather zany French scientist. I asked Hans Otto if he would mind if, during my five years in JET, I dictated a diary of my life in the project."

Dr Watson waved a thick volume entitled *The Torus*, even thicker than the piece of hull from that heavy ferry! When he can find time he hopes to publish it as a book.

Dr Watson was asked to stay on at JET after the construction phase but, having served five years, he chose to move to Harwell instead, but agreed with the Atomic Energy Authority that he could continue his academic contacts with Merton.

He had five years working for the AEA on offshore technology, and then in 1989, moved to research nuclear robotics.

Dr Watson explained: "We all know the destructive effect of exposure to massive radiation on the human body, but it is equally damaging to a normal robot. The challenge

was to make a robot that was radiation tolerant.

"This, and working with the Marine Technology Support Unit in Harwell on offshore oil and gas projects (1982-88) eventually lead me to become involved in the decommissioning of nuclear submarines in the Russian fleet."

Dr Watson was dispatched to Russia to help them dispose of their nuclear submarines.

"The Russians had a fleet of 250 nuclear submarines but the need for these had decreased because of the end of the Cold War.

"Safely cutting up 40,000 tons of metal 50 meters in length with a nuclear core was not easy," Dr Watson said.

"They had been using oxyacetylene hot cutters, but that was hazardous in many ways. I helped them to develop a new technology — very high pressure water jets which can slice through the hull like butter.

"This enables them to cut the subs into three parts — removing the two ends, which can be recycled, and leaving the central nuclear compartment for long-term storage."

At this point Dr Watson produced some fascinating photographs of himself with Russian colleagues standing next to the shaft of a rocket launcher from a decommissioned sub.

One of them, Evgeny Antoshin, a former nuclear weapon testing expert, has become a good friend and took Dr Watson to visit a Museum of Bombs in the Urals, including a 100 megaton bomb.

Post Cold War, Dr Watson has continued to be interested in the verification of nuclear weapon dismantling.

Since assisting in the decommissioning of the submarines Dr Watson, became a regular visitor to Eastern Europe.

He was a business development manager for AEA in Russia, Romania and Bulgaria between1992-2002 — and jokingly describes his role as that of a travelling salesman.

Dr Watson's musical interests include membership of the enigmatic Anonymous Singers, a madrigal group for philosophers and their partners.

Dr Wason modestly says he was allowed to be a founder member on account of some lectures he gave on the philosophy of physics. I asked him about the origin of the group's name.

"Oxford City Library would only lend sets of scores to properly constituted groups, so I presented myself as a representative of the Anonymous Singers and the name stuck," he explained. Their first concert took place in Balliol College in February, 1972.

One of his trips to Russia, inspired another desert island choice connected to his passion for music.

"During one of my trips to Russia I saw Tchaikovsky's The Queen of Spades at the Bolshoi and was surprised that it was so rarely performed in England. I suggested we put it on our repertoire and set about acquiring the scores," Dr Watson said.

"There were no loan sets available and it appeared to be out of print. This put me in an embarrassing position, but thought that I could easily buy a copy in Russia and adapt it myself.

"In Moscow, I contacted the Conservatoire bookshop and all the other Moscow music shops but each time the answer was 'niet'. I was getting desperate.

"In St Petersburg I tried again and still 'niet'. I was now in trouble but just as I was about to leave, I passed an old man on the pavement outside the Conservatoire selling scores.

"Not expecting anything I asked if he had a copy. This time the answer was 'yes, but it will cost you a lot'.

"A 'lot' turned out to be 500 roubles and after a little haggling we settled for 400 rubles — about £8."

That was not the end of the story of the score, as Dr Watson revealed.

"My luggage was searched at Moscow airport and the customs officer pulled out the score of The Queen of Spades, saying: 'This looks more than 50 years-old to me. You will need a special export license.' So my precious score was impounded.

"Before my next trip to Russia, to rescue it, we discovered that Welsh National Opera owned a set of scores and were prepared to lend them to us," Dr Watson said.

He had the satisfaction of seeing The Queen of Spades performed at Oxford's Holywell Music Room in June, 2002.

In the meantime, armed with his export license he had become the proud owner of a rare first edition of The Queen of Spades — a score dated June 2,1890 — six months before the first performance of the opera. He will forever associate it with The Anonymous Singers and Russia.

Sholto Kynoch founded the Oxford Lieder Festival in 2002. When in 2004, they decided to form a charitable trust they approached Dr Watson to become its chairman.

"I agreed and as a result was subject to a few 'take me to your Lieder' jests," he laughed. "The priority was to sort out the finances and ensure it operated profitably and that involved a lot of work."

The festival has gone from strength to strength so I wondered what delights lay in store for this year's event.

"There is a problem about what constitutes Lieder, but we are expanding the repertoire to make it more international in flavour," Dr Watson said.

"This year's programme will include French, Scandinavian and Russian songs. In 2013-14, the festival hopes to perform all Schubert's Lieder.

"I own a set recorded by the distinguished accompanist Graham Johnson and it would be hard to leave that behind."

So out of all his interesting suggestions for the island what would be his final choice if he could only take one?

"I think it will have to be Graham Johnson's set of recordings of Schubert Lieder."

I could not help seeing Christopher cast an admiring eye at his treasured cello, which he plays in a string quartet called the Thursday Quartet — named after the day of the week they meet on.

"Yes, it would be hard to leave that behind," he said.

46

Michelle Dickson

Director of The Oxford Playhouse

The Oxford Playhouse has a well-earned reputation as one of Britain's leading theatres. From its foundation in the 1920s, it has been associated with the launch of many stellar careers and acclaimed productions.

Famous names such as Richard Burton, Elizabeth Taylor, John Gielgud, Judi Dench, Ian McKellen, Ronnie Barker and Dirk Bogarde have all enjoyed the limelight on the Playhouse stage.

It remains thriving and vibrant, despite the difficult economic climate. The air of enthusiasm in the building is palpable and at its heart is the theatre's director, Michelle Dickson.

After gaining experience in the commercial sector, she was appointed director in 2008. Her motto is 'a Playhouse for everyone' and on the day I met Michelle, a friendly sing-song workshop for pre-school children and their families was in full swing.

As a teenager Michelle had 'an impossible dream'. Or so she thought. To her surprise, her dream came true. Will it be drama that inspires her choices for the desert island?

"I was born in 1975 in Stourport, on the banks of the River Severn, in Worcestershire. As a child I loved a print of a street scene by Ken Law, which hung on our living-room wall.

"It got lost at some point, but on a recent visit to the Oxford University Language Centre, I saw the print again. I shall have to consider taking it to the island, not only because it would remind me of my childhood home, but also because I saw it on the day that a Blue Plaque was unveiled at the original home of the Oxford Playhouse at what is now the Oxford University Language Centre in Woodstock Road."

I asked Michelle about her childhood. "My father, Ian, was a teacher of maths, geography and PE at Windmill Middle School in Stourport, where, aged nine, I went as a pupil.

"My introduction to amateur dramatics was via my mother, Jackie. I did take part in the village pantomime but never had any ambition to become an actress.

"A school visit to the Royal Shakespeare Theatre at Stratford-upon-Avon ignited my passion for theatre."

Michelle saw Mark Rylance in *Hamlet*.

"He was amazing and cemented my love of English, but it was another event at the same time that had me asking questions.

"My teenage tastes were catholic and, aged 14, I went to the recently opened Birmingham Symphony Hall to a concert by Deacon Blue. I suddenly realised that it was actually someone's job to put on these shows and run theatres. From then on, my ambition began to take root. I was interested in the stage from the audience point of view, not walking the boards."

In 1993, Michelle was one of the few students from her school to gain admission to Oxford University.

"I watched a lot of drama while I was reading English at Wadham. After my degree, I knocked on the door of the Playhouse and asked for work experience," Michelle recalled.

"I started in the marketing department and from there managed to get paid work backstage helping Tim Boyd, the technical manager.

"For a while I worked as a dresser, starting on *Henry IV*. The wardrobe mistress had a sheet with a grid listing all the characters and every change of costume. I had to dress Timothy West, and one quick change was into armour. The last piece to fix was a buckle, but I could not have fastened it properly, because it came undone on stage!

"Timothy was so kind and generous. I thought he would be angry but instead he said. 'Come on let's practice so it will be all right tomorrow.'"

"He has been to The Playhouse many times since, and I always remind him of our first encounter and what a difference it made that he was kind to me."

Michelle's next backstage job saw her working with the stage lights — on the 'follow spot'.

"This is the light up in 'the gods' that needs the least technical experience but it is the most obvious if you make a mistake," Michelle explained.

"The old heavy spotlight had weights to balance it. For pantomimes, I had to light the baddie in green and the fairy in pink. I did all 75 performances of Dick Whittington sitting on a bridge wearing headphones that tuned into everything backstage.

"It was a great learning experience in understanding the technicalities of putting on a show."

In 1999, Michelle left Oxford to work at the British Council Drama Department.

The British Council works across all forms of drama — from live art and theatre to classic and text-based drama to reflect contemporary Britain to the rest of the world. Michelle was asked to focus on Western Europe and Africa — no small task.

She explained: "In Western Europe, I worked with festival directors who knew what they wanted. Africa was different, with the projects exploring exchange and skills development.

"One project in South Africa was particularly memorable. I was lucky enough to go to Durban, in 2000, to run a British Dance Festival. Part of it was working with two teachers from London Contemporary Dance School, delivering a week-long workshop for aspiring dancers.

"It was held at the Market Theatre in Johannesburg. This theatre had stayed open during the time of apartheid and was legendary for the quality of its productions and for keeping black culture alive and thriving.

"I went to see a show, without any knowledge of the company. It was Handspring Puppet Theatre's production of The Chimp Project and it was phenomenal. The craft and mastery of the artists was exceptional, and the play was deeply moving. I left in tears.

"The company will be making their first visit to the Oxford Playhouse with a production of Woyczeck on the Highveld in November.

"I have a real love of South Africa and its theatre so a picture from this show would be a great reminder of that exciting show," she said.

"My first encounters with contemporary dance happened in Oxford and my passion for it developed while I was with the British Council. My manager was Gregory Nash, who had been a dancer and choreographer, and he was responsible for my dance education. Gregory encouraged me to see as much British and international dance as possible. Companies such as Ultima Vez, Pina Bausch and Merce Cunningham were fantastic to experience.

"I find dance a wonderful release — uplifting and inspiring. On the desert island, Jackson Pollock's painting Summertime (1948) would recreate the sense of watching dance."

Until 2002, Michelle's experience was entirely within subsidised arts — and so she decided to apply for a post with the Ambassador Theatre Group (ATG). She was successful, and was involved in programming seven regional theatres, including Milton Keynes.

"At ATG I had to think about popular shows that thousands of people wanted to see. Big musicals, ballet and international companies are part of it. I had to learn how to negotiate and do deals. Milton Keynes was the most popular theatre in the country at the time.

"A lot of my work was on the phone and computer but it was a great pleasure to stand in the foyer and see 1,600 people arriving to see a show each evening. I also liked to be there at the close — to see their faces — hoping their experience had been special. "

In 2004, Michelle rejoined the Playhouse as deputy director. So, what is it about Oxford that draws people back here?

"Hedda Beeby had left, so my job was supporting Tish in programming and producing. I read scripts, watched DVDs and travelled to see shows. I took a lot of time choosing, trying to think about the preferences of different audiences. We wanted shows for different age groups including ones that appeal to young children.

"The Playhouse has a tradition of supporting new writing and experimental shows, which is less commercial but is the way new talent can emerge along side the amazing people like Michael Palin and Alan Bennett, who also come here."

In 2008, Tish Francis announced that she was stepping down and Michelle was appointed director of the Playhouse.

She said: "I was clear what I thought we realistically could achieve and had a plan. All the staff are passionate about the theatre and the board have given me wonderful support.

"The theatre could not function without them or our 100 volunteers. You can feel the energy in the building.

"Funding is an issue in these difficult economic times. While grants from the university and the city and county councils have decreased, we are fortunate that the Arts Council has increased our grant to enable us to produce more shows here in Oxford."

Michelle is particularly proud of the Playhouse Plays Out project. She said: "The idea is to take unconventional shows out of the building into unusual locations, and attract newcomers to theatre.

"I ought to take a picture of the French dance company who performed with a dancer and a digger on the rugby pitch at Cherwell School. A little more conventional are our annual Shakespeare productions in the quadrangle at the Bodleian.

"We had a production of *The Three Sisters* on a narrowboat in September and we took three shows to the Truck Festival this year, where we also ran family workshops and a tea tent.

"The idea is to show people what The Playhouse and live performance is all about, and hopefully, they will discover that the Playhouse has something for them."

Then she told me the story of an experimental show *One Small Step* which illustrated some risk taking with a new writer.

"David Hastings was a student at Ruskin College on their MA in Creative Writing and worked on our stage door.

"He wrote an unusual play as part of the course and came to see me to talk about taking it to Edinburgh. I read it and asked if we could produce it. The play was about the history of the space race from both the Russian and American perspective," Michelle explained.

"There were 30-40 characters all played by just two actors. We made it on a shoestring in terms of the props and design.

"We set it in an attic filled with 1950s junk and the two actors used the objects to tell the story. A beach ball becomes the sputnik and a sugar bowl the lunar module.

"They put buckets on their heads and cardboard boxes on their backs and climbed down a filing cabinet onto the moon, the surface of which was white Styrofoam.

We took *One Small Step* to Edinburgh, which was financially risky. It played to rave reviews and was chosen by the British Council for their showcase the following year (2009).

"It became the most popular show with promoters, and last year we toured it to 20 countries, beginning with the Sydney Festival and including Singapore, China, India, Armenia and the Gaza Strip.

"The little Lego man (*pictured above*) that represented American astronaut Alan Shepard (the first American in space) would be a great souvenir to take to the island."

But if Michelle can only take one thing, what would it be?

"It would be great to have some of the posters of the shows that had such an influence on me," she said. "But I would want to take the Jackson Pollock. It is full of movement, energy and, to me, is endlessly fascinating."

47

Dr Chris Wright

Chemist and businessman

In the course of his career Dr Chris Wright has made many trips to Japan. One one such trip he visited a Buddhist temple and had his fortune told — and his polite Japanese hosts were very disturbed by what it revealed.

"They had never seen such a bad fortune, Chris recalled. "It compared my future to a cork, perpetually tossed on stormy seas. In effect I was to be doomed to bad luck in every sphere."

His 'fortune' was written on a piece of paper in elegant Japanese calligraphy — and he was told to burn it.

"Instead I brought it home with me and had it framed," he smiled.

Maybe the bad luck was counteracted by the arched frame threaded with rags and absinthe seeds — which he was given on a visit to Iran.

Chris has certainly brought good fortune to many. Most of the 46 castaways on our desert island are creative but joining them this month is a man who is not just creative himself, but encourages entrepreneurial enterprises, especially among researchers, in the academic world.

Chris was the first chief executive officer of IP2IPO, a company whose aim was to commercialise Oxford University's intellectual property.

"There was often an adversarial relationship even antagonism between so -called vulture capital companies and universities. We were able to change that perception in Oxford, by working in long term partnership with the Department of Chemistry," he explained.

"That year, IP2IPO raised £20m towards the building of the chemistry laboratory on the corner of Mansfield Road and South Parks Road in Oxford. In return, the company would share the equity from spin-off companies and technology licenses created over a 15 year period.

"The company bore the financial risk with no guarantee of any return but with the aim of being a catalyst for developing ideas and creating value from real science in labs."

IP2IPO was not just successful creating wealth and opportunity in Oxford — at least a dozen UK universities then wanted to be in on the act.

Chris studied chemistry at Oxford so for him it was as if his life had come full circle.

When IP2IPO went public in the alternative investment market, Chris decided to retire — but somehow could not stay retired. He missed the buzz of seeing seeds of ideas blossom into life-changing technologies, so he now uses his personal chemistry to help grow young enterprises.

He is part-time CEO of Faradion, based at Leafield, near Witney, which is working on the next generation of batteries for electric cars and renewable energy storage.

Chris explained: "By 2016, the cost of EV batteries should be down to a third of its present price"

He is also chairman of Covesion Ltd, a firm that is developing 'picoprojector' technology which will allow images to be projected from mobile telephones onto flat surfaces.

Another of his projects will enable cell-based biological assays in nano-volumes, thus reducing the cost of drug development.

As a chemist, Chris understands the role of a catalyst but what I wondered was the root of his entrepreneurial curiosity?

"I was born in Yorkshire in 1947, but have spent most of my life in the Thames Valley. My father, John Wright, was pulled out of university during the Second World War to work on operational radar systems for the Navy.

"Aged 11, I was a boarder at the direct grant grammar school in Reading, when my parents were stationed in Washington. By the time I was reading chemistry at St John's here in Oxford, my father was managing the

Devonport dockyard in Plymouth."

As a student at Oxford, Chris was responsible for the JCR fine-art collection, with a seemingly fabulous purchasing budget, and treasurer of the University Opera Club.

When in charge of props for a production of *The Rise and Fall of the City of Mahagonny* by Bertold Brecht at the Oxford Playhouse, he met assistant stage manager Annie Metherell.

They married, in 1968, when Chris was only 21. One of his suggestions for the desert island says it all.

"I have a collection of Valentine cards — the ones Annie and I have given each other every year since we met," he said.

"My interest in materials began with my PhD when I used neutrons to uncover some of their mysteries. The large Isis facility at the Rutherford Appleton Lab has developed from such beginnings.

"After a Royal Society Fellowship in Italy, I went to Manchester to learn about polymers and then was given a Fellowship at the research establishment at Harwell. Those experiences served me well.

"I learned a small amount about a wide range of different technologies — it was my first introduction to selling intellectual property and from then on I was always fascinated by the power of inventions and the interplay with design and function," Chris said.

Chris used his fireplace to illustrate how the basic principle of creating value from an idea is not new.

"This fireplace is described in patent Number 102 of 1637 and was granted by Charles 1 to the Earl of Berkshire even though he probably was not the inventor," Chris said.

"In those days patents were monopolies for production. The earl was a pretty incompetent soldier in the English Civil War, but had good contacts.

"Even then they were concerned with the efficient use of energy. This fireplace was designed so that the fire could heat the room but also dry malt in another room at the same time.

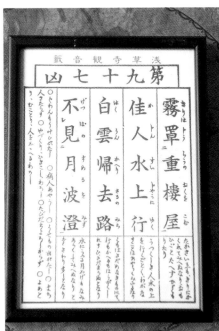

Chris showed me a botanical print, contemporary with the fireplace, dated 1620, by a Dutch artist called Crispin Van de Passe.

"I think he is a very fine, much under appreciated engraver. One of the reasons I like this print is that this is, in effect, an advertisement from a catalogue, showing Dutch capabilities, at that time, in flower growing; the knowledge of how to develop new bulbs especially tulips.

"Today these new varieties would definitely be seen as intellectual property. This engraving is of autumn crocuses. As well as having an attractive print with a story behind it, it would remind me of home."

I had noticed these very plants blooming under a tree in Chris and Annie's garden.

His next suggestion was a small framed print, dated 1809.

"This will also have resonance for me. There was an explosion of interest in discovering new materials in the 18th century lead by entrepreneurs such as Wedgwood and Boulton. By the end of the century, 30 chemical elements had been identified. This print predates Dalton's symbols; — it lies somewhere between alchemy and modern chemistry.

"The symbols were the work of Lavoisier who, in 1794, at the height of his intellectual ability, was executed during The French Revolution."

Tragedy and stupidity and the growth of scientific knowledge all in one table of symbols — no wonder it is a possibility to have on the island. Chris left Harwell for the private sector in 1984.

"Harwell was the Atomic Energy Authority`s research establishment which had

been created for a purpose that had largely been achieved.

"It was a massive national resource and needed new objectives, but there were too many different views as to what these should be. The simplicity of purpose in the private sector was very refreshing.

"When I left, for what turned out to be a brief spell in the food industry, I had not envisaged that I would return and have an influence on the outcome of those discussions.

As a memento of the food industry and an illustration of how patents were used in 19th century advertising as a mark of quality, Chris showed me his patented Gourmet Pie Cup.

Those of you familiar with those ceramic 'pie birds' used for holding up pastry will understand its use. What was inventive about this one was that it had holes under the rim which redirected the steam and gravy so the pie crust was not spoilt.

"My next post, at the British Oxygen

Company, was managing technical sales," Chris said. "We were demonstrating, proprietary processes which ran the whole gamut of industrial technology from arc furnaces to food freezing via memory chips. I was now selling intellectual property on a global basis."

Returning to Harwell when privatisation was suggested, Chris had ideas to help it develop — but chance plays a part in the history of institutions as well as individuals.

Although the government was interested in privatisation it looked like falling by the wayside as there was no Parliamentary time available to debate the issue.

Then Michael Hesteltine's attempt to privatise the Post Office failed and suddenly they needed something to fill the gap —thus AEA Technology was born.

In due course Chris became group operations director of the newly-formed company.

He showed me what looked like a framed photograph with amazing light effects.

"This unique object would remind me of Harwell and also about how some things are frozen in time. It is a neutron radiograph of a pelargonium. Everyone is familiar with x-rays but the neutron radiograph can pick out light materials," he explained.

"It was built for physics purposes but we occasionally made use of it to detect fluids in engines. With the pelargonium it reveals the tracery of its veins and leaves because it is picking up the water. The machine has long been decommissioned as the research came to its natural end, so this picture really is unique."

During the 1990s at Harwell Chris was involved in licensing what is now the ubiquitous lithium battery.

"On the island this would be quite nostalgic," said Chris, holding up an ancient looking mobile phone.

"The Motorola Startac was the first clam-shell phone and one of the first to use a lithium battery. The lithium battery science was invented in Oxford in the inorganic chemistry lab and then commercialised by AEA Technology. "It illustrates the potential to create value from ideas and inventions. I was responsible for the team which was marketing the battery all over the world and now the technology is all-pervasive.

"The clam shell is a classic design and this early one was installed in my car, so it has to be a possibility for the island," Chris said

In 2000, Chris's life-long interest in design, function and intellectual property all came together. He was able to lead IP2IPO and be an initiator of long-term investment support for developing new companies from scientific research.

Looking back on his career, Chris showed quiet satisfaction at being in on the beginning of so many technologies.

"My suggestions so far all relate to items that were once cutting-edge new designs that we now take for granted. I have been thinking about life on a desert island and I may want a little comfort and colour.

"Annie and I love Persian rugs and once went on a trip to Iran and saw them made by families in remote villages. Colourful, thick but coarse rugs made from spring wool are called Gabbeh and we have one — not on the floor but hanging on the wall — and we love it.

"If I took that, I could sleep on it, use it as a blanket or hope it is a magic carpet that could transport me home.

"Alternatively, I have a nomad`s tacheh, a kind of donkey blanket, which I could use for transporting my firewood on the island, except it is much more than that.

"The decorative, carpeted side panels are designed to prevent injury to the donkey from the rocks on steep climbs. The inside has panniers and pockets which can hold a family's possessions — so it is a good example of the unity of design and function," Chris said.

"I will also need some reading material and amusement. This natural history book could provide that and possibly be useful at the same time."

"It was published, in 1855, and written by Rev JG Wood who was curate of St Thomas the Martyr (Osney). It was a very popular description of most of the world's animals known at that time, but it is nothing like a modern day natural history book.

"He does not describe the animals and birds with facts — it is mostly full of anecdotes. The description of the swallow is about how small boys throwing stones could bring down two at once! His description of homo sapiens as a species wrestles with all the issues of the day."

I pointed out that Chris had made rather a lot of intriguing suggestions but the time had come to make a decision and choose just one of them.

"I will choose the hand-knotted donkey blanket, because with all its pockets it should hold everything apart from the fireplace! If you won't let me do that, well then it will have to be the Valentine cards."

It seemed a reasonable request, so the cards and book are packed in the side pocket while the Gabbeh rug in the middle wraps around the pictures. But I suggested he leave the phone behind because it would not do for our castaways to be rescued too quickly.

48

Marcus and Alix Hodge

Artist and founder of the Ten for Ten charity

In 2010, artist Marcus Hodge found himself in a war zone. He was commissioned by the The Third Battalion Rifles to paint a scene of Sangin market in Afghanistan, to mark the end of the regiment's six month tour in the region.

After completing a four-day military training, he spent ten days with soldiers in Sangin, going out on foot patrol with them into the bazaar.

The ten days Marcus was with the regiment proved to be terrible for the battalion. Six men died — making the period the worse for casualties during the regiment's entire time in Afghanistan.

The experience proved life-changing for Marcus and also for his wife, Alix.

She was deeply affected by her husband's account of returning to Camp Bastion after patrols and finding the regiment had suffered yet another casualty. Alix wanted to do something to show respect for the bravery of these young men and their comrades.

She said: "I realised that the tenth anniversary of the war in Afghanistan was approaching. I wanted to embark on ten days of fundraising — in other words Ten for Ten."

Alix teaches at Cothill House, near Abingdon, and initially involved her school in the campaign.

"I aimed to get ten schools involved but the idea spread. With the support of The Soldiers' Charity and Help for Heroes, it was eventually taken up by 173 schools and involved more than 54,000 children!

"We were even supported by three schools from overseas, two near Forces bases in Germany, one in France and one in Akrotiri in Cyprus," she said.

Alix described a particularly moving visit to Cothill by five young soldiers, from Three Rifles, two of whom had lost limbs.

"When the time came to thank them all the children stood up and cheered. Without

any prompting from the staff, each pupil went up and shook their hands. The soldiers were overwhelmed, saying this was the first time they had been thanked in this way and had so much respect shown to them."

"The experience also enabled the pupils to talk of personal loss — and it was one boy's avenue to express his feelings about his sister dying. This spontaneous reaction has led to some wonderful writing in the school and a national schools writing project called *Missing You*," Alix added.

Marcus believes in serendipity, that chance experiences change lives — just as his time in Sangin changed him and Alix.

So what will determine their choice for the desert island and will their ideas about the single object, work of art or book they would like to see washed up on the beach be very different?

Despite having built a formidable reputation as a portrait artist, Marcus, 45, did not start out in life with the aim of becoming a painter.

"Although my father, Spencer Hodge, is a wildlife artist, I was brought up by my grandparents on the south coast and a career in art had not occurred to me," he said.

"I studied business and economics at Queen Mary College, University of London, but I think I knew right away that it was not for me. I was even briefly sent down, but did return to get my degree."

So, Marcus decided to take a working gap year. "I drifted around doing things like managing an ice cream parlour in LA. I worked on a stud farm in Kentucky and as a deckhand on a yacht in Monaco. Then my father told me about this great little art school in Palma and suggested I go there for a while until I decided what I wanted to do."

That 'little while' turned into five years studying art at the Escuela Libre del Mediterraneo in Palma (under J Torrents

Llado), one of only two remaining art schools in Europe to teach traditional art techniques.

Alix, born in Gloucestershire, in 1965, had trained as a teacher at Homerton College in Cambridge. She was introduced to Marcus at a May ball. They became friends and flatmates — but their relationship was purely platonic.

While Marcus was away travelling, Alix worked for an advertising and PR company, in London, until she was struck down by a debilitating virus. Then Marcus happened to get in touch and, as a result, she went to Palma to visit him and convalesce.

She recalled: "I was completely washed-up and weighed just eight stone, but it was love at first sight. We married in 1992 and bought a house in the dusty backstreets of old Palma for very little money in those days. We loved it."

A small shell encrusted with more shells from the Lido in Venice, where the couple went for their honeymoon, is their first choice for our island.

"It cost nothing but it is beautiful, said Marcus. "We had no money, but my father was living in Venice with his second wife."

Alix added "Some days we only had enough money to buy one pizza between us but it didn't matter — we were young and the Lido was magical."

From Marcus's studio at the bottom of their Oxfordshire garden, Alix fetched a small bronze head of a dog — another idea for the island.

"This would encapsulate those years in Palma — Marcus made this model of one of our two dogs. We called him Llamp (Mallorquian for lightning) because he was small, white and very fast — until the day he was hit by a motorbike and lost a leg — thereafter coping well with just three."

After five years in Palma, the couple decided to return to England.

Marcus said: "It was idyllic, but not a viable place to develop a career. Back in England, I was able to find an agent and a gallery and exhibited with the Royal Society of Portrait Painters."

He also entered competitions and, within just a year, was named one of the 'A' list of portrait painters by *Harpers and Queen*.

"I asked Marcus to donate something for an art show at the school where I was teaching, Thomas's in Battersea," said Alix.

"He made a charcoal portrait of a little boy called Jack Bartholomew, which so delighted Jack's mother that she rolled it up and took it with her everywhere, including to dinner parties.

That picture is on Marcus's website but, if I could only take one of Marcus's pictures to the island and, assuming our children could not come with us, it would have to be the charcoal sketch he made of me with our two children, Clara and Freddie."

Clara is the couple's eldest child. Marcus said: "We named her after the street we lived on in Palma — Santa Clara. I will always remember the first time Alix left me alone to look after her for an hour when she was five-days old. I made this . . .

Marcus showed me a small but exquisite plaster head, which Alix brought along for our photoshoot at the Ashmolean Museum.

I asked Marcus which portrait painter he most admired and if he could take one portrait by another artist, what would it be?

"The Rembrandt self-portrait, in old age, that hangs in the Wallis Collection in Hertford House, London.

"When he painted it, he had lost everything — it is such an honest portrait. It is inspiring because, however bad things got, he kept on working," Marcus said.

"I am usually commissioned to paint a person I have never met before. It is another thing doing a portrait of someone you have known for a long time — like a near neighbour of ours in Appleton, the High Sheriff of Oxfordshire, Richard Dick — someone you like enormously and, as well as getting the physical likeness you want to capture that special thing about him. That is the reason for the institutional commissions too.

"Then I need to get to know who they are quickly, if I am to achieve that sense of them on the canvas," Marcus added.

"Portraiture is only one part of my life. I like to travel and paint in places like India. There is someone there we would want to remember — her name is Sita and she lives in Jaipur, the pink city of Rajasthan in India.

"We first met her when we travelled to India in search of family history. Both Alix and I have strong connections with the country. My grandfather lived there until he was six. I wanted to trace my great-grandfather who, we were told, had managed a flying school just north of Delhi," Marcus said.

"Alix has family links to India too, through the military. While there, we visited this

orphanage for girls and met and sponsored Sita. Since then, other members of our family and friends have sponsored girls and, between us, we are supporting ten of the 22 in the orphanage. This Christmas our family will spend three days in Rajasthan celebrating with them."

Alix said, "It was strange and amazing that we felt immediately connected, almost as if India was in our blood."

Marcus added: "I would love to be able to spend more time in India painting the people, the landscape and wildlife. I admire the dancing Ganesh in the South Asian galleries of the Ashmolean. Ganesh's mother was Sita so that would remind me of our Sita and travels in Northern India."

Marcus's first solo exhibition in London's Cork Street, in 2001, featured paintings from India. I wondered whether it was his attachment to the sub–continent that led to his time in Afghanistan.

He said: "I had done military commissions before — but this painting was intended to be something different — something that would reveal more than just the immense bravery of the soldiers in the toughest conditions.

"I experienced walking around in heavy body armour in seething hot conditions — bedding down in a sleeping bag on the floor. I saw them in the thriving market talking to stallholders and building a school.

"Meeting the local people and seeing the progress that the bazaar made every day, set against the most casualty-strewn week the regiment had experienced, gave birth to my painting."

The memory of one of the men killed during Marcus's time with the Third Battalion was particularly poignant. Corporal Richard Green was shot by a sniper at the checkpoint where Marcus was due to sit and sketch a few hours later. Alix explained how it affected her.

"When Marcus told me his stories of men he had met now dead or injured I was determined to do something.

"Marcus took part in the Reading half marathon along with 23 members of Richard Green's family, in his memory. It was then the idea of Ten for Ten crystallised. Ten days fundraising — one day for each year we have been in Afghanistan.

"Initially, I began in the school where I teach, Cothill. Bringing injured soldiers to the school invoked such an amazing response. It is so much easier responding to an individual than to mass casualties. That is why I always wear this and would continue to wear it on the desert island."

Alix showed me the wristband she wears in memory of Corporal Green.

We were getting close to the moment when they would have to make that decision of what would be their final choice to take on the island if they could only have one thing

Marcus's first thoughts were set in the Cast Gallery of the Ashmolean.

He said: "The Belvedere Torso is an incredibly powerful sculpture — maybe more impressive because it is incomplete.

"There is also a cast of a horse's head from the front corner of the Parthenon. The makers of these fabulous pieces would not have been regarded as artists but as artisans, so we have no idea who made them. But their work is still as fresh after thousands of years."

I was not surprised by the choice of subject matter because Marcus is adept at catching the spirit of people and horses in paint, bronze and in clay. He is also one of the first artists to be commissioned by the Jockey Club.

But then Marcus changed his mind and decided to go with something practical — a professional coffee-maker. The one in the museum café would be fine, he said.

I envisage our island as rather different to that of Radio 4's *Desert Island Discs*. I do not think our castaways will be alone. I expect a coffee-maker will prove rather popular. I hope

the scientists on the island will manage to generate the power to run it.

Alix wanted something much less practical.

"I think I would like a book — Laurie Lee's *Cider with Rosie*," she said.

"There is a character in the book, a fierce teacher called Crabby B, who reminds me how not to do it.

"It is a wonderful story written with such a wealth of evocative images from a bygone age. The characters, however, are as true to life now as they were then."

49

Nicola Blackwood
MP for Oxford West and Abingdon

Should you ever happen to stray into the courtyard beneath the Speaker's Chambers during a late-night sitting at the Houses of Parliament, you may be transported by the sublime sounds of Bach, played on the only piano in the Palace of Westminster, accompanied by a beautiful mezzo-soprano voice which wafts from an open window.

That voice belongs to the Honourable Nicola Blackwood, MP, for Oxford West and Abingdon.

Nicola's talent for music might well have seen her career take a very different path, away from politics. By the age 12, she was practicing piano, flute and singing for four hours-a-day.

Then, from the age of 14, she trained as a classical singer at London's Trinity College of Music. After achieving a first in music, at St Anne's here in Oxford, and an M Phil, in musicology at Emmanuel College, Cambridge, she decided to take a gap year before doing a D Phil.

"I intended heading for South East Asia, starting with Australia, but the 2004 tsunami put a stop to my plans. My sister, Anneliese, suggested I work as an intern at Conservative campaign headquarters for a couple weeks while I decided what to do instead," Nicola said. "I ended up staying five-and-a-half-months, and later working for Andrew Mitchell, who is now Secretary of State for International Development."

Nicola attributes her political ambition to being firmly grounded in ideals of public service by her parents. Her father, Roger is a cardiologist and mother Libby a nurse.

Nicola said: "Their eyes met over an operating table at the Radcliffe Infirmary when my mum was the scrub nurse and my dad the surgeon. Oxford has always played an important role in my life."

Nicola was not actually born in Oxford, but in Johannesburg, South Africa, in 1979.

When working at the Baragwanath Hospital, her father angered the apartheid leadership by speaking up for the health needs of the black community. This resulted in the family returning to Oxfordshire, living for a few years in Charlbury.

"If I had gone, as expected, into a career in

music, I would hope to provide audiences with moments of delight and inspiration, but I saw that politics can effect practical change — my experience volunteering in Africa showed me how it is possible to transform people's lives and opportunities. Combined with the intellectual engagement, all these factors coalesced."

The ambition formed, Nicola put herself forward as a potential Conservative candidate for Oxford West and Abingdon.

Most MPs start their political career as a candidate in an unwinnable seat, learning how to campaign before getting the opportunity that can lead to electoral success.

Evan Harris had held Oxford West and Abingdon for the Lib Dems comfortably since 1997 — but while this seat was not one the Conservatives expected to win, it was far from a hopeless ambition.

So, at 5.30am on Friday, May 7, 2010, the returning officer announced that she had topped the polls.

Recalling that night Nicola said: "I felt shock followed by delight — this is such a wonderful constituency — the field of candidates was very strong. I had not expected to win. I was so fortunate that I had four years to get to know all the communities before the election."

Nicola took her seat -one of only 144 women MPs in a parliament of 650. She is not however, the youngest — that honour goes to 26-year-old Pamela Nash, MP for Airdrie and Shotts.

Commenting on her first days as an MP, Nicola said: "The learning curve is like the north face of the Eiger. You arrive without office and staff .

"You are assigned an e-mail address, but almost a week goes by before you have the means of accessing them. About 700 people e-mailed me, thinking I had received their messages! At least, I knew my way around the building, not all new members do."

I wondered whether it would be music, politics, her constituency or Africa which would inform her choices for our desert island. Her wish to be photographed at the Sheldonian seemed to suggest Oxford and music.

She said: "I played flute in an orchestra accompanying the scola cantorum in Merton College Chapel while I was an undergraduate.

"I cannot for the life of me remember which term it was or anything else about the performance, but that concert led to a lifelong passion for Bach's Magnificat. It is pure musical joy and it cannot fail to lift my mood.

"If I take the score — maybe a fine manuscript from the Bodleian — then I would be able to sing on the island. If I can take my flute I could play it as well," Nicola added.

"Another musical choice would be the manuscript of Copland's 12 Poems of Emily Dickinson — The World Feels Dusty. I was introduced to this song cycle by my singing teacher Meriel Dickinson when I was an undergraduate. She was a very successful mezzo who had performed this song cycle accompanied by Aaron Copland himself, and I was incredibly lucky to have been taught by her.

"This song is all about priorities and about remembering what is important to you in the face of your own mortality. I recently lost a very close friend very unexpectedly and it certainly reminds you what matters and what really does not."

Nicola's African connections combined with music for her next choice.

"Mozart's Clarinet Concerto is used in the soundtrack to my favourite film, Out of Africa, which I just love for its beautiful filming of African landscapes. The fabulous soundtrack stops my heart and makes me homesick every time I hear it. But unless there is a battery-powered CD player on the desert island, there is no purpose in taking recorded music.

"So perhaps I should take Lucy Wiles' Seascape. This oil on canvas is hanging in my living room and was a gift to me from my parents when I turned 16," Nicola said.

"Lucy Wiles is a well-known artist on the south coast of South Africa who lives near my grandmother — who is also a portrait artist.

Her pieces are always on sale in local galleries in the area. This painting is of the beach below my grandmother's house. We used to visit every summer when I was growing up and I remember it as the most innocent, safe, joyful time. Really terribly Enid Blyton — just a bit more African!"

Nicola described how, as a child, she and her sister Annaliese would sit on giant boulders in the garden and play house — then run down to the beach together.

"But our joyful childhood experiences alone on the beach would not be safe now," she said. "It feels like a loss of innocence."

"If I wanted a reminder of England, I think I would take John le Carré's Smiley novels. My greatest indulgence is to snuggle down under a blanket in the winter with a good spy novel, oranges and a hot water bottle. For my money no-one has topped John le Carré yet, and no character has stolen my heart quite as completely as George Smiley."

Nicola and Smiley may have something in common — the fact that both the fictional character and the MP sometimes have to make difficult decisions.

"No-one can tell you how to vote," Nicola said. "When you go to bed at night, you have to justify your decision to yourself. It is quite isolating, but I am lucky — I have a close and supportive family and locally everyone has been great."

Nicola's next desert island suggestion was the result of an encounter in New York.

"I saw Jackson Pollock's Number 1A 1948 in New York at the Museum of Modern Art (MOMA) when I went in February to the launch of UN Women.

"MOMA was a revelation, firstly because they let you take photographs, which completely confused me — and secondly because I had never seen such a significant collection of abstract expressionism in one place.

"I am a fan of the genre — much to my family's bemusement. I took a photo of this Pollock on my iPhone and it is now my screensaver — a real democratisation of high art if ever there was one," Nicola said.

"It felt odd that Pollock was painting this during the year they were signing the Universal Declaration of Human Rights, but on the other hand it speaks deeply to me of the turmoil and inequality that the declaration was trying to fix, and reminds me we still have a long way to go."

Since 2006, Nicola has been actively involved in the Conservative Party Human Rights Commission. It was set up to find ways the UK can help combat abuses in countries like Burma and the Democratic Republic of Congo.

Nicola is particularly concerned by the way women suffer disproportionately since the abuse of women has become a characteristic of 21st-century warfare.

She explained: "Sexual violence has become a weapon of war and the United Nations recognised this in 2000 and called upon the world to do something to protect women.

"It also recognised something else that I have witnessed. All the women I come across who have been victims of appalling abuse do not behave as victims. They are incredibly brave and stand up and speak out, but are not always heard.

"They are resource for change, but are not getting the chance of a seat at the peace table. Without that opportunity, it is hard to see how lasting conflict resolution and

reconciliation can take place."

Nicola reflected that perceptions and reactions to women do not seem to have moved on a great deal. She showed me an image of John Sergeant's Portrait of Mme X which at the time in which it was painted —1883 — was rather avant guard.

She said: "The finished portrait is in the Metropolitan Museum of Art, but an unfinished sketch is held in the collection of the Tate Britain just minutes away from my office in Parliament.

"I always wanted to be elegant like that when I was growing up, what I did not realise was that this portrait sparked scandal because her open posture and exposed shoulders was seen as rather unladylike.

"Knowing what I know about the critical reception of this work makes me love it even more now. It says a lot about our complicated relationship with how we, particularly women, choose to appear to the world."

We had arrived at that difficult moment when the castaway has to look dispassionately at her suggestions and choose just one.

"It has to be the manuscript of Bach's Magnificat. If I am worried or upset and I put in my earphones and listen to the Magnificat, I can cope with anything that the world can throw at me.

"I know I will not have a recording of it but, as there are so many musical people on the island, and with Marios Papadopolos (who was cast away on our desert island a while ago) at the piano and to conduct us, I am sure we can do a Gareth Malone and get everyone involved.

"I have learned every soprano solo in it. Using the score, we can perform our own *Magnificat* when the going gets tough."

50

Andrew Smith
MP for Oxford

Labour MPs are a rare commodity in the south of England but Andrew Smith continues to hold the Oxford East seat since first taking it, against the odds, in 1987. And at the last election, while the Labour vote shrank dramatically almost everywhere else in the country, Andrew increased his majority.

Andrew was born in Wokingham in 1951 and was brought up in Burghfield, where his mother, Ena, still lives. When he visited his village primary school, the children empathised when he joked: "An early challenge for a child growing up here is learning how to spell Burghfield."

Andrew won a place a Reading Grammar School and from there came to Oxford to read Politics, Philosophy and Economics (PPE) at St John's College. That choice suggested an early interest in politics.

"My parents were not involved in politics, but talked about current affairs. Like a lot of people, I can point to an inspiring teacher. Frank Terry at Reading School taught A-Level history and encouraged us to think for ourselves and to have aspirations. My success in ,getting into Oxford was, in large part thanks to him."

Andrew says his PPE was focused mainly on economics and politics, and he went on to study for a BPhil including statistics, maintaining a practical interest in the subject ever since. "Not all my colleagues share my fascination with analytical spreadsheets," he said.

"I flirted with the idea of a career in academia and worked for the Open University and taught at tutorial colleges, but a chance encounter changed my life."

That encounter was with his wife, Valerie. They first met over the juke box at The Crown pub in Jericho (which used to be opposite St Barnabas' Church), in 1972.

"Val was born in Salford and, aged just 16, wanted to embark on an adventurous new life on the south coast. But the lorry which gave her and her friend a lift was not going that far, so dropped them in a place they had never heard of, called Oxford," Andrew said.

"She had not seen anywhere so beautiful so, after bumping into an acquaintance, ended up staying and meeting me."

Valerie and Andrew married in March 1976, and have a son, Luke. Andrew showed me a picture of Valerie "the love of my life" with their granddaughter, Mirai.

"Mirai is bilingual since her mother is Japanese. I keep this photograph of Val reading to her on my desk and cannot imagine being without it on the island.

"Something else which would be very nice, if you can track it down, is that juke box. I can still remember the push-button code for our special songs."

Meeting Val was not the only time chance played a role in his life.

"At first, we lived in the Donnington ward and I put myself forward to be one of three Labour candidates contesting three city council seats. I was selected, but it was a terrible year for Labour. Tony Williamson was a popular councillor and we expected he would hold onto his seat, but neither of the other two Labour candidates were expected to win.

"Tony's daughter made the rosettes for us. She laid three out on a table — two were the same and one rather different in style," Andrew remembered.

"Tony chose first and I decided to pick the one identical to his. I am not superstitious but, as I won by just 11 votes, I have never been able to forget that coincidence — and that rosette is somewhere in my attic."

In 1978, he became acting agent for the then Labour MP for Oxford, Evan Luard. The following year he became members' relations officer for the Oxford and Swindon Co-operative Society.

The years 1979 and 1980 saw Labour back in control of Oxford City Council. Andrew was chairman of the recreation and amenities committee. He later also chaired the race and community relations committee and the planning committee.

Andrew said: "I formed friendships then, especially in the ethnic minority communities, which are still close and important me. I am unusual in that I actually enjoy canvassing and meeting people on the doorstep."

That is fortunate, because during the week I interviewed Andrew he had been out and about in his constituency on three previous evenings. His team knocked on 40,000 doors in the run-up to the last election in 2010.

"Doing that, you get a sense of the amazing diversity of the people of Oxford. I am at home in different environments — in fact I relish the opportunity of mixing with people from different backgrounds."

For Andrew, the pivotal moment in his political career came when Evan Luard left the Labour Party to join the newly-formed SDP, and the Labour Party had to find a new candidate for the Oxford seat.

"There were many factions in the Labour Party at that time with quite a sectarian bite — it is not like that now. It resulted in a long and tense selection process in a room packed with 160 people. One candidate was eliminated at each ballot. I eventually won on the fifth ballot," Andrew explained.

A candidate aged just 30 was a rarity in 1982. But there was another young hopeful wanting to become the Labour candidate — his name was Tony Blair.

Andrew described the encounter: "We first met at the Headington branch before an interview at the Headington Labour Club. He introduced himself to me as we waited in the bar for our turn to be interviewed. He beamed that famous smile at me across a tiled table."

Also in the race was a young woman called Cherie Booth. "I beat them both," said Andrew.

"Later, Tony and I were twinned — a kind of parliamentary support mechanism. I sent him my maiden speech for comment."

Tony Blair went on to be selected for, and to win, Sedgefield.

Andrew represented Labour in the 1982 election, which he lost to the Conservative candidate Steve Norris by 1,200 votes.

"If I want a reminder of razor-edge election nights on the island, I would take one from the election in 1987 — my black dustbin! In the centre of the hall were plastic bins labelled with the name of a candidate. Each bundle of 50 votes per candidate was placed in the relevant bin and we watched the piles grow.

"As the count was drawing to an end, dismay spread among my supporters. My votes reached the rim of the bin, but Steve Norris had a little mountain of bundles above the rim," Andrew recalled. But that was not the end of the story.

"When all the votes were sorted, the bundles were laid out in rows on tables. Once the bins were emptied, a roar came from the balcony from my supporters —I had an extra row. My bundles had been pressed down more firmly in the bin than Steve's! I will never forget the image of that bin."

Andrew took his place as one of the youngest MPs in the Parliament of 1987. A friend rang him, suggesting he approach the Houses of Parliament via Earl's Court.

Andrew said: "There was a huge hoarding that had been awaiting an advertisement and a graffiti artist had availed himself of the blank canvas. Sprayed across it was the slogan —'Independence for Scotland, Wales, the North and Oxford East!' My photograph of the hoarding would be a good souvenir."

At the time the Conservative Government was bringing in the Baker Bill, changing the governance of polytechnics.

Andrew's colleagues in the Labour Party were impressed that he was aware of all the details of the changes — as a result of being chairman of the governing body of Oxford Polytechnic, now Oxford Brookes University. He was made Shadow Minister for Higher Education and worked with long- time friend, Jack Straw.

The sudden and tragic death of John Smith in 1994 caused another leadership election.

"When Gordon decided not to stand against Tony Blair, I joined the team that helped Tony formulate his campaign strategy and became Shadow Chief Secretary at the Treasury, working with Gordon. It was a demanding and difficult job. I had to work closely with Gordon to police spending commitments. To be trusted on managing the economy, we had to be careful about promising only what was deliverable within financial constraints."

Andrew contested the 1997 election and, after 13 years in the political wilderness, Labour found itself in government. He became a Minister for Employment, working with David Blunkett.

"David was a wonderful person to work with. I was responsible for developing the New Deal programme — which I found fulfilling. We were able to deliver on our promise of taking a quarter of a million young people off benefits and into work," Andrew said.

I sensed that this was probably the achievement of which Andrew is most proud.

In 1999, Andrew was appointed to the cabinet, as Chief Secretary to the Treasury, where he served two-and-a half-years, managing public spending, and focusing on how to increase spending on the National Health Service and International Development.

"The 2001 election occurred during that period and Gordon put me up against Michael Portillo in the television debates on the economy," Andrew said.

"A year later, I became Secretary of State for Work and Pensions. My main task was to introduce pension credits to lift more than a million pensioners out of poverty, to bring in the Pension Protection Fund to help people whose firms had gone bust, depriving them of their pensions, and to introduce disability equality legislation."

Andrew resigned his Government post in 2004. "The reason given in the media was true — that I wanted to spend more time with my family and on the constituency work I enjoy," he explained. "Rumours suggested that I resigned before being pushed but, in his memoir, Tony confirmed that he had no intention of sacking me. I intensely dislike the culture of 'negative briefing' and there was a lot of it around at that time. Personally I like Gordon Brown, get on with him well and count him a friend.

A serious man for serious times, but with a lighter side which didn't always come through in public," Andrew said.

"I really enjoy leading and working on constructive projects and believed the infighting was a distraction. I also felt I did not have enough space for home or for constituency commitments at that time," he added. "It may have been an unusual decision, but choosing to concentrate on working in Oxford East, as we sought to rebuild trust and support after a difficult period with the controversy of the Iraq war, suited me."

Andrew's instincts proved right — the 2005 election was close, with his majority reduced to 963. If he had stayed in the Cabinet rather than throwing himself into constituency work, he believes that there would have been a real chance he would have lost the seat.

Five years on and the 2010 general election saw swings against Labour all over the country, but particularly in the south.

Andrew said: "I have lived my whole life within ten miles of the Thames and I think it does give me a better natural understanding of local people."

In the polls the Lib Dems were showing well and the boundary changes did not favour Labour — so another close contest was on the cards. Yet again, Andrew defied expectations and won when Labour seats were being lost all over the country.

"There were counts going on in the main hall and Assembly room. In the hall where nearly all the wards were being counted it really was too close to call.

"In the other room they were counting the Blackbird Leys votes ,and that is where the winning majority was."

It turns out that Andrew would be a reluctant castaway on our desert island.

"If I took the book *Papillon* by Henri Charrière and Patrick O'Brien, it would bolster my determination to get away from the island," he smiled. "I would really want to get off the island and back to Oxford."

Andrew said: "There is something very special, about Oxford East, with its amazing diversity and excellence. There is a complete range of backgrounds, incomes and social situations. Visit the Cowley Road and St Clements and you discover cuisines of the world in miniature.

"With its range of industry, employment and culture, Oxford is a place of excellence. I would want to get back to all that — but most of all to Val and all the friends I have in the constituency.

"I would also really miss our cats. I would be a bit lost too without my Mini and my bike.

"I would want to take some tools to make a kayak as a means of escape. Garden tools are another possibility because of the need to survive — I would want to grow things."

His fellow castaways will probably appreciate those garden tools.

Life on the island of

Oxtopia

The long-running BBC Radio 4 programme *Desert Island Discs* strands its guests alone upon an imaginary island. I envisage a significant difference for my castaways on my island — they will not be alone. Imagine the prospect of 50 of the illustrious people profiled in this book working together to create a unique society. The historians, Bettany Hughes, Helen Rappaport, and Rita Ricketts will have plenty of work to do recording the developments and disagreements in Oxtopia.

With Christopher Brown's experience masterminding the creation of the new Ashmolean museum, I can imagine him chairing the building committee. But knowledge of the ideas of Buckminster Fuller will be an essential as the only architect on the island, Ray Foulk, is a devotee of that visionary thinker. The two creative scientists Christopher Watson and Chris Wright will be needed to arrange the energy supply and I expect Ray will ensure their system is environmentally-friendly.

I hope the other castaways will not be wary of the two lawyers, the two politicians, and the journalists (Mick Smith and John Lloyd) on the island. Since one of the lawyers is Shami Chakrabarti, I do not think they need be too concerned for their liberty and Nicola Blackwood MP will surely charm them in the evening singing popular arias. Indeed, she voiced the ambition of turning them into a choir ready to perform Bach's *Magnificat*, under the guidance of conductor and genius at the piano, Marios Papadopolous.

There are two pianos, a cello and a wind- up gramophone on the island and many of the castaways have taken part in amateur dramatics and choral societies. With Marios Papadopolos, the Director of Oxford Philomusica, as impresario for the classical music and the founder of the original Isle of Wight Festival, Ray Foulk and Robin Bennett of Truck to organise a contemporary rock festival — they are in for some treats. It would be interesting to see Robin on his guitar and Marios collaborating on something new — possibly to lyrics written by Jenny Lewis?

John Forster wanted to take the Blenheim Palace organ to play, but was concerned about the lack of power supply. Presuming the two CWs, (Watson and Wright) can take care of that problem, there could be a magnificent fourth instrument.

Andrew McLellan, with his Pitt Rivers knowledge of the natural materials used in the making of more primitive musical instruments, could create some timpani and woodwind. I feel sure that the one thing that will not be lacking is entertainment.

Christopher Ball arrives suitably equipped with his story telling blue marble. Fellow poet, Jenny Lewis is also a dramatist as is Patrick Collins. Put them together with screen writer, John Ballam, theatre director, Michelle Dickson, and designer Brigit Hegarty, they should create the most amazing productions. Imagine a backdrop painted by Korky Paul and murals by Weimin He and Marcus Hodge, add the atmospheric music — what masterpieces will emerge?

Journalist John Lloyd could exercise his lifelong dream of writing novels and plays. Brian Aldiss, MG Harris and Jane Tranter can provide them with a stream of futuristic ideas. How about Bill Heine? Will he set up a radio station and a cinema?

With four artists, three museum directors and two gallery directors, the visual arts are bound to flourish but will the island look like a new Athens or new Oxford? Will Gothic, Palladian or something startlingly contemporary dominate the skyline? I am sure Helena Whall and Debbie Dance will prevent any urban sprawl.

Dame Jessica Rawson is experienced in administration and together with two other former college wardens, Sir Roger Bannister and Sir Christopher Ball and a university vice chancellor, Janet Beer, leadership will not be in short supply. Charles Swaisland, who administered a province, could consider the island rather small.

There is no shortage of teachers from every level of the education system and the devotees of life-long learning abound, both with practical experience and inspiration from their own lives. Christopher Watson is just one example of someone embarking on an ambitious venture later in life; he learned to play the cello aged 63.

The night classes and lectures will be incredible mind- expanding experiences. Weekend courses could include Professor Jim Kennedy leading fossil hunting expeditions and George McGavin exploring the wild life and encouraging them to crawl inside logs and cherish the insect world.

The castaways need not be unduly concerned about their health given the presence of two medical doctors, a nurse and a counselling psychologist and their spiritual needs can be catered for by a nun and a bishop. Sir Roger Bannister, John Baugh and Sir Christopher Ball will surely encourage a benign fitness regime. The only thing I worry about for them is food production. There are no career farmers on the island but John Ballam, with his years of experience on the family farm in Harmony, USA, could be put in charge of agriculture.

The two Andrews, Smith and McLellan have ensured there are tools on Oxtopia. Andrew Smith has added his garden tools to a Pitt Rivers machete. Jim Bennett, with his knowledge of the history of science, is likely to have intermediate technology solutions for many technical difficulties. But will they construct a tool shed to preserve the spades and will it become the preserve of the men only?

I image my island to be very fertile, with plenty of fruit, nuts, herbs and spices — and of course the fruit of the sea is all around. Presuming the castaways can hunt, fish and grow vegetables, there will be plenty of scope for a chef. Simonetta Angelo Hornby's best-selling memoir(in Italy) of her Sicilian childhood is filled with recipes and I know there are other castaways who dabble in the culinary arts. Will they establish a communal kitchen and will the women be put in charge?

I hope Oxtopia is situated in a peaceful region but, if attacked by pirates, the three castaways with military experience could organise their defence and see them off.

If the fictional crime of the Inspector Morse series rears its ugly head, Colin Dexter will be on hand to solve the mystery as well as devise crossword puzzles to keep his fellow islanders busy.

Having been treated to a glimpse into their lives and attitudes, Oxtopia will certainly not be a version of the Australian outback's *I'm A Celebrity . . . Get Me Out of Here*. During their lives our 50 castaways have achieved remarkable things and would, I believe, be horrified to be described as celebrities.

Despite that, having a secret camera filming them at work creating a model society would be compulsive viewing.

Given the atmosphere of learning and creativity which informs their lives, surely they will have innovative solutions. After a few years would disagreements arise, will they need to create democratic institutions?

I certainly wish them all well. It has been such a privilege interviewing them and I am sure that having read this book, you will be impressed by this amazing group of people. Perhaps, after a few years, they will have built boats and be ready to receive tourists to visit who will see what kind of society has blossomed.

Location, location, location

A model aeroplane on a piece of the Berlin Wall, a blue marble, a Steinbeck piano, the Alfred Jewel, a 1950s comic, arrowheads, a ceremonial sword and a machete, Buckminster Fuller's iconic map, a barometer, a jade turtle, a Chinese bronze wine vessel, and a miniature Japanese cabinet are just a few of the intriguing choices made by our 50 castaways.

The venue for their photoshoot is also the choice of the castaway. For convenience many have opted for their home or office but others went for some of the most beautiful locations in Oxfordshire, the Ashmolean Museum being the most popular.

When I interviewed its director, Christopher Brown, for the first in the castaway series, his museum was in the process of being transformed. The first stage of the rebuild opened in November 2009 and castaway number 24, the historian Bettany Hughes spoke at the evening opening.

We photographed her on that day with the object of her choice, a 3,500 year-old model of a Minoan baby.

Author Colin Dexter also chose the Ashmolean as the location for his photographs.

Stage two of the renovation of the museum was the attractive new cast gallery opened in 2010 and used as a location by Marcus and Alix Hodge our 48th castaways.

I like to say to my grandchildren: "Where shall we go today? How about India, China or Egypt?" Whatever their choice, I can take them to the Ashmolean!

Egypt is a children's favourite and, in December 2011, the stunning new Egyptian and Nubian gallery opened.

I met the artist who designed the cover of this book at an exhibition at the Ashmolean which he co-curated. *Chinese Prints* had to be shown in two parts because the exhibition rooms were so small.

Colin Dexter outside the Ashmolean Museum

Now the Ashmolean can mount events of international calibre in its spacious exhibition rooms. So if you have not visited this treasure house, do go. Admission to the museum is free, charges are sometimes made for special exhibitions. It is open Tuesday to Sunday from 10am to 6pm (also Bank Holiday Mondays).

But the Ashmolean is not the only wonderful museum in Oxford.

The University Museum of Natural History, and The Pitt Rivers Museum just behind it, are among the most family-friendly museums in the country.

Every weekend the buzz of children having a good time echoes around one of my favourite buildings. The attraction for me is the grandeur of the dinosaurs beneath that soaring Gothic Revival roof. The two museums have been the venue for four castaway photo-shoots.

The Museum of the History of Science in Broad Street was the original home of the Ashmolean. Its director, Jim Bennett and George McGavin were pictured there.

Just next door is Oxford graduate Christopher Wren's magnificent Sheldonian Theatre — the chosen location for the director of Oxford Philomusica, Marios Papadopoulos, who is sensitive to its beauty and its acoustics and by the MP for Oxford West and Abingdon, Nicola Blackwood, who sang there as a student.

Scientist Christopher Watson was for many years chairman of the Oxford Lieder Festival, so nearby Holywell Music Room was the scene of memorable musical moments in his life. It is the oldest custom-built concert hall in Europe and opened its doors to the public in 1748.

Helen Rappaport wanted to stand beneath Edward Burne Jones' windows in Christ Church Cathedral and Dame Jessica Rawson chose Merton College which, for her, is the most beautiful place on earth.

St Edmund Hall is small in comparison to Merton but is a gem and was the choice of poet Jenny Lewis.

The University of Oxford Botanic Garden is the oldest botanic garden in the country, Designer Brigit Hegarty was pictured with natural design as a backdrop as was Bill Heine with John Buckley's embrace. Artist in residence, Weimin He, chose the iconic Radcliffe Observatory, now within Green/Templeton College which is at the heart of central Oxford's largest redevelopment project.

Most chosen locations are part of the University of Oxford but town venues include the Covered Market, Oxford Castle, Blackwell's bookshop, Blackbird Leys and Cowley Road.

Just eight miles from Oxford is World Heritage Site, Blenheim Palace.

It was the obvious location for its archivist, John Forster, but was also chosen by Professor Janet Beer. The palace was a gift from Queen Anne and a grateful nation to the Ist Duke of Marlborough, following his world changing victory at The Battle of Blenheim (1704). The palace was also the birthplace of the great statesman Winston Churchill.

The experience of Blenheim is more than admiring the splendour of the buildings- an essential ingredient is savouring the glorious gardens and the parkland landscaped by Capability Brown.

Blenheim Palace

Compton Verney

Entering by the town gate, the view of palace, lake, bridge and park is one of the greatest sights in England. Your entrance ticket can be converted into an annual pass.

For opening times and more information vist the website to www. blenheimpalace.com

Not far north of Banbury, lies the only venue beyond the county boundary.

Back in 1993, our sixth castaway, Sir Peter Moores, bought Compton Verney House. The Grade I listed 18th century building was in a run down state, the roof about to collapse and he restored it converting the interior into a superb contemporary gallery capable of hosting international exhibitions.

The collections include Neapolitan art from 1600 to 1800; Northern European medieval art from 1450–1650; British portraits paintings of Henry VIII, Elizabeth I and Edward VI and works by Joshua Reynolds; a world class collection of Chinese bronzes including objects from the Neolithic and Shang periods; British folk art and more.

The Canaletto chosen by its director, Steven Parrisien (Castaway 28) hangs in the permanent collection.

The house is set in Arcadian-style landscaped gardens, also designed by Capability Brown.

For opening times and more information vist the website: www.comptonverney.org.uk

My thanks to Weimin He

Two generations — (left) the mother as a child in 1989, and (right) her daughter, aged eight, s ketched by Weimin He in 2011

I first met Weimin He, in 2007, when I reviewed the Chinese print exhibition at the Ashmolean Museum for *The Oxford Times*. Weimin jointly curated the superb display with Shelagh Vainker and the attractive book *Chinese Prints: 1950 – 2006*.

You will have noticed that most of the 50 castaways are people of many talents and Weimin is no exception. Weimin is as quiet and modest as his talent is prodigious.

To master English well enough to write, lecture and teach using it is no small achievement. When I asked him to be Castaway number 40 I discovered that his first experience living outside of China was in Belfast during the troubles — yet he adapted and was awarded a Ph.D. in Fine Arts at the University of Ulster, in 2005.

His depth of knowledge applies to both Western and Chinese art. The result of that insight, and his achievements as a practicing

artist, is the respect of his fellow Chinese artists around the world.

During 1989, he wandered like a travelling minstrel around Loess plateau — his music coming not from guitar or lyre but flowing from his brush and pen.

In 2011 Weimin returned to the same district in Shanbei, and once again was inspired by the people and sites. Recently I was privileged to see Weimin's latest sketches — and hear his stories — from this trip China.

While sketching an old man in the small town of Tongzhen in Jia County, Shannxi province, curiosity drew an eight-year-old girl to peer over Weimin's shoulder.

A few days later, in a village where the people live in rather elegant caves, he was surprised to see the child again and even more surprised to discover that he had sketched her mother at the same age on his 1989 trip.

Those sketches are reproduced here. You will notice the holes in the mother's shoes. Rural

Self portrait, 1989

China is still poor compared with the rapid development in the towns and cities, but even there people are better off than in 1989.

From this revelation an idea blossomed. Weimin is now planning a 'then and now' project, which I believe will be both moving and illuminating.

There is a warmth and empathy about his portrait sketches, but the profound changes occurring in China also come to light with deserted villages where beauty was combined with sadness.

Visit Weimin's website (www.heweimin.org) and you will be transported by the gallery of his work. As well as the portrait sketches you can see the impressive *Rhyme of Loess Plateau* and *Fantasy of Ancient Ruins*.

Indulge in a bit of the 'then and now' by comparing his self portrait painted in 1989 with the photographs in his castaway feature.

In Oxford he has been prolific and is producing energetic and charismatic images of work on the site of the Radcliffe Observatory Quarter, where he works as artist in residence.

In the not too distant future, I hope we shall have the pleasure of seeing an exhibition of all the work he has produced.

Weimin He is not the first Chinese artist to create his own particular impressions of our city.

In the 1940s, an artist called Chiang Yi used delightful pictures to illustrate his book called *A Silent Traveller in Oxford*.

The sketches on this page are from the artist's current work on the Radcliffe Observatory site in Oxford. Weimin designed the cover for this book and has also provided various illustrations. I have been privileged to see him at work over the past few years and feel honoured by his contribution to Oxford Castaways

Behind the lens

Professional photographers are not used to having the camera turned on them. I would like to pay tribute to the staff and freelance photographers who have worked on the castaway features for *Oxfordshire Limited Edition* magazine.

There are seven staff photographers employed by Newsquest Oxfordshire. Their knowledge of the area and where to park can rival that of taxi drivers!

Each day they are given a programme and may have to attend many jobs. Sometimes, for no fault of their own, a previous photoshoot can overrun and the half to three-quarters of an hour allocated for a castaway photoshoot becomes 20 minutes. Then their professionalism shines through. Despite this pressure of work, attractive images always grace the pages of *Oxfordshire Limited Edition*.

Many of the castaways have told me that they do not photograph well — but most are surprised and delighted with the results.

I like to have the portrait picture with their final choice of item, but when that object or work of art is in a distant museum or gallery that is not possible, so I have to adapt. The castaways seem reassured if I am present to suggest alternatives. Whether the photographers feel the same is another matter, but they are a tolerant group used to putting subjects at their ease and so are kind to me too.

I am now trusted to hold the equipment at the required angle.

The photographers:

Antony Moore photographed 13 castaways beginning with Christopher Brown, followed by George McGavin, Charles and Cecillie Swaisland, Sister Francis, Bettany Hughes, Michael Smith, Diana Sanders, Steven Parrisien, Ray Foulk, Brian Aldiss, Christopher Watson and Michelle Dickson.

Despite his modesty, Antony's vast experience and cultural awareness cannot always be hidden. He put Brian at ease reminding him of a train journey they just happened to share after returning from seeing the same play in London, as well as showing extensive knowledge of his books.

Jon Lewis photographed eight castaways, starting with Jim Bennett at the Museum of the History of Science, followed by the Bishop of Oxford and Air Commodore Bob Martin.

Jon's own experience in the armed forces was revealed through the empathy with which he handled this commission. Deborah Dance, Marios Papadpolous, John Lloyd, Patrick Collins and Alix and Marcus Hodge also came under his respectful lens.

Ed Nix is the youngest photographer on the team. My first encounter with him was at Bill Heine's photoshoot at John Buckley's evocative studio near Wallingford where we carried John's sculpture, *Embrace,* to a field. The sculptor recognised Ed's artistic bent.

Ed has also photographed Simonetta Hornby, Colin Dexter, John Baugh, Dame Jessica Rawson and Robin Bennett.

Damian Halliwell is another staff photographer to capture our castaways. Rita Ricketts and John Ballam came under his expert eye.

Of the freelancer photographers given assignments for Oxfordshire Limited Edition by photo-editor Jessica Mann, Mark Bassett has been the most prolific, being involved in six features, including Helena Whall, Andrew McLellan, and Sir Christopher Ball.

To earn a living as a freelance photographer, you not only have to be good at what you do but need to be dedicated to your art and craft.

Freelancer Mark Hemsworth had great locations for each of his castaway shoots. He made glorious pictures of the vice-chancellor of Oxford Brooks University, Janet Beer in Blenheim Palace and colourful impressions of publisher David Fickling in the basement of his offices in Beaumont Street. Sounds gloomy? Not if the room is papered with contemporary comics. He photographed Jenny Lewis in the grounds of St Edmund Hall.

Andrew Walmsley had an inspiring, if challenging time, taking wonderful pictures of artist Dr Weimin He looking down from the stairs of the fabulous Radcliffe Observatory and of Oxford West and Abingdon MP, Nicola Blackwood in and around the Sheldonian.

Freelancers, David Fleming and Marc West photographed Brigit Hegarty and Sir Roger and Lady Moyra Bannister, while the Witney-based photographer Denis Kennedy caught entrepreneur Chris Wright in relaxed mood.

I would like to thank them all and I hope you share my admiration for their work.

From the editor's chair

Oxfordshire Limited Edition, which first saw the light of day in 1986, recently published its 300th issue. I am proud to have been involved in commissioning, editing and designing more than 200 issues of this award-winning magazine.

For four years in a row (until 2008, when the awards fell victim to the credit crunch) it was named Regional Colour Magazine of the Year in the annual Newspaper Awards – a success due largely to the knowledgeable and talented group of freelance writers, including the author of this book, who regularly contribute to the magazine.

Published free with *The Oxford Times*, the county's weekly newspaper (which this year celebrates its 150th anniversary), Oxfordshire Limited Edition brings together features on the county's history and heritage, its natural environment, and the fascinating people who have chosen to make Oxfordshire their home.

Which is where this book has its genesis. The 50 people profiled here have very different stories to tell – but all have a love of Oxford and Oxfordshire in common. From academics to scientists, musicians and writers, all have taken inspiration from their surroundings.

I owe a lot to Oxford too. It is where I found my feet professionally, and developed journalistic skills which allowed me to work on both regional and national magazines, meet some very special people (many of whom I am happy to be able to call friends), and travel to some exciting parts of the world.

One of the first of the special people I have encountered over the years was archaeologist, the late and sadly-missed Peter Reynolds, who would have made a perfect castaway for this book.

When I was following a journalism course at Highbury College in Cosham, Portsmouth, I had to produce a feature article about a subject of my choice.

I was living with relatives in the village of Hambledon at the time, and Peter Reynolds was in the process of setting up an Iron Age village at Butser Hill, not far away. It was the perfect subject.

I spent a fascinating sunny summer afternoon with Peter at Butser talking about the lives of Iron Age people and how they developed farming methods – and watching as a large roundhouse was constructed.

Peter also had some very strong views about journalists and the press – many of which have been proved true in recent times and which have informed my career ever since. In fact I think I learned more from that encounter than during the three terms at college.

Butser Ancient Farm is still operating, albeit at a different location, and even has a Facebook page which I urge you to visit.

I am also lucky that Oxfordshire Limited Edition allows me to indulge my own interests in local history, music, the arts, amd the environment.

Fortunately it appears there are still enough people out there who share those passions and continue to support the magazine by buying *The Oxford Times* on the first Thursday of each month.

Journalism is going through a tough time at the moment, with inquiries, scandals, redundancies and cost-cutting creating a roller-coaster for all who work or are connected with the business.

I sometimes feel sorry for those young people starting out in the trade – but recall that in my early years as a young reporter in Hertfordshire we seemed to spend most winters on picket lines with banners and Thermos-flasks full of hot tea and the odd hip flask, holding out for a tiny percentage rise in wages.

One year I remember a group of striking reporters making a giant snowman to hold one of our placards in the grounds of Hertford Castle.

Not much had changed in the world of industrial relations by the time I came to work in Oxford. More picket lines in Osney Mead, but this time the police had been called in by management to manhandle us out of the way of delivery vans.

But I would not have wanted to follow any other career. It is something I always wanted to do from teenage years and remains a passion in the brave new world of the Internet and 24-hour news.

Peter Reynolds' prescient views about journalism may well have proved accurate. But I would ask those of you concerned by the excesses of the News of the World and other tabloid newspapers, to recall the words of Gerald Priestland, the celebrated former foreign and religious affairs correspondent for the BBC, who wrote: "Journalists belong in the gutter because that is where the ruling classes throw their guilty secrets.

What I would take with me to our desert island?

I would find it hard to live without a radio —another great love since my youth — so a wind-up or solar powered radio would be essential. To remind me of home, my small flock of Ryeland sheep and the wonderful Oxfordshire village of Wolvercote, I would want to take my shepherd's crook.

I am sure there will be goats on the island, so perhaps I could adapt my shepherding skills and create a new flock in our tropical paradise.

Tim Metcalfe,
Editor, Oxfordshire Limited Edition

The author

Sylvia Vetta likes to think that she is embarked on a third career, after teaching and running antique centres. In 1998, she began writing about art and antiques in Oxfordshire Limited Edition magazine and in various specialist magazines, including the opinion page in *The Antiques Dealer Magazine* and hopes that was not the reason it ceased production!

She is a keen walker and with the help of Tim Metcalfe wrote and produced *Oxfordshire Rambles*, a book of ten walks originally led by Margaret and Jack Ibbott, fundraising for development projects supported by the villagers of Kennington. It is still on sale in Oxford and the profits go to Kennington Overseas Aid.

Sylvia is a member of the Oxford Writers Group and has successfully completed the Diploma in Creative Writing at Oxford University Department of Continuing Education. That course and her passion for art and history — including a life-long interest in China and India is the inspiration for a novel she is writing focusing on The Stars Art Movement of 1979 (when Ai Wei Wei began his career). The novel, *Little Winter Paints the Stars* is based in China 1960-1993 and in California to the present day.

She is married with three sons and six grandchildren.